The Technique of the Mystery Story

The Technique of the Mystery Story

Carolyn Wells

MINT EDITIONS

The Technique of the Mystery Story was first published in 1913.

This edition published by Mint Editions 2021.

ISBN 9781513284224 | E-ISBN 9781513289243

Published by Mint Editions®

 MINT
EDITIONS

minteditionbooks.com

Publishing Director: Jennifer Newens
Design & Production: Rachel Lopez Metzger
Project Manager: Micaela Clark
Typesetting: Westchester Publishing Services

Contents

I

The Eternal Curious

The Inquisition into the Curious is Universal
Early Riddles
The Passion for Solving Mysteries

Why is the detective story? To entertain, to interest, to amuse. It has no deeper intent, no more subtle raison d'être than to give pleasure to its readers.

It has been argued that its "awful examples" (sometimes very awful!), are meant as cautionary pictures to restrain a possible bent toward the commission of crime. It is held by some that the habit of analytical and synthetical reasoning, requisite to appreciate the solving of these fictional mysteries, is of value in training the mind to logical and correct modes of thinking; the practical application of which, in the everyday affairs of life, proves a valuable asset in the worldly struggle for success.

According to Mr. H. E. Dudeney, in the "The Canterbury Puzzles":

"There is really a practical utility in puzzle-solving. Regular exercise is supposed to be as necessary for the brain as for the body, and in both cases it is not so much what we do as the doing of it, from which we derive benefit. Albert Smith, in one of his amusing novels, describes a woman who was convinced that she suffered from 'cobwigs on the brain.' This may be a very rare complaint, but in a more metaphorical sense, many of us are very apt to suffer from mental cobwebs, and there is nothing equal to the solving of puzzles and problems for sweeping them away. They keep the brain alert, stimulate the imagination and develop the reasoning faculties. And not only are they useful in this indirect way, but they often directly help us by teaching us some little tricks and 'wrinkles' that can be applied in the affairs of life at the most unexpected times, and in the most unexpected ways."

There is an interesting passage in praise of puzzles, in the quaint letters of Fitzosborne. Here is an extract: "The ingenious study of making and solving puzzles is a science undoubtedly of most necessary acquirement, and deserves to make a part in the meditation of both sexes. It is an art, indeed, that I would recommend to the encouragement of both the Universities, as it affords the easiest and shortest method of conveying some of the most useful principles of logic. It was the maxim of a very wise prince that 'he who knows not how to dissemble knows not how to reign;' and I desire you to receive it as mine, that 'he who knows not how to riddle knows not how to live.'"

But though all this may be true as a vague result, it is not the author's real purpose. He writes solely for entertainment; presumably the entertainment of his audience, but often equally for the entertainment of himself.

1. Inquisition into the Curious is Universal

THE DETECTIVE STORY, AND NOW we include the whole range of mystery or riddle stories, is founded on a fundamental human trait, inquisitiveness. Man is an incarnate interrogation point. The infant's eyes ask questions before his tongue can do so, and soon the inquiring eyes are supplemented by a little outstretched hand, trying to satisfy a curiosity by the sense of touch. But, once having achieved a vocabulary, however small, he uses it almost entirely to make inquiries, until so prominent becomes this trait, that his conversation is cut off altogether, and he is condemned to be visible but not audible.

Attaining further intelligence, his inquiries become more definite and thoughtful, though no less numerous and eager. He seeks books, whether in or out of running brooks; he inquires of authorities, or he reasons out answers for himself, as he grows in body and brain. He meets a friend in the street, he pours out questions. In his business he progresses by one question after another. Is he an inventor? He questions of Nature till he probes her various secrets. Is he a philosopher? He questions his soul.

To quote Mr. Dudeney again:

"The curious propensity for propounding puzzles is not peculiar to any race or to any period of history. It is simply innate in every intelligent man, woman, and child who has ever lived, though it is always showing itself in different forms; whether the individual be a Sphinx of Egypt, a Samson of Hebrew lore, an Indian fakir, a Chinese philosopher, a mahatma of Tibet, or a European mathematician makes little difference.

"Theologian, scientist, and artisan are perpetually engaged in attempting to solve puzzles, while every game, sport, and pastime is built up of problems of greater or less difficulty. The spontaneous question asked by the child of his parent, by one cyclist of another while taking a brief rest on a stile, by a cricketer during the luncheon hour, or by a yachtsman lazily scanning the horizon, is frequently a problem of considerable difficulty. In short, we are all propounding puzzles to one another everyday of our lives—without always knowing it."

An orator makes his best effects by questions. The Book of Job is impressive largely because it is written in interrogative form.

Many trite quotations are questions. "What is truth?" or "Is life worth living?" arrest our attention because they are debatable queries. Who is not more interested in the Questions of the Day than in the known facts?

According to Mr. George Manville Fenn, the man who invented a wondrous and mysterious plot for a story deserves a palm.

"He must have been a deep thinker, one well versed in the philosophy of goose quill, knowing that his story would thrill the reader, and that he had achieved the great point of seizing upon that reader's imagination, and holding it, so that he would follow the mystery of the fiction to the very end. It may have been the result of some haphazard lucky thought, but still he must have been a careful student of everyday life, and must have duly noted how largely curiosity or the desire to fathom the unknown is developed in the human brain."

As with other human traits, inquiry is inherent to a greater extent and also more largely developed in some minds than in others. Some people say "How do you do?" and wait interestedly for your answer. Others say "How are you?" and without pausing for reply, go on to remark about the weather. But it is the people who are interested in answers who care for detective stories. It is the people who care for the solution of a problem who write and read mystery tales.

One who has studied these questions from many points of view, and, above all, noted how a story will "catch on," and almost electrically seize the imagination of the reading world, will constantly see that in the majority of cases the most popular fiction of the day is that in which mystery plays a prominent part—a mystery which is well concealed. This is no secret. It is the natural desire for the weird and wonderful— that hunger for the knowledge of the unknown which began with the forbidden apple; and the practiser of the art in question merely grows for those who hunger, a fruit that is goodly to the eye, agreeable to the taste, and one that should, if he—or she—be worthy of the honored name of author, contain in its seeds only a sufficiency of hydrocyanic poison to make it piquant in savor. It is no forbidden fruit that he should offer, merely an apple that is hard to pick—a fruit whose first bite excites fresh desire, whose taste brings forth an intense longing for more, and of which the choicest and most enticing morsel is cleverly held back to the very end.

As Mr. Dudeney observes:

"It is extraordinary what fascination a good puzzle has for a great many people. We know the thing to be of trivial importance, yet we are impelled to master it, and when we have succeeded there is a pleasure and a sense of satisfaction that are a quite sufficient reward for our trouble, even when there is no prize to be won. What is this mysterious charm that many find irresistible? Why do we like to be puzzled? The curious thing is that directly the enigma is solved the interest generally vanishes. We have done it, and that is enough. But why did we ever attempt to do it? The answer is simply that it gave us pleasure to seek the solution—that the pleasure was all in the seeking and finding for their own sakes. A good puzzle, like virtue, is its own reward. Man loves to be confronted by a mystery—and he is not entirely happy until he has solved it. We never like to feel our mental inferiority to those around us. The spirit of rivalry is innate in man; it stimulates the smallest child, in play or education, to keep level with his fellows, and in later life it turns men into great discoverers, inventors, orators, heroes, artists and (if they have more material aims) perhaps millionaires."

But the kernel of their interest is resolution.

A mystery and its solution designedly set forth in narration, implies a previous sequence unknown to the reader.

It is this re-solution that attracts the alert brain, and stimulates the reader to solve for himself a problem whose answer he will shortly learn. But he wants to learn that answer as corroborative proof of his own solution, and not as a revelation.

It is this instinct, great in some, small or perhaps even entirely lacking in others, that makes a mind interested in puzzles or mysteries.

2. Early Riddles

THE ENJOYMENT OF PUZZLES OR mysteries is as old as humanity itself.

First there is the ancient Riddle, that draws upon the imagination and play of fancy. Readers will remember the riddle of the Sphinx, the monster of Bœotia, who propounded enigmas to the inhabitants and devoured them if they failed to solve them. It was said that the Sphinx would destroy herself if this one of her riddles were ever correctly answered: "What animal walks on four legs in the morning, two at noon, and three in the evening?" It was explained by Oedipus, who pointed out that man walked on his hands and feet in the morning of life, at the noon of life he walked erect, and in the evening of his days he supported his infirmities with a stick. When the Sphinx heard this explanation, she dashed her head against a rock and immediately expired. Puzzle solvers may be really useful on occasion.

Then there is the riddle propounded by Samson. It is perhaps the first prize competition in this line on record, the prize being thirty sheets and thirty changes of garments for a correct solution. The riddle was this: "Out of the eater came forth meat, and out of the strong came forth sweetness." The answer was, "A honeycomb in the body of a dead lion."

The classic "Riddle of the Sphinx" is mythological rather than historical, and belongs to the Grecian deity, not the Egyptian Sphinx. Its date is unauthenticated, but at least it wears the halo of antiquity, for Sophocles wrote of it in the Fourth Century B.C.

Samson has been called the Father of Riddles, but merely because his famous riddle was among the first to creep into print. Doubtless older and better ones were buried in an oblivion from which they can never be disinterred.

"Out of the eater," propounded 1200 B.C., does not strike us as an exquisitely clever conceit, but it embodies the true principle of the riddle and of the riddle story. The asker already knew the solution, and that was why the guessers strove to attain a re-solution.

In those days riddles were proposed at wedding feasts and other social gatherings, a practice still obtaining to a degree.

The Queen of Sheba came to visit Solomon, "to prove him with hard questions." And Solomon, in his turn was addicted to the giving of riddles to Hiram, King of Tyre, who was fined for those he failed to guess.

Among the Egyptians, puzzling was a religious rite and the Sphinx was their goddess. We are told that such was the esoteric religion of the Egyptians that all the priests were riddlers and their religion one vast enigma.

Other recorded ancient riddles are of interest to the antiquarian, but enough has been said here to prove the inherent love of Question and

Answer in man's mind from the earliest ages. From earlier than Samson to later than Sam Lloyd the puzzle has held its own among mental activities.

And puzzle, in its broader sense includes all branches of mystery or detective stories as well as mere riddles or conundrums.

The Century Dictionary defines puzzle as "A riddle, toy or contrivance which is designed to try one's ingenuity."

3. The Passion for Solving Mysteries

THIS IS THE CRUX OF the mystery story. It is designed to try the reader's ingenuity at re-solution. The exercise of this tried ingenuity is what gives the entertainment or amusement found in a mystery story.

The type of mentality or the kind of mental bias that gives pleasure in puzzling is the same in author and reader. The talent that knits is the same talent that unravels. The propounder uses the same kind of acumen as the guesser, and his pleasure in doing so is of the same sort.

It is difficult to say just what this mental faculty is, but we who possess it know that its exercise gives us exquisite enjoyment.

As the athlete rejoices in his muscular prowess, as the musician rejoices in the melodies he makes, as the artist glories in his painted masterpiece, yea, even as the clam is notoriously happy in his own element, so the mental acrobat revels in concentrating all his brain power on an analytical problem.

Lowell declared that Poe had two of the prime qualities of genius— "a faculty of vigorous yet minute analysis and a wonderful fecundity of imagination." These two qualities are present to a greater or less degree in every lover of mystery fiction; and it is the degree that determines the intensity of the call of the author and the response of the reader.

II

THE LITERATURE OF MYSTERY

The Rightful Place of the Mystery Story in Fiction
The Mystery Story Considered as Art
The Claims of Antagonists and Protagonists

What makes for worthwhileness in mystery fiction of any kind is the puzzle and its answer—not the gruesomeness of a setting or the personality of a hero or the delineation of a character.

A liking for mystery fiction is not a mark of poor taste or an indication of inferior intellect. Its readers form an audience greatly misunderstood by other literary people whose mentality lacks this bent. But what especial audience is not misunderstood? Do not many people say to music lovers, "I don't see how you can sit through Parsifal"? Do not some scoff at people who trail through art galleries, catalogue in hand?

Let us concede that a taste for mystery fiction is not universal. We will even admit that in its nicer points the riddle story may be "caviar to the general," but we will not agree that it is unworthy a place in literature or that it is outside the pale of art.

1. The Rightful Place of the Mystery Story in Fiction

DR. HARRY THURSTON PECK SAYS IN "Studies In Several Literatures":

"Supercilious persons who profess to have a high regard for the dignity of 'literature' are loath to admit that detective stories belong to the category of serious writing. They will make an exception in the case of certain tales by Edgar Allan Poe, but in general they would cast narratives of this sort down from the upper ranges of fine fiction. They do this because, in the first place, they think that the detective story makes a vulgar appeal through its exploitation of crime. In the second place, and with some reason, they despise detective stories because most of them are poor, cheap things. Just at present there is a great popular demand for them; and in response to this demand a flood of crude, ill-written, sensational tales comes pouring from the presses of the day. But a detective story composed by a man of talent, not to say of genius, is quite as worthy of admiration as any other form of novel. In truth, its interest does not really lie in the crime which gives the writer a sort of starting point. In many of these stories the crime has occurred before the tale begins; and frequently it happens, as it were, off the stage, in accordance with the traditional precept of Horace.

"The real interest of a fine detective story is very largely an intellectual interest. Here we see the conflict of one acutely analytical mind with somother mind which is scarcely less acute and analytical. It is a battle of wits, a mental duel, involving close logic, a certain amount of applied psychology, and also a high degree of daring on the part both of the criminal and of the man who hunts him down. Here is nothing in itself 'sensational' in the popular acceptance of that word.

"Therefore, when we speak of the detective story, and regard it seriously, we do not mean the penny-dreadfuls, the dime-novels, and the books which are hastily thrown together by some hack-writer of the 'Nick Carter' school, but the skillfully planned work of one who can construct and work out a complicated problem, definitely and convincingly. It must not be too complex; for here, as in all art, simplicity is the soul of genius. The story must appeal to our love of the mysterious, and it must be characterized by ingenuity, without transcending in the least the limits of the probable."

This is a clear and rational definition of the Detective Story as we propose to consider it, and it seems to justify the acceptance of such stories as literature.

But even in the complete absence of necessity for apology, we must consider the rightful place of the Mystery Story in fiction.

It is neither below nor above other types of story, but side by side with character studies, problem novels, society sketches or symbolic romances; and in so far as it fulfils the requirements of the best literature, just so far it is the best literature.

There are bigoted and thoughtless critics who deny the Mystery Story any right to be considered as literature at all. But better judges are better pleased.

To quote from a personal letter of Mr. Arlo Bates:

"As to whether a Detective Story is literature, it seems to me that the question is not unlike asking whether a man with blue eyes is moral. No story ever took a place as literature on the strength of its plot. I am in the habit of telling my classes that one can no more judge the literary value of a novel from its plot, than one can judge of the beauty of a girl from an X-ray photograph of her skeleton. To exclude detective tales would be greatly to diminish the world's literary baggage."

Professor Brander Matthews tells us in "Inquiries and Opinions" that "Poe transported the detective story from the group of tales into the group of portrayals of character. By bestowing upon it a human interest, he raised it in the literary scale."

But Mr. Matthews continues:

"Even at its best, in the simple perfection of form that Poe bestowed on it, there is no denying that the Detective Story demanded from its creator no depth of sentiment, no warmth of emotion, and no large understanding of human desire. There are those who would dismiss it carelessly, as making an appeal not far removed from that of the riddle and of the conundrum. There are those again who would liken it rather to the adroit trick of a clever conjurer. No doubt, it gratifies in us chiefly that delight in difficulty conquered, which is a part of the primitive play-impulse potent in us all, but tending to die out as we grow older, as we lessen in energy, and as we feel more deeply the tragi-comedy of existence. But inexpensive as it may seem to those of us who look to literature for enlightenment, for solace in the hour of need, for stimulus to stiffen the will in the never ending struggle of life, the detective tale, as Poe contrived it, has merits of its own as distinct and as undeniable, as those of the historical novel, for example, or of the sea-tale. It may please the young rather than the old, but the pleasure it can give is ever innocent; and the young are always in the majority."

Perhaps with his inerrant sense of terminology, Professor Matthews struck the right word when he called the Mystery Story inexpensive. It is that, but it is not necessarily cheap.

The indiscriminate critic who pronounces all detective stories trash, would be quite as logical and veracious should he call all love stories trash or all historical novels trash. The matter of a detective story is definite and easily invoiced; the manner allows scope as high as poetry or as deep as philosophy or as wide as romance. There is as true literature in Poe's detective stories as in Bacon's Essays, though of a different sort.

A recent well-known author published a book of clever detective stories anonymously. Asked why, he said that he considered the admission of its authorship beneath his literary dignity. "Because," he explained, "they are false to life and false to art."

As a generalization, nothing could be more untrue. A detective story may be these things, but so may stories in any other field of fiction. It depends on the author.

But to imply that a detective story is necessarily false to life and is false, per se, to art, is a mistake.

To quote Julian Hawthorne's very able essay on this subject:

"Of course 'The Gold Bug' is literature; of course any other story of mystery and puzzle is also literature, provided it is as good as 'The Gold Bug,'—or I will say, since that standard has never since been quite attained, provided it is a half or a tenth as good. It is goldsmith's work; it is Chinese carving; it is Daedalian; it is fine. It is the product of the ingenuity lobe of the human brain working and expatiating in freedom. It is art; not spiritual nor transcendental art but solid art, to be felt and experienced. You may examine it at your leisure, it will be always ready for you; you need not fast or watch your arms overnight in order to understand it. Look at the nice setting of the mortises; mark how the cover fits; how smooth is the working of that spring drawer. Observe that this bit of carving, which seemed mere ornament, is really a vital part of the mechanism. Note, moreover, how balanced and symmetrical the whole design is, with what economy and foresight every part is fashioned. It is not only an ingenious structure, it is a handsome bit of furniture, and will materially improve the looks of the empty chambers, or disorderly or ungainly chambers that you carry under your crown. Or if it happen that these apartments are noble in decoration and proportions, then this captivating little object will find a suitable place in some spare nook or other, and will rest or entertain eyes too long focused on the severely sublime and beautiful."

2. The Mystery Story Considered as Art

Yes, the detective story at its best is primarily and integrally a work of art. It is like those Chinese carved balls, referred to by Tennyson as, "Laborious orient ivory, sphere in sphere," and as the mystery story originated in the Orient, there may be some correlation.

The detective story has been called "ingenious but somewhat mechanical." Here the stigma lies in the "but." The detective story is ingenious and mechanical. On these two commandments hang all the laws of mystery fiction writing. Also ingenious and mechanical are the

Fixed Forms of verse. Who denies the beauty and art of sonnets and rondeaux, and even sestinas, because they are ingenious and mechanical?

As the mosaic worker in Florence picks out his colored bits with utmost skill, care and patience, so the worker in Fixed Forms selects his words and fits them into his inexorable pattern until he achieves his perfect and exquisite result.

Heraldic devices are not "artistic" in the accepted sense of the word, but they are an art in themselves; ingenious and mechanical, but still art. The Heraldic lions in front of the New York Public Library may not be true to nature's lions, may not be true to a poetic imagination of a lion, but they are true to the laws of the conventional lion of heraldry, and are therefore art.

Oriental embroidery is art as much as an impressionist picture, though of a different type, and characterized by ingenuity and mechanism.

If, as Lowell says, "genius finds its expression in the establishment of a perfect mutual understanding between the worker and his material," then we can exclude no serious endeavors from the possibility of being art.

And the qualities of ingenuity and mechanism are peculiarly fitted to bring about the establishment of just such an understanding.

3. The Claims of Antagonists and Protagonists

ONE REASON FOR A SWEEPING denouncement of the detective story is the innate propensity of the human mind for bluffing at intellect. Many people would be glad to admit a taste for mystery fiction, but tradition tells them that such things are but child's play, while a love of ethics or metaphysics betokens a great mind. Ashamed then, of their honest liking for puzzle solving, they deny it, and pretend a deep interest in subjects which really mean little or nothing to them.

"How can you read such stuff?" they ask in shocked tones of the puzzle lover, who, with alert brain and bright eyes, is galloping through "The Mystery of the Deserted Wing," and then they turn with a virtuous yawn, back to the uncut pages of the erudite tome through which they are plodding their weary way.

To the truly great intellect who understands and knows whereof he thinks, the above does not apply. But so long as men are unwilling to be caught in a liking for "child's play," and so long as women yearn after that smattering of abstruse literature which represents to them "a breadth of culture," so long will the detective story be ostentatiously denounced on the corners of the streets, and eagerly devoured behind closed doors.

Of course there are plenty of people of real intelligence who have no taste for Mystery Stories. This proves nothing, for there are also plenty of people of real intelligence who like them. Again we might as well ask, "Does a blue eyed man like cherries?"

But, as many people are fond of the authority of the good and great, let us be definite.

In a personal letter, President Woodrow Wilson writes:

"The fact is, I'm an indiscriminate reader of detective stories and would be at a loss to pick out my favorites. On the whole I have got the most authentic thrill out of Anna Katharine Green's books and Gaboriau's."

Dr. William J. Rolfe, the famous Shakespearian editor, was exceedingly fond of Mystery Stories and puzzles of all sorts. He especially revelled in the books of charades written by his friend and colleague, Professor William Bellamy.

Indeed, the hasty and inconsiderate judgment that relegates all detective fiction to the trash-pile, might be modified by the knowledge of the college professors and deep-thinking scholars who turn to detective stories for recreation and enjoyment.

A well known member of the English Parliament has such a taste for detective literature that his friend speaks thus of him:

"The weighty work in which the eminent statesman is so deeply engrossed," he said, "is called 'The Great Rand Robbery.' It is a detective novel, for sale at all bookstalls."

The American raised his eyebrows in disbelief.

"'The Great Rand Robbery?'" he repeated, incredulously. "What an odd taste!"

"It is not a taste, it is his vice," returned the gentleman with the pearl stud. "It is his one dissipation. He is noted for it. You, as a stranger, could hardly be expected to know of this idiosyncrasy. Mr. Gladstone sought relaxation in the Greek poets, Sir Andrew finds his in Gaboriau. Since I have been a member of Parliament, I have never seen him in the library without a shilling shocker in his hands. He brings them even into the sacred precincts of the House, and from the Government benches reads them concealed inside his hat. Once started on a tale of murder, robbery, and sudden death, nothing can tear him from it, not even the call of the division-bell, nor of hunger, nor the prayers of the party Whip. He gave up his country house because when he journeyed to it in the train he would become so absorbed in his detective stories that he was invariably carried past his station."

Perhaps such an inordinate relish is not to be entirely commended, but the fact remains that an analytical mentality gets an intense enjoyment out of the solving of puzzles or mysteries, that a differently constituted brain cannot in the least understand or appreciate.

It all comes back to the incontrovertible philosophy:

> *"Different men are of different opinions,*
> *Some like apples, some like inions."*

And this same thought Henry James voices thus:

"In a recent story, 'The Beldonald Holbein,' it is not my fault if I am so put together as often to find more life in situations obscure and subject to interpretation than in the gross rattle of the foreground." One could not find a more luminous comment upon his short stories than these words contain. The situations that he prefers are, as he says, "obscure" but "subject to interpretation." Hawthorne's situations, however, even when obscure, are always vital. We cannot imagine Hawthorne saying, as James says, "It is an incident for a woman to stand up with her hand resting on a table and look out at you in a certain way."

If, then, Mr. James gets exquisite satisfaction out of the careful consideration of this incident, why may not another equally great intellect become absorbed in finding out who stole the jewels?

The curiosity aroused by Mystery Fiction is not then, a mere idle curiosity but an intellectual interest.

III

THE HISTORY OF MYSTERY

Ancient Mystery Tales

To trace the origin and history of the mystery story is simply to trace the origin and history of man's mind. Mystery stories were told and wonder tales invented before the days of old Rameses, before the Sphinx was hewn or Samson born. And indeed the rousing of latent curiosity, the tempting with a promise to divulge, which is the vital principle of the mystery story, began no later than with the subtlety of the Primal Serpent.

There is no country which has not its quota of traditional and folk-lore tales, founded almost invariably on some element of mystery, surprise or suspense. And why? Because the interest of the eternal audience is "gripped" by a desire to know the unknown. Because the ancients told and retold stories of mystery with never failing success. These tales lived. Translated, rewritten, paraphrased, they are still living, because of their ever new appeal to the very human trait of curiosity.

1. Ancient Mystery Tales

TAKE THE STORY OF "THE Clever Thief." It comes from the Tibetan, from an ancient Buddhist book that goes back nearly a thousand years. But even then it was not new. Missionaries had carried it thither from India in an odd corner of their bags, or in some chamber of the memory not filled with the riddles of being. Where did they get it? Who can say? It was old when Herodotus wandered through sun-lit Egypt twenty-four centuries ago, gleaning tales from the priests of Amen and of Ptah. He tells it, point for point, as did those Buddhist missionaries, but lays it in the days of Rameses, nigh four thousand years ago. Everything is there; the cutting off of the head to elude detection, the tricks by which the relatives mourn over the headless trunk, the snare set for the thief and his outwitting it. And that same tale, like good merchandise, was carried both east and west. It found its way to India, over the vast Himalayas, to the gray roof of the world. It came with equal charm to the Mediterranean isles, up the Adriatic coasts, and as far as Venice. There Ser Giovanni told it, transmogrifying Pharaoh of the Nile into a worshipful Doge, as he had already been made over into a Buddhist magnate, but in no way altering the motive, the suspense, the artfulness of the tale. What is this story then? Is it Venetian? Is it Pharonic? Is it Greek? Is it Tibetan? It is all these, and perhaps something more, vastly older than them all. Its craft, mayhap, goes back to that primal serpent who, more subtle than all the beasts of the field, has ever inspired darkling feints and strategies.

Stories whose motive is a subtly discerned clew are not less primordial. The most vivid of these tales of deduction are, perhaps, those which come to us through the Arabs, in their treasure store, "The thousand and one nights." The Arabs gleaned them from every land in southern Asia, and from most ancient Egypt, in those days when Moslem power overshadowed half the world. And then they retold them with a charm, a vivid freshness, a roguishness, and a dash of golden light through it all that make them the finest story-tellers in the world.

Can we fix the dates of these Arabian stories? Only in a general way. Some of them came from Cairo, some from Syria, some from the Euphrates and Tigris Valley, some from Persia and India and China; and they were gathered together, it would appear, in the century before Shakespeare was born, by some big-hearted, humorous fellow, among the great anonymous benefactors of mankind. But he made no claim of inventing them. If he had he would have been laughed at for his pains. For old men had heard them from their grandfathers, generation after generation, and the gray grandsires always began to tell them, saying: "So 'twas told to me when I was such a tiny child as thou art."

Though many of these tales excite merely wonder and surprise, others have the germ of that analytic deduction from inconspicuous clues, that we call ratiocination, or the detective instinct.

There is an Arabic story, called "The Sultan and his Three Sons." From this we quote two illuminative passages which employ the principle of deductive analysis.

And they stinted not faring till the middle way, when behold they came upon a mead abounding in herbage and in rain-water lying sheeted. So they sat them down to rest and to eat of their victual, when one of the brothers, casting his eye upon the herbage, cried, "Verily a camel hath lately passed this way laden half with Halwa-sweetmeats and half with Hamiz-pickles." "True," cried the second, "and he was blind of an eye." Hardly, however, had they ended their words when lo! the owner of the camel came upon them (for he had overheard their speech and had said to himself, "By Allah, these three fellows have driven off my property, inasmuch as they have described the burden and eke the beast as one-eyed") and cried out, "Ye three have carried away my camel!" "By Allah we have not seen him," quoth the Princes, "much less have we touched him"; but quoth the man, "By the Almighty, who could have taken him except you? and if you will not deliver him to me, off with us, I and you three, to the Sultan." They replied, "By all manner of means; let us wend to the sovereign." So the four hied forth, the three princes and the Cameleer, and ceased not faring till they reached the capital of the King.

Presently, asked the Sultan, "What say ye to the claims of this man and the camel belonging to him?" Hereto the Princes made answer, "By Allah, O King of the Age, we have not seen the camel much less have we stolen him." Thereupon the Cameleer exclaimed, "O my lord, I heard yonder one say that the beast was blind of an eye; and the second said that half his load was of sour stuff." They replied, "true, we spake these words"; and the Sultan cried to them, "Ye have purloined the beast, by this proof." They rejoined, "No, by Allah, O my Lord. We sat us in such a place for repose and refreshment and we remarked that some of the pasture had been grazed down, so we said: This is the grazing of a camel; and he must have been blind of one eye as the grass was eaten only on one side. But as for our saying that the load was half Halwa-sweetmeats and half Hamiz-pickles, we saw on the place where the camel had knelt the flies gathering in great numbers while on the other were none; so the case was clear to us (as flies settle on naught save the sugared) that one of the panniers must have contained sweets and the other sours." Hearing this the Sultan said to the Cameleer, "O man, fare thee forth and look after thy camel; for these signs and tokens prove not the theft of these men, but only the power of their intellect and their penetration."

Later Voltaire used this method for his "Zadig," Poe for his "Dupin," and Gaboriau for his "M. Lecoq"; while later still it reappeared as the basis of the "Sherlock Holmes" stories.

The story of "The Visakha" is nearly a thousand years old, but the following quotation will prove that the element of acute observation is the same as that described in a previous story proving the wisdom of Solomon.

After she had taken charge of the boy the father died. A dispute arose between the two women as to the possession of the house, each of them asserting that it belonged to her. They had recourse to the King. He ordered his ministers to go to the house and to make inquiries as to the ownership of the son. They investigated the matter, but the day came to an end before they had brought it to a satisfactory conclusion. In the evening they returned to their homes. Visakha again questioned Mrgadhara, who told her everything. Visakha said, "What need is there of investigation? Speak to the two women thus: 'As we do not know to which of you two the boy belongs, let her who is the strongest take the boy.' When each of them has taken hold of one of the boy's hands, and he begins to cry out on account of the pain, the real mother will let go, being full of compassion for him, and knowing that if her child remains alive she will be able to see it again; but the other, who has no compassion for him, will not let go. Then beat her with a switch, and she will thereupon confess the truth as to the whole matter. That is the proper test."

Mrgadhara told this to the ministers, and so forth, as is written above, down to the words, "The king said, 'The Champa maiden is wise.'"

IV

Ghost Stories

A Working Classification
The Ghost Story
Famous Ghost Stories
The Humorous Ghost Story

In "The Technique of the Novel," Prof. Chas. F. Horne thus discusses the mystery story:

"This is the tale of the Improbable, the story that depends chiefly upon plot, external or action plot. It deals with surprise, with mystery, with the unexpected. It sees truth perhaps, but only the oddities of truth, where verity fixes a feeble hope upon coincidence, or upon ignorance, and usually gropes blindly toward that comfortable travesty of material payment for immaterial efforts which man miscalls 'poetic justice.' Such a novel may be either:

"1. The story of fear, which holds the excited reader shivering in darkness, by means of hinted horrors or by spectres frankly visible. Such visions haunt the 'Castle of Otranto' and Mrs. Radcliffe's more elaborate work.

"2. The story of intrigue, of cunning bad folks and rather idiotic good ones, of subtle schemes, intricate knaveries, and surprising secrets coming to light at just the dramatic moment needful for the triumph of virtue and defeat of vice. If one may do so without seeming to belittle the work, I would suggest 'Tom Jones' as showing the perfection of this sort of plot.

"3. The detective story, in which the plot is deliberately presented upside down. Consequences are first shown, and then worked backward to their causes, the steps being all suggested, yet made as unexpected as possible, that the reader may exercise his own wits and join the detective in an effort to solve the riddle.

"4. The novel of the unknown, the story of strange suggestion, which reaches beyond man's knowledge of his cosmos, not to terrify and amaze, but to analyze and understand, to suggest possibilities and questions, to see human nature in new lights, as Hawthorne does in "Septimius Felton," or Mr. Wells in his 'War with Mars'."

1. A Working Classification

BUT IT IS OBVIOUS THAT the various types or kinds of mystery story cannot be classified with exactness; so they may be generally divided into three groups—a broad classification which will best suit our purpose: Ghost stories, Riddle stories, and Detective stories.

Among the earliest literature the supernatural was a strong element. Its appeal was not only to curiosity, but equally if not more to wonder, awe, and terror.

In safe surroundings, people like to be frightened. The baby crows with delight when we jump at him and say, "boo!" Children huddle together in ecstasy when listening to bugaboo tales; and grown-ups read and write ghost stories with intense enjoyment of their inexplicable horror.

Though detective stories may receive an unjust opprobrium, yet ghost stories are admitted to the inner circles of literature and art.

From the days of the Witch of Endor, the superhuman personage has had an exalted place in literature.

Shakespeare, Dickens, and Washington Irving number among their characters ghosts who became famous. And in latter days, Henry James, Rudyard Kipling and F. Marion Crawford have given us ghosts well worthy of their literary predecessors.

The story founded on the supernatural is a distinct branch of the Mystery Story, and except for the principle of Question and Answer, has little in common with the other two branches.

2. The Ghost Story

THE FASCINATION OF THIS REALM of experience, which is traditional from age to age, yet always elusive, is undeniable. Few men have seen ghosts, or will confess that they have seen them. But almost everybody knows someone of the few. Haunted houses are familiar in all neighborhoods, with the same story of the roistering sceptic who will gladly pass the night alone in the haunted chamber, and give monsieur the ghost a warm welcome; but who, if not found dead in the morning, emerges pale and haggard, with a settled terror in his look, and his lips sealed forever upon the awful story of the night.

Mansions in country places are advertised for sale or hire, with the attraction of a well regulated ghost, who contents himself until driving up at midnight with a great clatter of outriders, and rumble of wheels, and brisk letting down of steps, and a bustling entrance into the house, and then no more. Staid gentlemen remember in their youth awaking in a friend's house in the summer night just in time to see the vanishing through the long window of a draped figure; a momentary pausing on the balcony outside; the sense of a penetrating, mournful look; then a vanishing; and at breakfast the cheery question of the host, "Did you see the lovely Lady Rosamond?" and a following tale of hapless love and woe.

As George William Curtis tells us, in "Modern Ghosts":

"The literature of ghosts is very ancient. In visions of the night and in the lurid vapors of mystic incantations, figures rise and smile or frown and disappear. The Witch of Endor murmurs her spell and 'an old man cometh up, and he is covered with a mantle.' Macbeth takes a bond of fate, and from Hecate's caldron, after the apparition of an armed head and that of a bloody child, 'an apparition of a child crowned, with a tree in his hand, rises.' The wizard recounts to Lochiel his warning vision, and Lochiel departs to his doom. There are stories of the Castle of Otranto and of the Three Spaniards, and the infinite detail of 'singular experiences,' which make our conscious daily life the frontier and border land of an impinging world of mystery.

"The most refined psychological speculation may extend the range of observation. But the 'mocking laughter' of desert places, the cry of the banshee, the sudden impression of a presence, the strange and fanciful popular superstitions, as they are called, in the same way that unapprehended physical conditions are sagely called nervous prostration—what is the key to them all? What is a hallucination? Who shall say conclusively that it is the thing that is not? And if it be, whence is it, and why?"

In the technical Ghost Story, as we shall now consider it, the question is certain to arise; "What was It?" And the answer must be "A ghost!"—that is an inexplicable supernatural manifestation of some sort. A rational and material explanation, as of a human being impersonating ghost, or, a mechanical contrivance responsible for mysterious sounds, takes the story out of this class at once.

Kipling's tale called "My own true ghost story" is not a ghost story at all; it is an exceedingly interesting riddle story. But "The Phantom Rickshaw" by the same author is one of the best of ghost stories.

And not only must the ghost be a real ghost, but the effect of the supernatural must permeate the whole story, the people being thus more real by contrast.

Although the reader be the strictest materialist, he must, to enjoy a ghost story, put himself in an attitude of belief in the supernatural for the time being.

As Julian Hawthorne says, in "The Lock and key library":

"A ghost story can be brought into our charmed and charming circle only if we have made up our minds to believe in the ghosts; otherwise their introduction would not be a square deal. It would not be fair, in other words, to propose a conundrum on a basis of ostensible materialism, and then, when no other key would fit, to palm off a disembodied spirit on us. Tell me beforehand that your scenario is to include both worlds, and I have no objection to make; I simply attune my mind to the more extensive scope. But I rebel at an unheralded ghostland, and declare frankly that your tale is incredible."

Miss Wilkins' story, "The Shadow on the Wall," is a perfect Ghost Story, told in a perfect way. There is no material explanation, the shadow on the wall has its own awful meaning, and the commonplace setting of the story throws into relief the weirdness of the plot.

With ghosts really seen by real people, the fictional Ghost Story has nothing in common. Hundreds of ghosts are annually brought to light in the dragnets of scientific spook catchers. But while these ghosts are interesting in and of themselves, they lack the setting of the Ghost Story of fiction, and without attempting to discuss the truth or falsity of their existence we fall back upon the assertion that a ghost belongs to the category of things naturally incredible. Notwithstanding the subconscious faith that all of us have in the possibility of phantoms, our reason refuses to accept them without proof much more conclusive than we should demand for the establishment of an everyday fact. So extreme is our reluctance to believe in such phenomena that the average man of education, if he saw a spectre with his own eyes, would, on referring the matter to his judgment, prefer to regard the apparition as an illusion, rather than accept it as a supernatural manifestation. The chances are, too, that he would be correct, inasmuch as hallucinations of vision are undeniably frequent.

Deep down in the heart of man there abides a firm belief in the power of the dead to walk upon the earth, and affright, if such be their pleasure, the souls of the living. Wise folks, versed in the sciences and fortified in mind against faith in aught that savors of the supernatural, laugh ideas of the kind to scorn; yet hardly one of them will dare to walk alone through a graveyard in the night. Or, if one be found so bold, he will surely hasten his footsteps, unable wholly to subdue the fear of sheeted spectres which may rise from the grass-grown graves, or emerge from moon-lit tombs, and follow on. For, strangely enough, the dead, if not actually hostile to the living, are esteemed dangerous and dreadful to encounter.

The real-life ghost story is largely made up of vehement protestations on the part of the narrator that "This really happened," and flat-footed inquiries as to "How do you explain it, if you don't believe in ghosts!"

But the Ghost Story of fiction tranquilly takes the belief in ghosts for granted, and goes on to create delightfully harrowing conditions, an atmosphere of deepest mystery and a problem unsolvable, except by the acceptance of a ghost.

The ghost need not be an actual character, not even an entity; it may be an impalpable shadow, or an invisible form. Or it may be, as in one story, a fearful pair of eyes that scared the hero of the tale,—and incidentally the reader,—much farther out of his wits than any conventional spectre clanking his chains might do.

And yet it is the strange fascination of this fear that attracts the reader to a ghost story.

3. Famous Ghost Stories

"What Was It?" by Fitzjames O'Brien, is a typical Ghost Story of horror. The dreadfulness of the experience is graphically pictured and the hold on the reader's attention is entirely that of the supernatural.

A parallel story is Maupassant's "The Horla."

This latter story is much longer and more elaborate, but the plots are almost identical. The Frenchman's story is told with a greater art, but is spun out to too great a length, and in some parts the horror is mere hysteria.

Among Ghost Stories with an occult moral, Kipling's "They" stands pre-eminent. This story has the element of beauty rather than horror, but it is a perfect Ghost Story none the less.

"The Turn of The Screw" is a wonderful Ghost Story. The supernatural element of its matter, aided by the supernatural element in Henry James' manner is a combination that makes a Ghost Story of distinguishment.

For stories of sheer hair-raising horror, F. Marion Crawford's Ghost Stories stand easily in the first rank. "The upper berth" is quite as terrifying a conception as the stories of O'Brien and Maupassant, but the descriptive details give an atmosphere of fright unattained by the other two. As an example of Mr. Crawford's awful word pictures we append the following extracts:

The light was growing strangely dim in the great room. As Evelyn looked, Nurse Macdonald's crooked shadow on the wall grew gigantic. Sir Hugh's breath came thick, rattling in his throat, as death crept in like a snake and choked it back. Evelyn prayed aloud, high and clear.

Then something rapped at the window, and she felt her hair rise upon her head in a cool breeze, as she looked around in spite of herself. And when she saw her own white face looking in at the window, and her own eyes staring at her through the glass, wide and fearful, and her own hair streaming against the pane, and her own lips dashed with blood, she rose slowly from the floor and stood rigid for one moment, till she screamed once and fell straight back into Gabriel's arms. But the shriek that answered hers was the fear shriek of the tormented corpse, out of which the soul cannot pass for shame of deadly sins, though the devils fight in it with corruption, each for their due share.

Sir Hugh Ockram sat upright in his deathbed, and saw and cried loud.

Slowly Nurse Macdonald's wrinkled eyelids folded themselves back, and she looked straight at the face at the window while one might count ten.

"Is it time?" she asked in her little old, far away voice.

While she looked the face at the window changed, for the eyes opened wider and wider till the white glared all round the bright violet, and the bloody lips opened over gleaming teeth, and stretched and widened and stretched again, and the shadowy golden hair rose and streamed against the window in the night breeze. And in answer to Nurse Macdonald's question came the sound that freezes the living flesh.

That low moaning voice that rises suddenly, like the scream of storm, from a moan to a wail, from a wail to a howl, from a howl to the fear shriek of the tortured dead—he who has heard knows, and he can bear witness that the cry of the banshee is an evil cry to hear alone in the deep night.

He was as brave as any of those dead men had been, and they were his fathers, and he knew that sooner or later he should lie there himself, beside Sir Hugh, slowly drying to a parchment shell. But he was still alive, and he closed his eyes a moment, and three great drops stood on his forehead.

Then he looked again, and by the whiteness of the winding-sheet he knew his father's corpse, for all the others were brown with age; and, moreover, the flame of the candle was blown toward it. He made four steps till he reached it, and suddenly the light burned straight and high, shedding a dazzling yellow glare upon the fine linen that was all white, save over the face, and where the joined hands were laid on the breast. And at those places ugly stains had spread, darkened with outlines of the features and of the tight-clasped fingers. There was a frightful stench of drying death.

As Sir Gabriel looked down, something stirred behind him, softly at first, then more noisily, and something fell to the stone floor with a dull thud and rolled up to his feet; he started back and saw a withered head lying almost face upward on the pavement, grinning at him. He felt the cold sweat standing on his face, and his heart beat painfully.

For the first time in all his life that evil thing which men call fear was getting hold of him, checking his heart-strings as a cruel driver checks a quivering horse, clawing at his backbone with icy hands, lifting his hair with freezing breath, climbing up and gathering in his midriff with leaden weight.

Yet presently he bit his lip and bent down, holding the candle in one hand, to lift the shroud back from the head of the corpse with the other. Slowly he lifted it. Then it clove to the half-dried skin of the face, and his hand shook as if someone had struck him on the elbow, but half in fear and half in anger at himself, he pulled it, so that it came away with a little ripping sound. He caught his breath as he held it, not yet throwing it back, and not yet looking. The horror was working in him, and he felt that old Vernon Ockram was standing up in his iron coffin, headless, yet watching him with the stump of his severed neck.

While he held his breath he felt the dead smile twisting his lips. In sudden wrath at his own misery, he tossed the death-stained linen backward, and looked at last. He ground his teeth lest he should shriek aloud.

Perhaps unique amongst Ghost Stories is the one by Mr. Crawford entitled "The Doll's Ghost." It would seem difficult to conceive a story of the ghost of a little girl's doll, that should be neither melodramatic nor ridiculous, but Mr. Crawford accomplished this, and the little sketch, while a true Ghost Story, is pathetic and charming.

4. The Humorous Ghost Story

RARELY, AND ONLY IN THE hands of a master, may a Ghost Story be treated with levity. The humorous touch is dangerous in connection with the supernatural. But the whimsical genius of Frank R. Stockton surmounted all difficulties and gave us two delicious humorous Ghost Stories, of which we quote a few lines.

The figure was certainly that of John Hinckman in his ordinary dress, but there was a vagueness and indistinctness about it which presently assured me that it was a ghost. Had the good old man been murdered, and had his spirit come to tell me of the deed, and to confide to me the protection of his dear—? My heart fluttered but I felt that I must speak. "Sir," said I.

"Do you know," interrupted the figure, with a countenance that indicated anxiety, "whether or not Mr. Hinckman will return tonight?"

I thought it well to maintain a calm exterior, and I answered:

"We do not expect him."

"I am glad of that," said he, sinking into the chair by which he stood. "During the two years and a half that I have inhabited this house, that man has never before been away for a single night. You can't imagine the relief it gives me."

As he spoke, he stretched out his legs and leaned back in the chair. His form became less vague, and the colors of his garments more distinct and evident, while an expression of gratified relief succeeded to the anxiety of his countenance.

"Two years and a half!" I exclaimed. "I don't understand you."

"It is fully that length of time," said the ghost, "since I first came here. Mine is not an ordinary case."

THE GHOST SMILED.

"I must admit, however," he said, "that I am seeking this position for a friend of mine, and I have reason to believe that he will obtain it."

"Good heavens!" I exclaimed. "Is it possible that this house is to be haunted by a ghost as soon as the old gentleman expires? Why should this family be tormented in such a horrible way? Everybody who dies does not have a ghost walking about his house."

"Oh, no!" said the spectre. "There are thousands of positions of the kind which are never applied for. But the ghostship here is a very desirable one, and there are many applicants for it. I think you will like my friend, if he gets it."

"Like him!" I groaned.

The idea was horrible to me.

The ghost evidently perceived how deeply I was affected by what he had said, for there was a compassionate expression on his countenance.

I drew my chair a little nearer to her, and as I did so the ghost burst into the room from the doorway behind her. I say burst, although no door flew open and he made no noise. He was wildly excited, and waved his arms above his head. The moment I saw him, my heart fell within me. With the entrance of that impertinent apparition, every hope fled from me. I could not speak while he was in the room.

I must have turned pale, and I gazed steadfastly at the ghost, almost without seeing Madeline, who sat between us.

"Do you know," he cried, "that John Hinckman is coming up the hill. He will be here in fifteen minutes, and if you are doing anything in the way of love-making, you had better hurry it up. But this is not what I came to tell you. I have glorious news! At last I am transferred! Not forty minutes ago a Russian nobleman was murdered by the Nihilists. Nobody ever thought of him in connection with an immediate ghostship. My friends instantly applied for the situation for me, and obtained my transfers."

V

Riddle Stories

Some Notable Riddle Stories
The Nature of the Riddle Story and Its Types

Riddle Stories, as we have chosen to designate them, are Mystery Stories concerned with a question and answer of absorbing interest, but one which in no way implies or includes the work of a detective, either professional or amateur. As a rule, Riddle Stories are not based upon a crime, but on some mysterious situation which is apparently inexplicable, but which turns out to have a most rational and logical explanation.

1. Some Notable Riddle Stories

"The Sending Of Dana Da," by Kipling, is one of the best stories of this type.

Here we have such a commonplace, ordinary medium as kittens, so employed as to make an unsolvable riddle.

When a man who hates cats wakes up in the morning and finds a little squirming kitten on his breast, or puts his hand into his ulster pocket and finds a little half-dead kitten where his gloves should be, or opens his trunk and finds a vile kitten among his dress shirts or goes for a long ride with his mackintosh strapped on his saddlebow and shakes a little sprawling kitten from its folds when he opens it, or goes out to dinner and finds a little blind kitten under his chair, or stays at home and finds a writhing kitten under the quilt, or wriggling among his boots, or hanging, head downward, in his tobacco jar, or being mangled by his terrier in the veranda—when such a man finds one kitten, neither more nor less, once a day in a place where no kitten rightly could or should be, he is naturally upset. When he dare not murder his daily trove because he believes it to be a manifestation, an emissary, an embodiment, and half a dozen other things all out of the regular course of nature, he is more than upset. He is actually distressed.

No one could know the truth until told and the explanation is entirely logical and satisfactory. Indeed, as the author says, finally: "Consider the gorgeous simplicity of it all."

A clever Riddle Story is one by Cleveland Moffett, entitled "The Mysterious Card."

In this story, a New Yorker, while in a Paris restaurant, is presented with a card by a charming and richly clad lady. The card bore some French words written in purple ink, but not knowing that language he was unable to make out their meaning.

He returned at once to his hotel to inquire concerning the message on the card.

In the words of the story:

Proceeding directly to the office and taking the manager aside, Burwell asked if he would be kind enough to translate a few words of French into English. There were no more than twenty words in all.

"Why, certainly," said the manager, with French politeness, and cast his eyes over the card. As he read, his face grew rigid with astonishment, and, looking at his questioner sharply, he exclaimed: "Where did you get this, monsieur?"

Burwell started to explain, but was interrupted by: "That will do, that will do. You must leave the hotel."

"What do you mean?" asked the man from New York, in amazement.

"You must leave the hotel now—tonight—without fail," commanded the manager, excitedly.

Now it was Burwell's turn to grow angry, and he declared heatedly that if he wasn't wanted in this hotel there were plenty of others in Paris where he would be welcome. And, with an assumption of dignity, but piqued at heart, he settled his bill, sent for his belongings, and drove up the Rue de la Paix to the Hotel Bellevue, where he spent the night. The next morning he met the proprietor, who seemed to be a good fellow, and, being inclined now to view the incident of the previous evening from its ridiculous side, Burwell explained what had befallen him, and was pleased to find a sympathetic listener.

"Why, the man was a fool," declared the proprietor. "Let me see the card; I will tell you what it means." But as he read, his face and manner changed instantly.

"This is a serious matter," he said sternly. "Now I understand why my confrère refused to entertain you. I regret, monsieur, but I shall be obliged to do as he did."

"What do you mean?"

"Simply that you cannot remain here."

With that he turned on his heel, and the indignant guest could not prevail upon him to give any explanation.

"We'll see about this," said Burwell, thoroughly angered.

The rest of the story is a succession of the hero's unfortunate experiences in endeavoring to solve the mystery of the card. He referred it to his dearest friend, to a detective agency, to the American Minister, and finally to his wife, but in every case the reader of the card turned from him in horror and dismay and refused to see or speak to him again. In the sequel to the story, called "The Mysterious Card Unveiled" the mystery is explained to the satisfaction of the reader.

Of course the best Riddle Story of its kind ever written is that masterpiece of Frank R. Stockton, "The Lady or The Tiger?" but this principle of leaving a question unanswered is not to be advised for any writer not possessing Stockton's peculiar genius.

As well as short-stories, there are many entire novels with a mystery interest but which are in no sense Detective Stories. "The Woman In White" is a good example. This book is said to have been the most popular serial story ever printed. On the publication day of the weekly in which the story was appearing in parts, the street in front of the office was thronged with people anxiously waiting for a new instalment of the adventures of Laura Fairleigh, Ann Catherick, the treacherous Baronet, and the diabolically fascinating Count Fosco.

The secret of Collins's power lies not in mere description but in suggestion. He excites us not by what he tells us but what he does not tell us. The compelling interest which holds the reader of "The Woman In White" is due less to the vivid description of dramatic incidents than to the artful suggestion of some impending fate.

2. The Nature of the Riddle Story and its Types

THE DISTINGUISHING FEATURE OF THE Riddle Story is that the reader should be confronted with a number of mysterious facts of which the explanation is reserved till the end. Now this reservation of the final solution, in order to pique the reader's curiosity, excite his ingenuity, and lead him on to an unexpected climax, is a quite legitimate artistic effect. The only question to be asked about it in any particular instance is whether it succeeds, whether the effect is really accomplished? And for its success two primary qualifications are necessary,—first, that the mystery should really be mysterious; second, that the explanation should really explain.

The Riddle Story, then, is based entirely on a puzzle whose solution is a clever trick of the author and usually not to be guessed by the reader. Unlike the Detective Story, there are no clues, either true or misleading. The reader goes swiftly from his first surprise to sustained wonder, and then to an intense and abiding curiosity that lasts until the solution is flashed upon him. The plot is meant to catch the reader napping, and seldom indeed is he wide awake enough to solve the riddle.

A distinct type of Riddle Story is that which describes a search for lost treasure. In so far as the searchers encounter mysterious conditions, or the reader is held in suspense concerning the meaning or outcome of the situations, in so far is the tale a Riddle Story. But to be a real Riddle Story, the mystery must be carefully built up, sustained and finally revealed with careful and coherent sequences.

Poe's story, "The Oblong Box," is one of the greatest Riddle Stories ever written. The mystery is seemingly inexplicable. The interest is intense and the conditions partake of all the elements of ghastliness and horror. The solution is unguessable but entirely logical, and Poe's inimitable workmanship makes the story a masterpiece of its kind.

Equally clever, in a totally different vein, is Kipling's "His Wedded Wife," and, different still, Aldrich's "Marjory Daw."

In both of these, the surprise is perfect, and so inherent a part of the plot, so skillfully and swiftly worked up, that all demands of the true Riddle Story are complied with.

In some Riddle Stories the interest is not in the unraveling of the web, but in the weaving of it. In De Quincey's "The Avenger" this is the case, and also in Bulwer's "A Strange Story." It is the strangeness of the story that captivates in these instances. The maze of mystery and hazard, and the confidence that it will all be made plain to us at last, provide sufficient charm to the lover of the Riddle Story. Crime and its detection have no part here, but mystery and paradox reign supreme.

Another sort of Riddle Story employs the cypher or cryptogram plot, but this is of such importance as to require a chapter to itself.

Poe's "Gold Bug" includes both the cryptogram and the buried treasure, and is of course the greatest story built upon either or both of these plots.

A novel by James DeMille is called "The Cryptogram," and the cypher is the main point of the story. But more often, cypher or secret writing is used as a side issue or a picturesque device in a stronger mystery plot.

VI

Detective Stories

1. What is a Detective Story?

The class of fiction which we shall group under this head must include all stories where the problem is invented and solved by the author and set forth in such a way as to give an astute reader opportunities for guessing or reasoning out the answer.

An actual detective need not necessarily figure in the story, but detective work must be done by some of the characters.

There must be crime or apparent crime or attempted crime. But whether the problem is one of murder, robbery or kidnapping,— whether it be solved by evidence, deduction or a cryptogram,—it is detected, not guessed, and this is the main element in our classification.

The average or typical Detective Story of today is the detailed narrative of the proceedings of an individual of unusual mental acumen in unraveling a mystery.

Strictly speaking, a detective is a member of the police organization or of a private detective agency. But for fictional purposes he may be such, or he may be anyone with what is called "detective instinct" or a taste for detective work.

It appears that in its earliest days the word "detective" meant merely a shadower or follower.

A curious old story in Harper's Magazine for 1870 begins thus:

The remarkable skill and penetration shown by our modern detectives in "shadowing" suspected persons until sufficient proof has been obtained to warrant their arrest is illustrated by the daily history of crime. By the term "shadowing" is meant that vigilant watch kept upon the culprit by someone who follows him like his own shadow, and to do this successfully indicates no small degree of skill on the part of the "detective." This last expression recalls to memory some strange facts which came to my knowledge in the early part of my life, and I can never meet the term in print or hear it in conversation without a painful reminiscence.

The story goes on to relate the harrowing experiences of a criminal who was shadowed by the ghost of his victim, and ends thus:

Such is the story in connection with the first use of the term "detective," and I never meet it, either in voice or in print, without thinking of Captain Walton, and the fearful retribution unfolded in his history.

But this old story is not a Detective Story according to our classification, it is a simple Ghost Story. It is only of interest in referring to the earliest use of our word "detective."

2. Rise of the Detective Story

THE DETECTIVE STORY AS WE know it was first written by Poe, yet he never used the descriptive word, nor was Dupin a detective, either professional or amateur, for when Poe wrote his immortal Dupin tales, the name "Detective" Stories had not been invented; the detective of fiction not having been as yet discovered. And the title is still something of a misnomer, for many narratives involving a puzzle of some sort, though belonging to the category which we shall discuss, are handled by the writer without expert detective aid. Sometimes the puzzle solves itself through operation of circumstance; sometimes somebody who professes no special detective skill happens upon the secret of its mystery; once in a while some venturesome genius has the courage to leave his enigma unexplained. But ever since Gaboriau created his Lecoq, the transcendent detective has been in favor; and Conan Doyle's famous gentleman analyst has given him a fresh lease of life, and reanimated the stage by reverting to the method of Poe. Sherlock Holmes is Dupin redivivus, and mutatus mutandis; personally he is a more stirring and engaging companion, but so far as kinship to probabilities or even possibilities is concerned, perhaps the older version of him is the more presentable. But in this age of marvels we seem less difficult to suit in this respect than our forefathers were.

The fact is, meanwhile, that, in the Riddle Story, the detective was an afterthought, or, more accurately, a deus ex machina to make the story go. The riddle had to be unriddled; and who could do it so naturally and readily as a detective? The detective, as Poe saw him, was a means to this end; and it was only afterwards that writers perceived his availability as a character. Lecoq accordingly becomes a figure in fiction, and Sherlock, while he was yet a novelty, was nearly as attractive as the complications in which he involved himself.

Detective Story writers in general, however, encounter the obvious embarrassment that their detective is obliged to lavish so much attention on the professional services which the exigencies of the tale demand of him, that he has very little leisure to attend to his own personal equation—the rather since the attitude of peering into a millstone is not, of itself, conducive to elucidations of oneself; the professional endowment obscures all the others. We ordinarily find, therefore, our author dismissing the individuality of his detective with a few strong black-chalk outlines, and devoting his main labor upon what he feels the reader will chiefly occupy his own ingenuity with,— namely, the elaboration of the riddle itself. Reader and writer sit down to a game, as it were, with the odds, of course, altogether on the latter's side,—apart from the fact that a writer sometimes permits himself a little cheating. It more often happens that the detective appears to be in the writer's pay, and aids the deception by leading the reader off on false scents. Be that as it may, the professional sleuth is in nine cases out of ten a dummy by malice prepense; and it might be plausibly argued that, in the interest of pure art, that is what he ought to be. But genius always finds a way that is better than the rules, and it will be found that the very best riddle stories contrive to drive character and riddle side by side, and to make each somehow enhance the effect of the other.

The intention of the above paragraph will be more precisely conveyed if we include under the name of detective not only the man from the central office, but also anybody whom the writer may, for ends of his own, consider better qualified for that function. The latter is a professional detective so far as the exigencies of the tale are concerned, and what becomes of him after that, nobody need care,—there is no longer anything to prevent his becoming, in his own right, the most fascinating of mankind.

Before Poe's or Gaboriau's stories, appeared the "Memoirs of Vidocq."

This work, thought by many to be largely fiction, is the history of a clever villain who became a detective, though never called by that name. He was a Secret Agent, and is called on his own title page, Principal Agent of the French Police. His memoirs are old-fashioned, dull and uninteresting, but they show glimmerings of the kind of reasoning that later marked the Fiction Detective.

Perhaps Gaboriau was the first author to use the terminology, since become so familiar, of detective, clues, deduction, etc.

Poe ascribed to his Dupin, "analytic ability," and this is all that is claimed for the conventional detective of fiction, though perhaps more acutely described by Brander Matthews as "imaginative ratiocination."

Poe goes further in saying Dupin's work was "The result of an excited or perhaps a diseased intelligence." This statement may have mirrored the author's own mind, for, while making no assertion, Professor Matthews observes that he should understand anyone who might declare that Poe had mental disease raised to the nth power, and we have long since been told that "great wits are sure to madness near allied."

3. The Detective-Fictive and Real

BUT IT IS THIS VERY principle that marks the difference between the detective in fiction and in real life. The cleverest detectives in life are not men of diseased intellect, however greatly developed may be their powers of ratiocination. It is just that touch of abnormality, of superhuman reasoning, that makes a Transcendent Detective.

Again, the work of the fiction detective is always successful. Naturally, because his work is planned to this end by the author. The fiction detective plays his game with marked cards. Though seemingly groping in the dark, he is walking a definite path laid straight to a definite end. He is pushed off on false scents, but pulled back and set right again by an adjusting power which does not exist in the case of real detectives.

Indeed, the sooner the writer of detective fiction realizes that the detective of fiction has little in common with the detective in real life, the better is that author equipped for his work.

The real detective, for one thing, is rarely a man of culture or high ideals. The fiction detective is usually an aristocrat, unfortunately impoverished, or working at his art for art's sake.

The real detective, however great his analytic ability, often finds that he cannot apply it to his case. The fiction detective never has this experience; he finds his case ready made and perfectly fitted to his powers.

The real detective finds little or nothing in the way of useful material clues. The fiction detective finds his properties laid ready to his hand at the right moment. Dropped handkerchiefs, shreds of clothing, broken cuff-links, torn letters,—all are sprinkled in the path ahead of him, like roses strewn before a bride.

Even Nature lends a helping hand to the favored detective of fiction. Usually "A light snow had fallen the evening before." This snow is declared by credible witnesses to have begun at one psychological moment, and stopped at another; thus allowing the inevitable display of footprints of certain sizes, shapes and superimposition. Indeed the laws of nature are willing to give way, at need, and vegetation takes on unusual qualities to help along the good work. Sherlock Holmes continually finds his indicative footprints on turf or grass plot, and of course the criminal is identified at once.

But the real detective seldom if ever finds these helpful footprints at the right time and place. In case of his need of them, the obstinate ground is hard and unimpressionable; or the snow is melting and shows only oblong holes; or the grass refuses to present a clear and definite impression; or even if fairly respectable muddy footprints appear on a nice, clean, hard-wood floor, they are so incomplete in outline that they might have been made by any well-advertised shoe.

The criminals and suspects in fiction must presumably wear shoes made for the purpose, with flat level soles that touch the floor at all points and leave an exact working diagram, instead of a shapeless blotch with ragged edges.

Similarly with finger-prints. Though carefully impressed in incriminating places by the fiction criminals, in real life they are rarely found where they can be of use. The finger-prints found on the discarded empty frame of the Mona Lisa have not yet led to the recovery of the picture; whereas in fiction they would long ago have put the thief behind bars.

No, the fiction detective is not a real person, anymore than the fairy godmother is a real person; but both are honored and popular celebrities in the realm of fiction.

And if one would realize the immense superiority of the fiction detective for fiction purposes he has only to read any of the occasionally published "true detective stories," or even those which are founded on actual cases.

4. Fiction versus Fact

MANY YEARS AGO, OLD-FASHIONED FAMILY papers published stories, beneath whose titles a line in parenthesis read, "Founded on fact." Such tales were invariably uninteresting, and at last the editors learned not to publish them.

A true tale of a criminal problem and its solution is uninteresting because it is not planned to be interesting. The technique of the detective story calls for the same kind of planning and preparation on the part of the author as does a successful act of legerdemain. The prestidigitator takes a rabbit out of a silk hat, but unless he had planned for it beforehand he couldn't do it. What he might take, unplanned, out of the hat,—its leather band or gilt stamped lining,—would be of no interest to his audience.

It is the old-fashioned or the inexperienced author who thinks that an incident which has come within his own experience or that of his friends, is necessarily available for a story.

One of Gelett Burgess' celebrated Bromides is, "Now this thing really happened!" And it is a fortunate writer who escapes the occasional, "I've something to tell you about my neighbor's mother-in-law; I know it to be true, and you can have it for one of your stories!" The enthusiastic generosity of the speaker causes his face to glow with the delight of "helping an author," and how can you tell him that not one in a million such anecdotes would be of use to you, and that moreover, your head and note-book are both crammed with material of the right sort waiting to be used?

Your helpful friend makes no claim save that his story is a fact, and he can never understand how apt is this quality to bar it from fiction. He can never understand the difference between fact and truth—truth, the wide universal element that must be adhered to; and fact, the petty and narrow incident that is rarely of interest, and often indeed contradicts truth.

Realism, according to its American master, Mr. W.D. Howells, is nothing more than the truthful treatment of material; and in Mr. Howells' hands this treatment has produced writings of absorbing interest. But it is an equally truthful treatment of material that appears in the Social and Personal column of the Miller's Corners Weekly Gazette, or in the Congressional Record, yet we are not interested in either.

But in the plot of a Detective Story, or in the mental makeup of the detective, realism finds little place—as much as you wish in the material details, in the clues, the inquest, or the suspected butler, but the keynote of the story itself is that of pure fiction.

It must seem to be true as fairy stories seem true to children. You must persuade your readers to believe it, as Peter Pan wheedled his audience into believing in fairies; but "Founded on Fact" or "Elaborated from the Records of a Real Detective," is fatal to the interest of a Detective Story.

Let the argument ring true, let the accessories be realistic, let the situations be logical and the conditions plausible; but let the magic of the unreal detective twinkle through it all as fairies dance in real moonlight. Sustain the interest by a subtly woven chain of events that leads unerringly to the climax in a way the uncertainties of real life can never do. Lead your readers on to the re-solution of the problem, whose terms have been stated in logical sequence straight through the book.

The uninitiate say, "You're so fond of detective stories, I suppose you read all the murder trials in the newspapers."

On the contrary, a true lover of detective fiction never reads detailed newspaper accounts of crime.

Why should he? He reads detective fiction for the enjoyment of the complete and finished entertainment therein provided. The statement of the problem, the interesting development, the breathless chase after false clues, the never tiring return to the right track and the final rounding up of the explanatory solution—he knows when he starts he will be disappointed in no particular. Every mystery will be explained and the fun is in trying to explain them himself. As an antagonist at chess, he pits himself against his opponent, the author, and endeavors to foresee and understand his feints and maneuvers. But to whatever degree he succeeds in this, a complete revelation awaits him at the end.

In real life a criminal case reported in the papers gives no assurance of ultimate solution, gives no assurance that all the developments are intentional and go to make up a complete and harmonious whole; that the whole story is so balanced and poised, so coherent and interdependent as to give only satisfaction to its readers.

In a word, the Detective Story of fiction is art; the accounts in the newspapers of the crimes of the day are merely the truthful treatment of material; and the latter, unless seen through the medium of an artist, is not of interest to the lover of the Detective Story.

Another argument against realism in this field of fiction, is the fact that from the nature of its plot the details of a Detective Story are often unlovely. The newspapers delight in realistic description of the gruesome elements of crime. The Detective Story writer in the interests of his art glosses these over, not only because they have no necessary bearing on his theme, "The riddle and its solution," but because they jar on the reader's taste and disturb his economy of attention.

Poe, whose imagination was beyond all bounds, thus speaks of realism:

"The defenders of this pitiable stuff uphold it on the ground of its truthfulness. Taking the thesis into question, this truthfulness is the one overwhelming defect. An original idea that—to laud the accuracy with which the stone is hurled that knocks us in the head! A little less accuracy might have left us more brains. And here are critics absolutely commending the truthfulness with which only the disagreeable is conveyed! In my view, if an artist must paint decayed cheeses, his merit will lie in their looking as little like decayed cheeses as possible!"

And so, the writer of detective fiction pictures as much cheese and as little decay as he may.

The tale of horror, or of gruesome interest, which not only paints the decayed cheese with realism, but with exaggeration, is not a Detective Story, it belongs in another class.

Of course all this applies to Detective Stories which are constructed in harmony with the unwritten but inexorable laws which require the aforementioned qualities. To be sure, plenty of Detective Stories are written which violate every requirement of true technique, but these are not in our argument.

This point is well discussed by Mr. Cecil Chesterton:

"I have read hundreds of such tales which made excellent reading so long as the mystery subsisted, but of which the conclusion was unspeakably weak and far-fetched and in some cases absolutely unintelligible. Nothing is more irritant in a detective story than that even one mysterious circumstance should remain at the end unexplained. Yet the writers appear to imagine that it is quite sufficient if they have thought of some sort of explanation of the central mystery, while a hundred attendant facts, introduced solely to puzzle or mislead the reader, are left without even a suggestion to illumine them.

"Indeed the conclusion ought to be not merely plausible, but in a sense inevitable. The reader ought not indeed to expect it, but he ought to feel afterwards that he ought to have expected it. To explain the problem at the last moment, as is often done, by introducing new circumstances at which he could not possibly have guessed, is merely to leave him labouring under a half-conscious sense of injury and resentment, and rightly so, for he has been cheated into attempting to solve a puzzle which, as it turns out, was for him quite insoluble. In an ideal detective story all the clues to the true solution ought to be there from the first, but so overlaid as to pass unnoticed. If anyone wishes to see how this can be done, let him read attentively the first two or three chapters of 'The Moonstone,' by Wilkie Collins. Here the all-important conversation between Franklyn Blake and the doctor is given at length, but in such a context as to appear a mere incident designed to throw light on a phase of Franklyn's temperament."

Recently there has been published a book of short true Detective Stories.[1] These are of so little interest as to be almost unreadable. The preface says, "Crime in itself, is painful and sometimes repulsive, but a study of the methods of criminal investigation by which difficult problems are solved and the guilty brought to justice is entertaining and may be profitable."

While the foregoing is true, the study of the methods of criminal investigation is not entertaining to the reader, unless written as literature,—indeed, as fiction.

A simple description of a crime and the methods pursued in regard to its investigation make dry reading. The setting, the characters, the atmosphere, of a well-constructed story are necessary to make it entertaining.

The preface we quote goes on to state frankly that the detectives they tell about, work in the most prosaic manner imaginable, but they somehow manage to get results, and that is what counts in the police world.

Here we have merely facts. Their work doubtless is prosaic, but a prosaic account of it entertains nobody.

Let us look at one of the stories of this book. It begins thus:

---

1. Adventures of the World's Greatest Detectives, George Barton.

One crisp December morning Louis Hanier, a Frenchman, the owner of a little wine shop on West Twenty-sixth street in New York City, was found dead in the hallway of his home. The bullet of a .38-caliber revolver was discovered in the man's heart.

He had been murdered.

Well, and suppose he had been. Outside of the impulse of common humanity, the reader has no interest in Louis Hanier. This is not the reader's fault. He cannot be expected to have an interest in a mere name. But the author of detective fiction will arouse such an interest in the reader's mind before announcing the murder.

Next we are informed that

> The problem was to find the man who had committed the crime—to pick him out of the millions of people in New York City. The newspapers were filled with the horrible story. The coroner's inquest attracted the usual crowd of morbid-minded people. The minor police officials became very busy—and accomplished nothing. After the hysterics were over, the puzzle finally made its way to the one man in New York City who had the genius and persistence to solve it.

The problem, as stated, rouses no thrill of expectancy. There is no cause for interest, wonder, or curiosity. It is all "The truthful treatment of the material," and has no art in presentation or implication. Now we come to the description of the detective:

In a few minutes the door opened and a strong, well-built man with square shoulders shambled into the room. He had gray hair, a thick nose, blue eyes, a smooth face and a perpetual smile. He glanced about him in a furtive way and realized that he was in the presence of the triumvirate of talent that ruled the under-world of Paris. He squared himself as a man would who was preparing to be on the defensive.

A commonplace description of a commonplace man, which does not in the least provoke our desire to know more of him.

And so, through the dull and prosy story, we read the uneventful proceedings which led to the conviction of the criminal.

Never would Detective Stories have a vogue if they were written thus. But it is not so much the presence of the facts as the absence of the fiction that is the trouble. The plain unvarnished statements leave us no room for expectation, no reason for surprise. Detective Stories are not built around truthful incidents.

Another volume of "True Stories of Crime," by Arthur Train, gives us this foreword:

"The narratives composing this book are literally true stories of crime. In a majority of the cases the author conducted the prosecutions himself, and therefore may claim to have a personal knowledge of that whereof he speaks. While no confidence has been abused, no essential facts have been omitted, distorted, or colored, and the accounts themselves, being all matters of public record, may be easily verified. The scenes recorded here are not literature but history, and the characters who figure in them are not puppets of the imagination, but men and women who lived and schemed, laughed, sinned and suffered, and paid the price when the time came, most of them, without flinching. A few of those who read these pages may profit perhaps by their example; others may gain somewhat in their knowledge of life and human nature; but all will agree that there are books in the running brooks, even if the streams be turbid, and sermons in stones, though these be the hearts of men. If in some instances the narratives savor in treatment more of fiction than of fact, the writer must plead guilty to having fallen under the spell of the romance of his subject, and he proffers the excuse that, whereas such tales have lost nothing in accuracy, they may have gained in the truth of their final impression."

The stories in this book may be interesting to a lover of human documents, but to the reader of "Detective Stories," they are dull and prosy, except where "the writer fell under the spell of romance."

5. The Interest of the Detective Story

POE SAYS, IN SPEAKING OF the writer's plan:

"A skillful literary artist has constructed a tale. If wise, he has not fashioned his thoughts to accommodate his incidents; but having conceived, with deliberate care, a certain unique or single effect to be wrought out, he then invents such incidents—he then combines such events as may best aid him in establishing this preconceived effect. If his very initial sentence tend not to the outbringing of this effect, then he has failed in his first step. In the whole composition there should be no word written, of which the tendency direct or indirect, is not to the one pre-established design. And by such means, with such care and skill, a picture is at length painted which leaves in the mind of him who contemplates it with a kindred art, a sense of the fullest satisfaction."

The interest of the Detective Story depends entirely on its rousing the reader's curiosity. Every detail of its plan must sustain and heighten an intense determination to know the solution of the riddle; and as this curiosity becomes keener, and this determination more inflexible, so much more necessary is it that the explanation shall be adequate and satisfactory.

But this result cannot be achieved if the author undertakes his work in the spirit shown by the authors of "The Wrecker," Robert Louis Stevenson and Lloyd Osbourne, when they say:

"We had long been at once attracted and repelled by that very modern form of the police novel or mystery story, which consists in beginning your yarn anywhere but at the beginning, and finishing it anywhere but at the end; attracted by its peculiar interest when done, and the peculiar difficulties that attend its execution; repelled by that appearance of insincerity and shallowness of tone, which seems its inevitable drawback. For the mind of the reader, always bent to pick up clews, receives no impression of reality or life, rather of an airless, elaborate mechanism; and the book remains enthralling, but insignificant, like a game of chess, not a work of human art. It seemed the cause might lie partly in the abrupt attack; and that if the tale were gradually approached, some of the characters introduced (as it were) beforehand, and the book started in the tone of a novel of manners and experience briefly treated, this defect might be lessened and our mystery seem to inhere in life."

The technique of the Mystery Story does not permit it to be a novel of manners, and yet the manners must not be neglected. If a Detective Story is to be literature, what may be called its manners must be looked after quite as carefully as its plot, though by no means with such conspicuous result. Intrinsic merit must be the real basis of its interest.

It is the care and artistic conscience that count, notwithstanding the ideas expressed in "The Wrecker."

Mr. Julian Hawthorne truly says, "You cannot make a riddle story by beginning it and then trusting to luck to bring it to an end. You must know all about the end and the middle before thinking, even, of the beginning; the beginning of a riddle story, unlike those of other stories and of other enterprises, is not half the battle; it is next to being quite unimportant, and, moreover, it is always easy. The unexplained corpse lies weltering in its gore in the first paragraph; the inexplicable cipher presents its enigma at the turning of the opening page. The writer who is secure in the knowledge that he has got a good thing coming, and has arranged the manner and details of its coming, cannot go far wrong with his exordium; he wants to get into action at once, and that is his best assurance that he will do it in the right way. But O! what a labor and sweat it is; what a planning and trimming; what a remodeling, curtailing, interlining; what despairs succeeded by new lights, what heroic expedients tried at the last moment, and dismissed the moment after; what wastepaper baskets full of futilities, and what gallant commencements all over again! Did the reader know, or remotely suspect, what terrific struggles the writer of a really good detective story had sustained, he would regard the final product with a new wonder and respect, and read it all over once more to find out how the troubles occurred. But he will search in vain; there are no signs of them left; no, not so much as a scar. The tale moves along as smoothly and inevitably as oiled machinery; obviously, it could not have been arranged otherwise than it is; and the wise reader is convinced that he could have done the thing himself without half trying. At that, the weary writer smiles a bitter smile; but it is one of the spurns that patient merit of the unworthy takes. Nobody, except him who has tried it, will ever know how hard it is to write a really good detective story. The man or woman who can do it can also write a good play (according to modern ideas of plays), and possesses force of character, individuality, and mental ability. He or she must combine the intuition of the artist with the talent of the master mechanic, but will seldom be a poet, and will generally care more for things and events than for fellow creatures."

Mr. Julian Hawthorne also discusses this question of interest as maintained by the inverse order of narration.

" . . . One charge, at least, does lie against the door of the riddle-story writer; and that is, that he is not sincere; he makes his mysteries backward, and knows the answer to his riddle before he states its terms. He deliberately supplies his reader, also, with all manner of false scents, well knowing them to be such; and concocts various seeming artless and innocent remarks and allusions, which in reality are diabolically artful, and would deceive the very elect. All this, I say, must be conceded; but it is not unfair; the very object, ostensibly, of the riddle story is to prompt you to sharpen your wits; and as you are yourself the real detective in the case, so you must regard your author as the real criminal whom you are to detect."

It is safe to say that Poe's conception of the interest-element in the Detective Story, as illustrated by his three great tales, "The Murders in the Rue Morgue," "The Purloined Letter," and "The Mystery of Marie Rôget," was that the great point was not the fascination of the mystery itself but the interest the reader would take in following the successive steps of reasoning by which the crime was ferreted out. The reader is thus turned into an analytical observer who not only delights in the mental ingenuity exhibited by the detective, but actually joins with him in working out the intricacies of a problem which, though at first seemingly insoluble, is at length mastered entirely. Thus his admiration for the "investigator" is happily coupled with his own delight in unraveling the skein which the author has woven expressly for the purpose, as Poe himself expresses it when he admits all the merits of the device, but modestly disclaims that his ingenious stories have real greatness. He speaks thus about them:

"They owe most of their popularity to being something in a new key. I do not mean to say that they are not ingenious—but people think them more ingenious than they are—on account of their method and air of method. In the 'Murders in the Rue Morgue,' for instance, where is the ingenuity of unraveling a web which you yourself (the author) have woven for the express purpose of unraveling? The reader is made to confound the ingenuity of the supposititious Dupin with that of the writer of the story."

Of course the ingenuity of the author and that of his character are identical, as they are in the case of Conan Doyle and Sherlock Holmes.

Doctor Doyle admits frankly his indebtedness to Poe, and though he claims another prototype than Dupin for his detective, yet he makes this acknowledgment:

"Edgar Allan Poe, who, in his carelessly prodigal fashion, threw out the seeds from which so many of our present forms of literature have sprung, was the father of the detective tale, and covered its limits so completely that I fail to see how his followers can find any fresh ground which they can confidently call their own. For the secret of the thinness and also of the intensity of the detective story is that the writer is left with only one quality, that of intellectual acuteness, with which to endow his hearer. Everything else is outside the picture and weakens the effect. The problem and its solution must form the theme, and the character drawing is limited and subordinate. On this narrow path the writer must walk, and he sees the footmarks of Poe always in front of him. He is happy if he ever finds the means of breaking away and striking out on some little side-track of his own."

6. A Summing Up

To SUM UP, THEN, WE must agree that for devotees the Detective Story sets a stirring mental exercise, with just enough of the complex background of life to distinguish it from a problem in mathematics. Whatever thrills of horror are excited come by way of the intellect, never starting directly in the emotions. The reader divests himself of sympathy, and applies to every situation the dry light of reason. It is only when one's reason is baffled, leaving the murder unexplained or the ghost at large, that one feels privileged to shudder. And such a shudder is remarkably different from a start that is unthinking. The Detective Story applies reason to some of the big half-mysteries of human conduct; and the result for the ordinary reader is not dissimilar to that felt by the philosopher when trying to square with his poor apparatus the secrets of Nature and Providence.

VII

The Detective

The all-important character of the Detective Story is, of course, the Detective. He is not only the Star Performer, but the reason for the Detective Story itself. What Mr. Hawthorne calls the Transcendent Detective is the detective of fiction. Such a one is made, not born.

As Mr. Vance Thompson puts it:

"Readers who pant breathlessly after Sherlock Holmes and his like should give thanks to Edgar Allan Poe; when he invented Dupin in the 'Murders in the Rue Morgue,' he created once for all the type of the detective in fiction. In all the years it has not changed very much. Sherlock Holmes still sits in his dark, superheated chamber; he is drugged with tobacco and opium; he maintains the 'profound silence' that distinguished Poe's cold analyst; indeed, one may be sure that the type will live for another eighty years."

1. The Real Detective and His Work

BUT WE HAVE ALREADY AGREED that this fiction detective has little or nothing to do with the real detective. When M. Goron, one of the greatest of French detectives, was asked concerning this, he replied:

"I dare say I have read nearly all the detective stories, those of Poe and Gaboriau, and 'Sir Doyle's' clever tales. Like everyone else I love to follow the twists and turns that lead to the end of these apparently inexplicable problems. It is a good intellectual sport—like playing chess. But do not imagine for a moment," and M. Goron was emphatic, "that it has anything at all to do with practical police work. Nothing at all. It is not by such subtle, opium-bred guesswork and fine-drawn deduction that criminals are detected."

M. Goron's theory is that in thief-taking, as in everything else, system is of prime importance; and after that the most effective auxiliary of the detective is Chance. Almost always it is by a lucky hazard that the shrewd criminal is brought down. For instance, the taking of Magne; it was tragically absurd—for the farce ended in the basket of wet sawdust under the guillotine.

In fact, detectives of real life invariably scorn the transcendent detective of fiction, and, in his turn, the story-book detective scoffs at the methods of the Central Office men.

Mr. Arthur C. Train, in "Courts Criminal and The Camorra," thus mildly satirizes our detective of fiction and sets him quite apart from the genuine article:

"The sanctified tradition that a detective was an agile person with a variety of side whiskers no longer obtains even in light literature, and the most imaginative of us is frankly aware of the fact that a detective is just a common man earning (or pretending to earn) a common living by common and obvious means. Yet in spite of ourselves we are accustomed to attribute superhuman acuteness and a lightning-like rapidity of intellect to this vague and romantic class of fellow-citizens. The ordinary work of a detective, however, requires neither of these qualities. Honesty and obedience are his chief requirements, and if he have intelligence as well, so much the better, provided it be of the variety known as horse sense. A genuine candidate for the job of Sherlock Holmes would find little competition. In the first place, the usual work of a detective does not demand any extraordinary powers of deduction at all.

"There are a very large number of persons who go into the detective business for the same reason that others enter the ministry—they can't make a living at anything else. Provided he has squint eyes and a dark complexion, almost anybody feels that he is qualified to unravel the tangled threads of crime.

"The real detective is the one who, taking up the solution of a crime or other mystery, brings to bear upon it unusual powers of observation and deduction and an exceptional resourcefulness in acting upon his conclusions. Frankly, I have known very few such, although for some ten years I have made use of a large number of so-called detectives in both public and private matters. As I recall the long line of cases were these men have rendered service of great value, almost everyone resolves itself into a successful piece of mere spying or trailing. Little ingenuity or powers of reason were required. Of course, there are a thousand tricks that an experienced man acquires as a matter of course, but which at first sight seem almost like inspiration.

"There is no more reason to look for superiority of intelligence or mental alertness among detectives of the ordinary class than there is to expect it from clerks, stationary engineers, plumbers, or firemen. While comparisons are invidious, I should be inclined to say that the ordinary chauffeur was probably a brighter man than the average detective. This is not to be taken in derogation of the latter, but as a compliment to the former. There is more reason why he should be.

"The telephone is the modern detective's chief ally, and he relies upon rapidity more than upon deduction. Under present conditions it is easier to overtake a crook than to reason out what he will probably do. In fact, the old-fashioned 'deductive detective' is largely a man of the past. The most useless operator in the world is the one who is 'wedded to his own theory' of the case—the man who asks no questions and relies only on himself. Interject a new element into a case and such a man is all at sea. In the meantime the criminal has made his 'get away.'

"In the story-books your detective scans with eagle eye the surface of the floor for microscopic evidences of crime. His mind leaps from a cigar ash to a piece of banana peel and thence to what the family had for dinner. His brain is working all the time. His gray matter dwarfs almost to insignificance that of Daniel Webster or the Hon. Benjamin F. Butler. It is, of course, all quite wonderful and most excellent reading, and the old-style sleuth really thought he could do it! Nowadays, while the fake detective is snooping around the back piazza with a telescope, the real one is getting the 'dope' from the village blacksmith or barber (if there is any except on Saturday nights) or the girl that slings the pie at the station. These folk have something to go on. They may not be highly intelligent, but they know the country, and, what is more important, they know the people. All the brains in the world cannot make up for the lack of an elementary knowledge of the place and the characters themselves. It stands to reason that no strange detective could form as good an opinion as to which of the members of your household would be most likely to steal a piece of jewelry as you could yourself. Yet the old-fashioned Sherlock knew and knows it all.

"There is no mystery about such work, except what the detective himself sees fit to enshroud it with. Most of us do detective work all the time without being conscious of it. Simply because the matter concerns the theft of a pearl, or the betraying of a business or professional secret, or the disappearance of a friend, the opinion of a stranger becomes no more valuable. And the chances are equal that the stranger will make a bungle of it.

"The national detective agency with its thousands of employees who have, most of them, grown up and received their training in its service, is a powerful organization, highly centralized, and having an immense sinking fund of special knowledge and past experience.

"This is the product of decades of patient labor and minute record. The agency which offers you the services of a Sherlock Holmes is a fraud, but you can accept as genuine a proposition to run down any man whose picture you may be able to identify in the gallery. The day of the impersonator is over. The detective of this generation is a hard-headed business man with a stout pair of legs."

Thus, the reader will observe that there are just a few more real detectives still left in the business—if you can find them. Incidentally, they one and all take off their hats to Scotland Yard. They will tell you that the Englishman may be slow (fancy an American Inspector of Police wearing gray suede gloves and brewing himself a dish of tea in his office at four o'clock!), but that once he goes after a crook he is bound to get him—it is merely a question of time. I may add that in the opinion of the heads of the big agencies the percentage of ability in the New York Detective Bureau is high—one of them going so far as to claim that fifty percent of the men have real detective ability—that is to say "brains." That is rather a higher average than one finds among clergymen and lawyers, yet it may be so.

Mr. John Wilson Murray, one of the noted detectives, says simply in his "Memoirs of a Great Detective":

"There is no magic about the detective business. A detective walking along the street does not suddenly hear a mysterious voice whisper 'Banker John Jones has just been robbed of $1,000,000.' He does not turn the corner and come upon a perfect stranger, and then, because the stranger has a twisted cigar in his mouth, suddenly pounce upon him and exclaim: 'Aha, villain that you are! give back to Banker Jones the $1,000,000 you stole ten minutes ago!' The detective business is of no such foolish and impossible character. Detectives are not clairvoyants, or infallible prophets, or supernatural seers. They possess no uncanny powers and no mantle of mysterious wonder-working. I remember a few years ago I was subpoenaed before a grand jury in the City of New York to testify on a matter pertaining to a prisoner, whose record I knew here in Canada. The foreman of that jury was a man prominent in New York's business life. When I was called he looked at me and suddenly said:

"'Inspector Murray, what crimes have been committed within the past hour in New York, and who committed them?'

"'I have not the slightest idea,' I replied.

"'Oh, ho! So you cannot go out and put your hands on every man who has committed a crime? You are a detective, yet cannot do that?' he said.

"'I am not that kind of detective,' I replied. 'When I get a guilty man it usually is by hard work or good luck, and often by both.'

"'Thank the Lord we've found a detective who is not greater than God,' he said.

"As a matter of fact the detective business is a plain ordinary business, just like a lawyer's business, a doctor's business, a railway manager's business. It has its own peculiarities because it deals with crime, with the distorted, imperfect, diseased members of the social body, just as a surgeon's business deals with the distorted, imperfect, diseased members of the physical body. But it is not an abnormal or phenomenal or incomprehensible business. There is nothing done in it, nothing accomplished by any detective, that is not the result of conscientious work, the exercise of human intelligence, an efficient system of organization and intercommunication, and good luck. A good detective must be quick to think, keen to analyse, persistent, resourceful, courageous. But the best detective in the world is a human being, neither half-devil nor half-god, but just a man with the attributes or associates that make him successful in his occupation.

"The best detective, therefore, is a man who instinctively detects the truth, lost though it may be in a maze of lies. By instinct he is a detective. He is born to it; his business is his natural bent. It would be a platitude to say the best detectives are born, not made. They are both born and made for the business. The man who, by temperament and make-up, is an ideal detective, must go through the hard years of steady work, must apply himself, and study and toil in making himself what he is born to be. Sandow was born to be a strong man, but, if he had not developed himself by hard work, he would not have become the strongest man of his time. As a detective advances in his business he will find that the more he studies and works, the stronger his powers of intuition, of divination, of analysis become. A very simple broad illustration will prove this. If a detective is chasing a criminal from country to country, and has learned, by study of the extradition treaties, that a certain country offers a better haven than another, he may save himself many a weary mile by going to the country where his common sense tells him his man is more likely to be. A mechanical knowledge of the use of tools, a knowledge of the effects of poisons, a knowledge of the ways of banking, of the habits of life of the various classes, in various callings, a knowledge of crooks, and, above all, a knowledge of human nature, in whatsoever way manifest, are invaluable elements of the equipment of a good detective."

2. Fictive Detective Material

THE USUAL WORK, THEN, OF a real detective does not demand the extraordinary powers of the fiction detective. But the plots selected by fiction writers for their stories are the cases that do demand it. And this, because it interests the reader's imagination, piques his curiosity and makes possible the solution of the problem.

The assertion of Sherlock Holmes founded on the aphorism that truth is stranger than fiction is in itself fiction.

"My dear fellow," said Sherlock Holmes, as we sat on either side of the fire in his lodgings at Baker Street, "life is infinitely stranger than anything which the mind of man can invent. We would not dare to conceive the things which are really mere commonplaces of existence. If we could fly out of that window hand in hand, hover over this great city, gently remove the roofs, and peep in at the queer things which are going on, the strange coincidences, the plannings, the cross-purposes, the wonderful chains of events, working through generations, and leading to the most outré results, it would make all fiction, with its conventionalities and foreseen conclusions, most stale and unprofitable."

"And yet I am not convinced of it," I answered. "The cases which come to light in the papers are, as a rule, bald enough, and vulgar enough. We have in our police reports realism pushed to its extreme limits, and yet the result is, it must be confessed, neither fascinating nor artistic."

"A certain selection and discretion must be used in producing a realistic effect," remarked Holmes. "This is wanting in the police report, where more stress is laid perhaps upon the platitudes of the magistrate than upon the details, which to an observer contain the vital essence of the whole matter."

The first-quoted remarks of Holmes are pure fiction and are introduced by the author to give an effect which he desires. But it is the truth that a certain selection and discretion must be used regarding plots, and it is this that makes or mars the interest of the Detective Story.

Poe's three masterpieces of detective fiction are perfectly conceived, constructed and completed, entirely in his imagination. But when he undertook "The Mystery of Marie Rôget" he worked upon a plot founded on fact; the story of a real murder of a real girl, with the result that there was no dénouement, and the editors of the magazine in which the story originally appeared, decided that it would be best to omit the latter half of the tale, and we are told that it was never printed in full. Though interesting in its statement of the problem, the solution never could be reached, and the story, as a Detective Story, was a failure.

3. The Transcendent Detective

THE STATUS OF THE FICTION detective is so well-defined that it is the habit of authors to scoff at it, and endeavor to convince us that their own detectives are true to life.

For instance, in a Detective Story of some merit, called "The House Opposite," by Elizabeth Kent, the detective says:

"I am aware that the detective of fiction is always supposed to be omniscient, but my profession, Doctor, is just like any other. There is no hocus-pocus about it. To succeed in it requires, in the first place, accurate and most minute powers of observation, unlimited patience, the capacity of putting two and two together. Add to this an unprejudiced mind, and last, but not least, respect, amounting to reverence, for any established fact."

Many authors of late think it argues themselves original to indulge in a fleer at the methods of Sherlock Holmes. A typical example of this often-used device is here quoted from "Midnight at Mears House," by Harrison J. Holt:

As I smoked, my gaze travelled idly about the room till it rested upon the big brass candlestick smeared with melted tallow which we had found that morning on the dining table.

"If I were only another Sherlock Holmes now," I thought, "I should be able to reconstruct the entire tragedy from that candlestick, supposing of course the murderer used it. An intelligent smell of the wick would tell me what particular brand of matches he used to light it, and it would only be necessary to visit the one dealer who kept them and get from him a photograph of the man, or a sufficiently accurate description of him, to make his arrest a matter of only a trifling difficulty." I chuckled at the absurdity of the notion. It seemed however, hardly more far-fetched and ridiculous than some of the great detective's marvellous exploits, which millions of readers have found plausible enough, I daresay, though I was never one of them.

Yielding to a sudden whim, I took down the candlestick from the mantelpiece.

"I should at least be able to deduce a few simple facts from a really scientific examination of it," I argued, facetiously—"whether the criminal was right or left-handed, for instance, or wore ready-made clothes, or if he was suffering from rheumatism or the whooping cough. It must be all here somewhere."

I proceeded gravely to smell of the wick. It had a decidedly burnt odour, due very likely, I imagined, to its having been lighted. It humiliated me, however, to be unable to decide how it had been lighted. I could not for the life of me make out whether the murderer had used wax vesta, safety-matches, ordinary parlour matches, or those infernal things tipped with sulphur commonly known as "hell-sticks."

He might even have lighted it with one of those self-igniting platinum-wire and alcohol devices, or with flint and steel, or by rubbing two sticks together, for all I could tell.

I began to feel discouraged. Doubtless there were imprints of his fingers as thick as flies and as plain as billboards all over the candlestick itself, if I could only find them. He would at any rate have left the damning mark of his thumb somewhere upon its shining surface: they were always considerate enough to do that—in the detective stories. It was part of the game. But again I was doomed to disappointment. We must have blurred the impressions through our inconceivable stupidity in touching the thing at all. We should have known enough, I reflected, to have left it alone till we had a chance to study it through a high-powered telescope.

This is good-natured satire, and the very fact that it contains the kernel of truth makes it effective.

4. Pioneer Detectives of Fiction

THOUGH LACKING THE TITLE, THE Transcendent Detective doubtless makes his earliest appearance in the person of M. Dupin.

The first allusion to Dupin's peculiar talents is found in "The Murders in the Rue Morgue":

"At such times I could not help remarking and admiring (although from his rich ideality I had been prepared to expect it) a peculiar analytic ability in Dupin. He seemed, too, to take an eager delight in its exercise—if not exactly in its display—and did not hesitate to confess the pleasure thus derived. He boasted to me, with a low chuckling laugh, that most men, in respect to himself, wore windows in their bosoms, and was wont to follow up such assertions by direct and very startling proofs of his intimate knowledge of my own. His manners at these moments were frigid and abstract; his eyes were vacant in expression; while his voice, usually a rich tenor, rose into a treble which would have sounded petulantly but for the deliberateness and entire distinctness of the enunciation. Observing him in these moods, I often dwelt meditatively upon the old philosophy of the Bi-Part Soul, and amused myself with the fancy of a double Dupin—the creative and the resolvent.

"Let it not be supposed, from what I have just said, that I am detailing any mystery, or penning any romance. What I have described in the Frenchman was merely the result of an excited, or perhaps of a diseased, intelligence."

Poe deliberately remarks on Dupin's diseased intelligence, thus providing a defence against any implication that the detective's powers were superhuman.

Analogous to this is Conan Doyle's characterization of Sherlock Holmes.

To quote from "A Study in Scarlet," where Holmes makes his first appearance:

"Well, I have a trade of my own. I suppose I am the only one in the world. I'm a consulting detective, if you can understand what that is. Here in London we have lots of government detectives and lots of private ones. When these fellows are at fault they come to me, and I manage to put them on the right scent. They lay all the evidence before me, and I am generally able, by the help of my knowledge of the history of crime, to set them straight. There is a strong family resemblance about misdeeds, and if you have all the details of a thousand at your finger-ends, it is odd if you can't unravel the thousand and first. Lestrade is a well known detective. He got himself into a fog recently over a forgery case, and that was what brought him here."

"And these other people?"

"They are mostly sent out by private inquiry agencies. They are all people who are in trouble about something, and want a little enlightening. I listen to their story, they listen to my comments, and then I pocket my fee."

"But do you mean to say," I said, "that without leaving your room you can unravel some knot which other men can make nothing of, although they have seen every detail for themselves?"

"Quite so. I have a kind of intuition that way. Now and again a case turns up which is a little more complex. Then I have to bustle about and see things with my own eyes. You see, I have a lot of special knowledge which I apply to the problem, and which facilitates matters wonderfully. Those rules of deduction laid down in that article which aroused your scorn are invaluable to me in practical work. Observation with me is second nature."

However, the later detective thus scorns the earlier one when Watson, thinking to flatter, compares Holmes to Dupin:

"No doubt you think that you are complimenting me in comparing me to Dupin," he observed. "Now, in my opinion, Dupin was a very inferior fellow. That trick of his of breaking in on his friends' thoughts with an apropos remark after a quarter of an hour's silence is really very showy and superficial. He had some analytical genius, no doubt; but he was by no means such a phenomenon as Poe appeared to imagine."

"Have you read Gaboriau's works?" I asked. "Does Lecoq come up to your idea of a detective?"

Sherlock Holmes sniffed sardonically.

"Lecoq was a miserable bungler," he said, in an angry voice; "he had only one thing to recommend him, and that was his energy. That book made me positively ill. The question was how to identify an unknown prisoner. I could have done it in twenty-four hours. Lecoq took six months or so. It might be made a text-book for detectives to teach them what to avoid."

But Dupin himself speaks with equal contempt of his predecessor in the profession. He says:

"Vidocq, for example, was a good guesser, and a persevering man. But without educated thought, he erred continually by the very intensity of his investigations. He impaired his vision by holding the object too close. He might see, perhaps, one or two points with unusual clearness, but in so doing he necessarily lost sight of the matter as a whole."

However, as Conan Doyle himself declares:

"In a work which consists in the drawing of detectives," he once wrote, "there are only one or two qualities which one can use, and an author is forced to hark back upon them constantly, so that every detective must really resemble every other detective to a greater or less extent. There is no great originality required in devising or constructing such a man, and the only possible originality which one can get into a story about a detective is in giving him original plots and problems to solve, as in his equipment there must be an alert acuteness of mind to grasp facts and the relation which each of them bears to the other."

The detectives who follow in the straight path trodden by these pioneers are legion.

Among the best known is The Thinking Machine, hero of two series of stories by the late Jacques Futrelle.

The Thinking Machine whose name was Professor Van Dusen was remotely German. For generations his ancestors had been noted in the sciences; he was the logical result of the master mind. First and above all he was a logician. At least thirty-five years of the half-century or so of his existence had been devoted exclusively to proving that two and two always equal four, except in unusual cases, where they equal three or five, as the case may be. He stood broadly on the general proposition that all things that start must go somewhere, and was able to bring the concentrated mental force of his forefathers to bear on a given problem. Incidentally it may be remarked that Professor Van Dusen wore a No. 8 hat.

5. Recent Detectives of Fiction

AMONG THE BEST OF LATELY-WRITTEN detective stories are two by Gaston Leroux, "The Mystery of the Yellow Room" and "The Perfume of the Lady in Black." In these stories two detectives figure. Though they are professional and amateur, they are not opposed, as is so often deemed necessary for dramatic effect, but have a far subtler contrast. Rouletabille is a delightful character and satisfactory in his procedure, while Larsan is a genius. And yet these detectives are little known to the reading public. It is perhaps because Sherlock Holmes was first in the modern field, and perhaps partly because his name appears in the titles of the collections of stories about him, that his name is so well known. Mr. Cecil Chesterton is right in saying:

"Sir Arthur Conan Doyle is at least entitled to claim the honour of being the only novelist since Dickens, one of whose creations has become a popular proverb. It is easy to test this. Mr. Rudyard Kipling is generally considered a popular writer. Mulvaney is probably Mr. Kipling's most popular creation. But let anyone say in an assembly of twenty average men chosen at random from the street—'That man is quite a Mulvaney.' Perhaps two men will understand the reference; perhaps one; quite possibly none. But let him say 'That man is quite a Sherlock Holmes.' The recognition will be instantaneous and unanimous. A man who had not heard of Holmes would be more singular than a man who could not sign his own name. Sir Arthur is the only writer of our time who has done this, and he has never done it twice. He has done more ambitious work than the Sherlock Holmes tales, but none of it has passed into the language."

Many series of really good detective stories have been published in magazines, and later in book form, but not one reader in ten remembers the detective's name.

Luther Trant and Craig Kennedy, Ledroit Conners and Eugene Valmont, are all first class fiction detectives yet their names are not household words like Sherlock Holmes. So with The Man in the Corner, Average Jones, Ashton-Kirk and Paul Beck. So with Scientific Sprague and Astro.

Though each of these is a real deductive detective, each has his own personal bent.

Sprague, Trant and Kennedy are scientific,—sometimes so much so that they run great danger of losing the popular interest.

This is Sprague's manner as the author, Francis Lynde, shows us:

"When my attention was first called to such things—it was on a case in the Department of Justice in which I was required to give expert testimony—I was very strongly impressed with the crudities of the ordinary detective methods. I said to myself that what was needed was someone who could apply good, careful laboratory practice; a habit of observation which counts nothing too small to be weighed and measured."

"Go on," said Maxwell.

"The idea came to me that I'd like to try it on, and I did. My theory is correct. Human beings react under certain given conditions just as readily, and just as inevitably, as the inorganic substances react in a laboratory experiment."

"I'M NOT SURE THAT I can explain it so that you will understand, but I'll try. In the first place, it is necessary to go at these little problems with a perfectly open mind—the laboratory mind, which is neither prejudiced nor prepossessed nor in anyway concerned with anything but the bare facts. Reason, and the proper emphasis to be placed upon each fact as it comes to bat, are the two needful qualities in any problem solving—and about the only two."

"I CAN NO MORE TELL you, Dick, than I can explain why, to a majority of people, white is white and black is black. For my own satisfaction I define the 'how' as a natural growth, favored by habit and training, of the scientific attitude; the mental slant which, if given free play, almost unconsciously notes, marks, deduces, reasons; deeming nothing too small or too trifling to go toward making up the whole of any conclusion. More than that, in my own case the faculty is able to hold itself workably aloof from the ordinary distractions of conversation and the like. It goes on, using the outward senses when it needs them, to be sure, but only as aids to the developing of its own little film in its own little dark room. Do you get the idea?"

6. The Scientific Detective of Fiction

THIS IS ALL LEGITIMATE, BUT tinged rather deeply with science. Craig Kennedy (created by Arthur B. Reeve) says:

"It has always seemed strange to me that no one has ever endowed a professorship in criminal science in any of our large universities."

Craig Kennedy laid down his evening paper and filled his pipe with my tobacco. In college we had roomed together, had shared everything, even poverty, and now that Craig was a professor of chemistry and I was on the staff of the Star, we had continued the arrangement. Prosperity found us in a rather neat bachelor apartment on the Heights, not far from the University.

"Why should there be a chair in criminal science?" I remarked argumentatively, settling back in my chair. "I've done my turn at police headquarters reporting, and I can tell you, Craig, it's no place for a college professor. Crime is just crime. And as for dealing with it, the good detective is born and bred to it. College professors for the sociology of the thing, yes; for the detection of it give me a Byrnes."

"On the contrary," replied Kennedy, his cleancut features betraying an earnestness which I knew indicated that he was leading up to something important, "there is a distinct place for science in the detection of crime."

"Colleges have gone a long way from the old ideal of pure culture. They have got down to solving the hard facts of life—pretty nearly all except one. They still treat crime in the old way, study its statistics and pore over its causes and the theories of how it can be prevented. But as for running the criminal himself down, scientifically, relentlessly— bah! we haven't made an inch of progress since the hammer and tongs method of your Byrnes."

"Doubtless you will write a thesis on this most interesting subject," I suggested, "and let it go at that."

"No, I am serious," he replied, determined for some reason or other to make a convert of me. "I mean exactly what I say. I am going to apply science to the detection of crime, the same sort of methods by which you trace out the presence of a chemical, or run an unknown germ to earth. And before I have gone far, I am going to enlist Walter Jameson as an aide. I think I shall need you in my business."

"How do I come in?"

"Well, for one thing, you will get a scoop, a beat,—whatever you call it in that newspaper jargon of yours."

However, Kennedy's methods and descriptions, though interesting to scientific minds, are often above the heads of a popular audience. For instance such a paragraph as this,—and in his stories they abound:

"This twelfth series is interesting. So far only radium, thorium, and uranium are generally known. We know that the radio-active elements are constantly breaking down, and one often hears uranium, for instance, called the 'parent' of radium. Radium also gives off an emanation, and among its products is helium, quite another element. Thus the transmutation of matter is, within certain bounds, well known today to all scientists like yourself, Professor Kennedy. It has even been rumored but never proved that copper has been transformed into lithium—both members of the hydrogen-gold group, you will observe. Copper to lithium is going backward, so to speak. It has remained for me to devise this protodyne apparatus by which I can reverse that process of decay and go forward in the table,—can change lithium into copper and copper into gold. I can create and destroy matter by protodyne."

7. The New Psychology in Detective Stories

ALL OF THE STORIES OF Craig Kennedy published under the title of "The Silent Bullet" are based upon the various chapters of Professor Hugo Münsterberg's delightful book called "On The Witness Stand." It is hoped and believed by Professor Münsterberg that these psychological experiments will yet become a practical means of the conviction of criminals.

They have not as yet obtained official sanction, but as Professor Münsterberg writes in a personal letter, "I myself did not expect such changes to come very soon, as on the one side there is still too much difference of opinion and of interpretation among the psychologists, and on the other side the whole problem of the experts before court is still in too confused a condition. An amateurish introduction of fancy experiments by lawyers who are dilettantists in psychology would certainly bring more confusion than help. All that has been gained is that evidently the lawyers and judges have become more conscious of the responsibilities which are involved wherever psychical functions are in play. I also think that the use of the brutal methods of extorting confessions and so on has been diminished."

A series of stories called "The Achievements of Luther Trant," by Edwin Balmer and William MacHarg, details the experiments of a detective who follows even more closely the experiments described in Professor Münsterberg's book. The Foreword of this series tells its own story:

"Except for its characters and plot, this book is not a work of the imagination.

"The methods which the fictitious Trant—one-time assistant in a psychological laboratory, now turned detective—here uses to solve the mysteries which present themselves to him, are real methods; the tests he employs are real tests.

"Though little known to the general public, they are precisely such as are being used daily in the psychological laboratories of the great universities—both in America and Europe—by means of which modern men of science are at last disclosing and defining the workings of that oldest of world mysteries—the human mind.

"The facts which Trant uses are in no way debatable facts; nor do they rest on evidence of untrained, imaginative observers. Innumerable experiments in our university laboratories have established beyond question that, for instance, the resistance of the human body to a weak electric current varies when the subject is frightened or undergoes emotion; and the consequent variation in the strength of the current depending directly upon the amount of emotional disturbance, can be registered by the galvanometer for all to see. The hand resting upon an automatograph will travel toward an object which excites emotion, however capable its possessor may be of restraining all other evidence of what he feels.

"If these facts are not used as yet except in the academic experiments of the psychological laboratories and the very real and useful purpose to which they have been put in the diagnosis of insanities, it is not because they are incapable of wider use. The results of the 'new psychology' are coming everyday closer to an exact interpretation. The hour is close at hand when they will be used not merely in the determination of guilt and innocence, but to establish in the courts the credibility of witnesses and the impartiality of jurors, and by employers to ascertain the fitness and particular abilities of their employees.

"Luther Trant, therefore, nowhere in this book needs to invent or devise an experiment or an instrument for any of the results he here attains; he has merely to adopt a part of the tried and accepted experiments of modern, scientific psychology. He himself is a character of fiction; but his methods are matters of fact."

A similar method is hinted at in "The Thinking Machine" stories. Mr. Futrelle says:

"Finally, with my hand on her pulse—which was normal—I told her as brutally as I could that her husband had been murdered. Her pulse jumped frightfully and as I told her the cause of death it wavered, weakened and she fainted. Now if she had known her husband were dead—even if she had killed him—a mere statement of his death would not have caused that pulse."

8. Other Types

"THE MAN IN THE CORNER," by Baroness Orczy, introduces himself in this way:

The man in the corner pushed aside his glass, and leant across the table.

"Mysteries!" he commented. "There is no such thing as a mystery in connection with any crime, provided intelligence is brought to bear upon its investigation."

A comparatively novel type of detective is Astro. This individual figures in a series of stories published in book form under title of "The Master of Mysteries." These stories are by Mr. Gelett Burgess, but are published anonymously.

The detective is a poseur, of a languid and self-conscious personality, who pretends to be a palmist and crystal-gazer, but who really is simply a clever sleuth detective. At his seances, conducted in draped and darkened apartments, he wears Oriental costume and is exceedingly bored. Instead of a Doctor Watson, he has for assistant a beautiful young woman named Valeska. The romance of these two runs through the book, and culminates on the last page with a "clergyman and witnesses." But the stories are properly constructed detective fiction of good technique.

VIII

DEDUCTION

Deduction, in a definite and restricted sense, is the motif of most of the detective stories of today. It is an unusually perspicacious analytic deduction from inconspicuous clues that we call ratiocination, or more familiarly, the detective instinct.

1. Ratiocination in Early Detective Stories

A STORY QUOTED IN ONE of the earlier chapters, called "The Sultan and his Three Sons," is a very ancient specimen of analytic deduction. Though it is, in turn, doubtless founded on an even older tale.

Centuries later the stories of the Sultan's sons reappeared almost verbatim in a story by the Chevalier de Mailly, entitled "Voyage et Aventure des Trois Princes de Sarendip," which appeared in 1719. De Mailly's version is substantially as follows:

The three princes, starting out on their journey, encounter a camel-driver who has lost one of his herd. They have noticed the tracks of such an animal though not seen him and when asked by the driver if they know of his whereabouts, the eldest replies: "Was he not blind?" The second: "Did he not have a tooth out?" The third: "Was he not lame?" The camel-driver assents with delight to the questions and continues on his way rejoicing. Not finding his camel, however he returns and accuses them of bantering with him. "To prove that what we say is so," said the eldest, "your camel carried butter on one side and honey on the other." The second: "And a lady rode the camel," etc. In the same manner they are arrested for theft and sentenced. And in the same manner the camel is refound and an explanation is given: "I judged that the camel was blind because I noticed that on one side of the road all the grass was gnawed down, while the other side was untouched. Therefore, I inferred that he had but one eye, else he would not have left the good to eat the poor grass." "I found in the road mouthfuls of half-chewed herbage the size of a tooth of just such an animal," etc.

Nearly thirty years later Voltaire practically repeated the story in his "Zadig," related thus:

Zadig found by experience that the first month of marriage, as it is written in the book of Zend, is the moon of honey, and that the second is the moon of wormwood. He was sometime afterward obliged to repudiate Azora, who became too difficult to be pleased; and he then sought for happiness in the study of nature. "No man," said he, "can be happier than a philosopher who reads in this great book which God hath placed before our eyes. The truths he discovers are his own, he nourishes and exalts his soul, he lives in peace; he fears nothing from men; and his tender spouse will not come to cut off his nose."

Possessed of these ideas he retired to a country house on the banks of the Euphrates. There he did not employ himself in calculating how many inches of water flow in a second of time under the arches of a bridge, or whether there fell a cube line of rain in the month of the Mouse more than in the month of the Sheep. He never dreamed of making silk of cobwebs, or porcelain of broken bottles; but he chiefly studied the properties of plants and animals and soon acquired a sagacity that made him discover a thousand differences where other men see nothing but uniformity.

One day, as he was walking near a little wood, he saw one of the queen's eunuchs running toward him, followed by several officers who appeared to be in great perplexity, and who ran to and fro like men distracted, eagerly searching for something they had lost of great value. "Young man," said the first eunuch, "hast thou seen the queen's dog?" "It is a female," replied Zadig. "Thou art in the right," returned the first eunuch. "It is a very small she spaniel," added Zadig; "she has lately whelped; she limps on the left forefoot, and has very long ears." "Thou hast seen her," said the first eunuch, quite out of breath. "No," replied Zadig, "I have not seen her, nor did I so much as know that the queen had a dog."

Exactly at the same time, by one of the common freaks of fortune, the finest horse in the king's stable had escaped from the jockey in the plains of Babylon. The principal huntsman and all the other officers ran after him with as much eagerness and anxiety as the first eunuch had done after the spaniel. The principal huntsman addressed himself to Zadig, and asked him if he had not seen the king's horse passing by. "He is the fleetest horse in the king's stable," replied Zadig; "he is five feet high, with very small hoofs, and a tail three feet and a half in length; the studs on his bit are gold of twenty-three carats, and his shoes are silver of eleven pennyweights." "What way did he take? Where is he?" demanded the chief huntsman. "I have not seen him," replied Zadig, "and never heard talk of him before."

The principal huntsman and the first eunuch never doubted but that Zadig had stolen the king's horse and the queen's spaniel. They therefore had him conducted before the assembly of the grand desterham who condemned him to the knout, and to spend the rest of his days in Siberia. Hardly was the sentence passed when the horse and the spaniel were both found. The judges were reduced to the disagreeable necessity of reversing their sentence; but they condemned Zadig to pay four hundred ounces of gold for having said that he had not seen what he had seen. This fine he was obliged to pay; after which he was permitted to plead his cause before the counsel of the grand desterham, when he spoke to the following effect:

"Ye stars of justice, abyss of sciences, mirrors of truth, who have the weight of lead, the hardness of iron, the splendor of the diamond, and many properties of gold: Since I am permitted to speak before this august assembly, I swear to you by Oramades that I have never seen the queen's respectable spaniel, nor the sacred horse of the king of kings. The truth of the matter was as follows: I was walking toward the little wood, where I afterwards met the venerable eunuch, and the most illustrious chief huntsman. I observed on the sand the traces of an animal, and could easily perceive them to be those of a little dog. The light and long furrows impressed on little eminences of sand between the marks of the paws plainly discovered that it was a female, whose dugs were hanging down, and that therefore she must have whelped a few days before. Other traces of a different kind, that always appeared to have gently brushed the surface of the sand near the marks of the forefeet, showed me that she had very long ears; and as I remarked that there was always a slighter impression made on the sand by one foot than the other three, I found that the spaniel of our august queen was a little lame, if I may be allowed the expression.

"With regard to the horse of the king of kings, you will be pleased to know that, walking in the lanes of this wood, I observed the marks of a horse's shoes, all at equal distances. This must be a horse, said I to myself, that gallops excellently. The dust on the trees in the road that was but seven feet wide was a little brushed off, at the distance of three feet and a half from the middle of the road. This horse, said I, has a tail three feet and a half long, which being whisked to the right and left, has swept away the dust. I observed under the trees that formed an arbor five feet in height, that the leaves of the branches were newly fallen; from whence I inferred that the horse had touched them, and that he must therefore be five feet high. As to his bit, it must be gold of twenty-three carats, for he had rubbed his bosses against a stone which I knew to be a touchstone, and which I have tried. In a word, from the marks made by his shoes on flints of another kind, I concluded that he was shod with silver eleven deniers fine."

This is only a single instance of Zadig's ratiocination, but Voltaire gives us many others.

Poe's stories follow precisely this same narrow path, and after him trail Gaboriau, Du Boisgobey, Conan Doyle and the rest of the long procession.

2. Deduction Used in Everyday Life

BUT THIS ADAPTATION FROM ORIENTAL lore is no disparagement of Poe's talent. He was the first to write a coherent and self-contained story whose interest depends solely on the application of human intelligence to the solution of a mystery. Others have done so since; and this peculiar trait of analytic deduction is by no means confined to detectives or to Detective Story writers. The average human being in everyday life, often without being definitely conscious of it, performs absolute ratiocination. It is only the extreme application of this principle, or an unusual demonstration of it in connection with interesting circumstances, that gives interest to a Detective Story.

As Professor Matthews says:

"Huxley has pointed out that the method of Zadig is the method which has made possible the incessant scientific discovery of the last century. It is the method of Wellington at Assaye, assuming that there must be a ford at a certain place on the river because there was a village on each side. It is the method of Grant at Vicksburg, examining the knapsacks of the Confederate soldiers slain in a sortie to see if these contained rations, which would show that the garrison was seeking to break out because the place was untenable."

Also it was the method of the North American Indian following a trail. It is the method of the housemother in dealing with her servants, her children, and perhaps her husband. In all walks of life it is more or less an available and practiced method, and this is one reason why it is of popular interest in a story, because it mirrors, though with the necessary exaggeration of art, the possibilities of everyday life and the working results of everyday philosophy.

For much philosophy goes to the make-up of a Detective Story. And it is to a great extent the truth and worth of this philosophy that determines the value of the story.

In Mr. Chesterton's opinion:

"The idea that you cannot put good philosophy into certain art-forms is as absurd and mischievous as the idea that you cannot put good workmanship into them. Mr. Shaw, for example, has put his philosophy into the form of ordinary melodrama in 'The Devil's Disciple.' Ibsen has put his into the form of pantomimic extravaganza in 'Peer Gynt.' There is no earthly reason why a man with a specific talent for the work should not put ideas as profound into the form of the detective story. For after all the essence of the detective story is the presence of visible phenomena with a hidden explanation. And that, when one comes to think of it, is the essence of all the philosophies."

3. The Analytical Element in the Detective Story

It is the invention and construction of the story, setting forth the puzzle in an attractive way, and continuing with sound reasoning and philosophy to a logical and satisfactory end, that arrests and holds the reader's attention. And the skilled author devises every circumstance of his tale with the one intent, to what the reader's desire to arrive at the author's solution simultaneously with, if not ahead of the author's detective.

To quote Poe himself:

"The mental features discoursed of as the analytical are, in themselves, but little susceptible of analysis. We appreciate them only in their effects. We know of them, among other things, that they are always to their possessor, when inordinately possessed, a source of the liveliest enjoyment. As the strong man exults in his physical ability, delighting in such exercises as call his muscles into action, so glories the analyst in that moral activity which disentangles. He derives pleasure from even the most trivial occupations bringing his talent into play. He is fond of enigmas, of conundrums, of hieroglyphics; exhibiting in his solution of each a degree of acumen which appears to the ordinary apprehension preternatural. His results, brought about by the very soul and essence of method, have, in truth, the whole air of intuition."

It is this air of intuition, even though we know it is absolutely not intuition, that we seek in Detective Stories. We wish to be amazed by the mysteries, sure that in due time they will be explained. We enjoy being confronted by absolute paradox.

As Maupassant says, "How weak our head is, and how quickly it is terrified and goes astray, as soon as we are struck by a small incomprehensible fact. Instead of concluding with these simple words: 'I do not understand because the cause escapes me,' we immediately imagine terrible mysteries as supernatural powers."

A very fine yet clear distinction is made by Poe which is not always carefully observed by his imitators or successors.

"The analytical power should not be confounded with simple ingenuity; for while the analyst is necessarily ingenious, the ingenious man is often remarkably incapable of analysis. The constructive or combining power, by which ingenuity is usually manifested, and to which the phrenologists (I believe erroneously) have assigned a separate organ, supposing it a primitive faculty, has been so frequently seen in those whose intellect bordered otherwise upon idiocy, as to have attracted general observation among writers on morals. Between ingenuity and the analytic ability there exists a difference far greater, indeed, than that between the fancy and the imagination, but of a character very strictly analogous. It will be found, in fact, that the ingenious are always fanciful, and the truly imaginative never otherwise than analytic."

4. Poe's Detective—The Prototype

THESE PRINCIPLES, MORE OR LESS clearly understood and adhered to, make up the conventional Fiction Detectives.

Stripped of their distinguishing characteristics, their morphine, knotted string, eccentric habits, or scientific appliances, they all depend for their right to exist, on their application of Poe's principles.

But notwithstanding that the later authors have followed so closely in the narrow path trodden by Poe, it is by no means sure that had Poe, Gaboriau and Conan Doyle never lived, others might not have been pioneers in this field of fiction, and even those who had never heard of Zadig and who knew no Oriental tales. For the detective instinct is not uncommon, and given its presence in combination with Nature's gift of a gray goose quill, a resulting Detective Story is inevitable.

It is Poe's assertion that analytic reasoning is oftenest the identification of the reasoner's intellect with that of his opponent, and he illustrates it thus, in "The Purloined Letter."

"I knew a schoolboy about eight years of age, whose success at guessing in the game of 'even and odd' attracted universal admiration. This game is simple, and is played with marbles. One player holds in his hand a number of these toys, and demands of another whether that number is even or odd. If the guess is right, the guesser wins one; if wrong, he loses one. The boy to whom I allude won all the marbles of the school. Of course he had some principle of guessing; and this lay in mere observation and admeasurement of the astuteness of his opponents. For example, an arrant simpleton is his opponent, and, holding up his closed hand, asks, 'are they even or odd?' Our schoolboy replies, 'odd,' and loses; but upon the second trial he wins, for he then says to himself, 'the simpleton had them even upon the first trial, and his amount of cunning is just sufficient to make him have them odd upon the second; I will therefore guess odd;'—he guesses odd, and wins. Now, with a simpleton a degree above the first, he would have reasoned thus: 'This fellow finds that in the first instance I guessed odd, and, in the second, he will propose to himself, upon the first impulse, a simple variation from even to odd, as did the first simpleton; but then a second thought will suggest that this is too simple a variation, and finally he will decide upon putting it even as before. I will therefore guess even;—he guesses even, and wins. Now this mode of reasoning in the schoolboy, whom his fellows termed 'lucky,'—what in its last analysis, is it?"

"It is merely," I said, "an identification of the reasoner's intellect with that of his opponent."

"It is," said Dupin, "and, upon inquiring of the boy by what means he effected the thorough identification in which his success consisted, I received answer as follows: 'When I wish to find out how wise, or how stupid, or how good, or how wicked is anyone, or what are his thoughts at the moment, I fashion the expression of my face, as accurately as possible, in accordance with the expression of his, and then wait to see what sentiments or thoughts arise in my mind or heart, as if to match or correspond with the expression.' This response of the schoolboy lies at the bottom of all the spurious profundity which has been attributed to Rochefoucauld, to LaBruyère, to Machiavelli, and to Campanella."

Perhaps spurious profundity is too harsh a term, for the profundity after all is only in the eye of the observer.

In similar case was the country boy who found a lost horse. After the owner of the horse and his friends had failed to find the animal that had strayed away, the bumpkin started off by himself, and soon returned bringing the horse with him. "How did you find him?" was the query. "Why," returned the rustic, "I thought if I was a horse, where would I go. And I went there, and he had."

This embodies much of the seemingly magical wisdom of the fiction detective.

5. The Detective in the Novel

SOME THIRTY YEARS AFTER POE'S Dupin, Gaboriau invented his Lecoq. As Gaboriau's stories are all novels, while Poe's are short-stories or novelettes, there is, of course, more setting, with more characters and more complex plot, in the French stories. But as a personality Gaboriau's detective stands out quite as clearly as Poe's.

An able critic thus compares Lecoq and Sherlock Holmes. He says: "The fact is that Sherlock Holmes was too perfect a detective for the stories of which he is the hero to be perfect detective stories. The conception of the ideal reasoner, the man in whom the powers of observation and deduction had become so acute that he saw instantly the remote causes and the remote consequences of every fact, was a fine one. Poe had conceived it before, but Sir Arthur amplified and popularized it. In one of his conversations with Watson, Holmes is, I remember, very severe on Lecoq, whom he pronounces 'a bungler.' Certainly Lecoq had no presence to the faultless insight of his critic. He was a clever and energetic detective, but no miracle worker. He made mistakes, he followed false scents, he led the reader astray. And so he made the story. In a word, Lecoq was a bungler because Gaboriau was an expert."

But is there not another and a better explanation why Holmes was forced to jump at his conclusions immediately, while Lecoq could blunder and retrieve his blunders? Is it not because all the Sherlock Holmes stories are short-stories, and all the Gaboriau stories are full-sized novels? To fill three hundred or more pages necessitates bungling, false leads, mistaken clues and fresh starts. While a Sherlock Holmes story, being told in a few thousand words, necessitates quick action.

But Lecoq's bungles are as interesting as his successful work. When need arises for the expanding of the story, Lecoq converses thus:

"But here I hesitate. I thought myself sure of the character of these murderers; but now—" He paused; and his contracted features clearly showed that he was engaged in a mental effort.

"But now?" asked M. Plantat.

M. Lecoq seemed to wake up. "I beg your pardon," said he. "I forget myself. I've a bad habit of reflecting aloud. That's why I almost always insist on working alone. My uncertainty and hesitation, the waywardness of my suspicions, compromise my reputation as an astute detective, for whom there's no such thing as a mystery." Worthy M. Plantat smiled indulgently. "I don't usually open my mouth," continued M. Lecoq, "until my mind is satisfied; then I speak in a peremptory tone, and say this is so or so. Today, however, I am working openly with a man who realizes that such a problem as this cannot be solved at the first attempt. This is why I allow you to see how I grope along. One can't always reach the truth at a bound; to realize it at times various calculations and deductions are necessary. Well, just now my logic is at fault."

And again in "File No. 113," Lecoq says:

"Our enemies are on the alert, and we must crush them instantly. I have made a mistake. I have been on the wrong track; it is an accident liable to happen to any man, no matter how intelligent he may be. I took the effect for the cause. The day I was convinced that culpable relations existed between Raoul and Madame Fauvel, I thought I held the end of the thread that would lead us to the truth. I ought to have been more mistrustful; this solution was too simple, too natural."

This is indeed proof that Lecoq is a bungler because Gaboriau is an expert.

In his own words Lecoq thus gives an account of his methods.

"A crime is committed—that is the prologue; I reach the scene; the first act begins. At a glance I note the scenery. Then I try to divine the motive of the crime; I group the various characters together, and link the different episodes to the central fact. The action soon reaches a crisis; the thread of my inductions enables me to name the guilty person; I search for him, arrest him, and deliver him up. Then comes the great scene; he struggles, resorts to every device in hopes of cheating justice; but the examining magistrate, armed with the weapons I have forged for him, overwhelms the scoundrel; he does not confess, but he is confounded. And then round the principal personage all kinds of secondary characters are grouped—accomplices, perhaps friends, enemies, witnesses of every description. Some of them may excite alarm, others claim respect, and others again are simply grotesque. The horrible always has its ludicrous side. My last scene is the assize court. The public prosecutor speaks, but his ideas are mine. His oratory is so much embroidery set round the canvas of my report. At last the presiding judge submits his questions to the jury; the fate of my drama is to be decided. Perhaps the jury answers, 'Not guilty,' and that means my piece was bad, and I must allow myself to be hissed; but if the verdict's 'Guilty,' then the piece was good, I am victorious, and receive my meed of applause. The next day I can go and see my hero, slap him on the shoulder, and say, 'You have lost, old fellow; I was one too much for you!'"

And yet this is not extraneous matter, it is an inherent part of the story of "The Mystery of Orcival." If this detective's tricks and manners are more dilatory, or described at greater length than those of Sherlock Holmes, it is entirely because he is a character in a book instead of in a short-story. Gaboriau had his faults, but they were in other respects than the art of his detective.

Reversing the more usual plan of having an amateur detective as a foil for the hero detective, Lecoq has Father Tabaret to whom he defers, as the secondary character.

Instead of Sherlock Holmes' assumption of superiority over his secondary character, we have Father Tabaret laying down the law to the humble hero detective. It is thus the picturesque old Frenchman admonishes Lecoq:

"Wait a little," said he, "before you disdain my praises. I said you had conducted the affair well, but you might have done it infinitely better. You have great gifts, I avow, you have the true detective's instincts, and a keen glance, you know how to sift the known from the unknown; only you are lacking in experience, and are too full of enthusiasm, and are apt to grow discouraged at a slight check. You hover round a fixed idea like a moth flutters; round the flame of a candle; but you are young, and will get over this; however, as I said before, you have made some successes."

Lecoq bent his head like a pupil receiving a reproof from his professor. Was not this old man the master, and he a mere scholar?

"I will point out all your faults to you," continued the old man, "and will show you how on three occasions, at least, you permitted a good chance to slip through your fingers, and so failed to clear up an affair which to outward appearances was so deeply bathed in obscurity, but which in reality was as transparent as crystal."

"And yet, sir—"

"Hush, hush, my boy, permit me to speak. On what principle did you start at the first going off? On this one—to mistrust all appearances, and to believe precisely the contrary to what appeared to be the truth or even the probability."

"Yes, that is just what I said to myself."

"And you did right in saying so. Taking this idea as lantern to light you on your way, you ought to have gone straight to the truth. But as I said before, you are young, and the first likely circumstances that you met with, made you entirely neglect your rule of action."

IX

Applied Principles

The Detectives of Poe, Doyle, and Gaboriau
Individuality of these Detectives
The Real Sherlock Holmes

1. The Detectives of Poe, Doyle, and Gaboriau

Conan Doyle's Detective Stories, being short-stories, more closely resemble Poe's tales than Gaboriau's novels do. Perhaps this is due more to a certain analogy of structure than to the actual working mentality of the detective. Dupin and his historian have rooms together, just as Holmes and Watson do. In each case the curiosity of the historian is first aroused by noticing the unconventional habits and studies of his companion. Dupin has his detractors among the official police, just as Holmes has his Greyson and his Lestrade, and Lecoq his Gevrol.

Perhaps the fatuous Watson chronicles his friend's exploits with even franker admiration than the nameless companion of Dupin, but they are equally earnest in their graphic and detailed recitals. It is to be regretted that so definite a character as Dupin's historian had no name for his better identification, that like Doctor Watson he might have "passed into the language."

Professor Brander Matthews gives this interesting dissertation upon the Teller of Poe's tales:

"Upon the preternaturally acute observer who was to control the machinery of the tale, the American poet be stowed a companion of only an average alertness and keen ness; and to this commonplace companion the romance: confided the telling of the story. By this seemingly simple device Poe doubled the effectiveness of his work, because this unobservant and unimaginative narrator of the unraveling of a tangled skein by an observant and imaginative analyst naturally recorded his own admiration and astonishment as the wonder was wrought before his eyes, so that the admiration and astonishment were transmitted directly and suggestively, to the readers of the narrative.

"In the 'Gold-Bug' the wonder-worker is Legrand, and in both the 'Murders in the Rue Morgue' and the 'Purloined Letter' he is M. Dupin; and in all three tales the telling of the story is entrusted to an anonymous narrator, serving not only as a sort of Greek chorus to hint to the spectators the emotions they ought to feel, but also as the describer of the personality and peculiarities of Legrand and Dupin, who are thus individualized, humanized, and related to the real world. If they had not been accepted by the narrator as actual beings of flesh and blood, they might otherwise retain the thinness and the dryness of disembodied intelligences working in a vacuum.

"This device of the transmitting narrator is indisputably valuable; and, properly enough, it reappears in the one series of detective tales which may be thought by some to rival Poe's. The alluring record of the investigations of Mr. Sherlock Holmes is the work of a certain Dr. Watson, a human being but little more clearly characterized than the anonymous narrators who have preserved for us the memory of Legrand and Dupin. But Poe here again exhibited a more artistic reserve than any of his imitators, in so far as he refrained from the undue laudation of the strange intellectual feats which are the central interest of these three tales.

"In the 'Gold Bug' he even heightens his suspense by allowing the narrator to suggest that Legrand might be of unsound mind; and in the 'Murders in the Rue Morgue' the narrator, although lost in astonishment at the acuteness of Dupin, never permits his admiration to become fulsome; he holds himself in, as though fearing that overpraise might provoke a denial. Moreover, Poe refrained from all exhibitions of Dupin's skill merely for its own sake exhibitions only dazzling the spectators and not furthering his immediate purpose."

Watson is doubtless fulsome, but like begets like, and the Reading Public, quick to take the cue, are also fulsome in praise of Sherlock Holmes.

According to Mr. Arthur Bartlett Maurice, Sherlock Holmes possesses the attributes of both Poe's and Gaboriau's heroes. Mr. Maurice asserts that, "If in one line we can trace the ancestry of Sherlock Holmes to Edgar Allan Poe's Dupin, in another we can work back to Gaboriau, not, however, to the great Lecoq, but to old Tabaret, better known to the official police who are introduced into the tales as Pere Tirauclair. From Dupin, Holmes derived his intellectual acumen, his faculty of mentally placing himself in the position of another, and thereby divining the other's motives and plans, his raising of the observation of minute outward details to the dignity of an exact science. Pere Tirauclair inspired him to that wide knowledge of criminal and contemporary history which enabled him to throw a light on the most puzzling problem and to find some analogy to the most outré case. With Lecoq, Holmes has absolutely nothing in common."

We object to this last clause. If nothing more, Sherlock Holmes certainly has methods of procedure in common with Gaboriau's detectives. Tirauclair, Lecoq's master and teacher, conducts his investigations after this manner:

As the old fellow spoke, his little gray eyes dilated and became brilliant as carbuncles. His face reflected an internal satisfaction even his wrinkles seemed to laugh. His figure became erect, and his step was almost elastic, as he darted into the inner chamber. He remained there about half an hour; then came out running, then re-entered and then again came out; once more he reappeared and disappeared again almost immediately. The magistrate could not help comparing him to a pointer on the scent, his turned up nose even moved about as if to discover some subtle odor left by the assassin. All the while he talked loudly and with much gesticulation, apostrophizing himself, scolding himself, uttering little cries of triumph or self-encouragement. He did not allow Lecoq to have a moment's rest. He wanted this or that or the other thing. He demanded paper and a pencil. Then he wanted a spade; and finally he cried out for plaster of Paris, some water and a bottle of oil. When more than an hour had elapsed, the investigating magistrate began to grow impatient, and asked what had become of the amateur detective. "He is on the road," replied the corporal, "lying flat in the mud, and mixing some plaster in a plate. He says he has nearly finished, and that he is coming back presently."

Sherlock Holmes when setting forth on a similar investigation conducts himself not dissimilarly. We quote from "A Study in Scarlet":

He whipped a tape measure and a large, round magnifying-glass from his pocket. With these two implements he trotted noiselessly about the room, sometimes stopping, occasionally kneeling, and once lying flat upon his face. So engrossed was he with his occupation that he appeared to have forgotten our presence, for he chattered away to himself under his breath the whole time, keeping up a running fire of exclamations, groans, whistles, and little cries suggestive of encouragement and of hope. As I watched him I was irresistibly reminded of a pure blooded, well trained fox-hound as it dashes backward and forward through the covert, whining in its eagerness, until it comes across the lost scent. For twenty minutes or more he continued his researches, measuring with the most exact care the distance between marks which were entirely invisible to me, and occasionally applying his tape to the walls in an equally incomprehensible manner. In one place he gathered very carefully a little pile of gray dust from the floor, and packed it away in an envelope. Finally he examined with his glass the word upon the wall, going over every letter of it with the most minute exactness. This done, he appeared to be satisfied, for he replaced his tape and his glass in his pocket.

The result by Gaboriau's man is announced in these words:

"The assassin then gained admission without difficulty. He is a young man, a little above the middle height, elegantly dressed. He wore on that evening a high hat. He carried an umbrella, and smoked a trabucos cigar in a holder."

While Sherlock Holmes triumphantly asserts:

"There has been murder done, and the murderer was a man. He was more than six feet high, was in the prime of life, had small feet for his height, wore coarse, square-toed boots, and smoked a Trichinopoly cigar. He came here with his victim in a four-wheeled cab, which was drawn by a horse with three old shoes and one new one on his off fore-leg. In all probability the murderer had a florid face, and the finger-nails of his right hand were remarkably long."

In "The Widow Lerouge," from which the above Gaboriau extracts are quoted, the discomfited Inspector, Gevrol, exclaims,

"Ridiculous! this is too much!"

While in the other case, Lestrade and Gregson content themselves with glancing at each other with an incredulous smile.

Mr. Maurice further observes: "The deductions of Dupin and of Sherlock Holmes we are ready to accept, because we feel that it is romance, and in romance we care to refute only what seriously jars our sense of what is logical; we take those of Lecoq, because they convince beyond all question, because when one has been forced upon us, we are ready defiantly to maintain that no other is possible."

However, Dupin himself refers to his own work thus:

"I said 'legitimate deductions;' but my meaning is not thus fully expressed. I designed to imply that the deductions are the sole proper ones, and that the suspicion arises inevitably from them as the single result."

2. Individuality of these Detectives

THE ATTITUDE OF THE TRANSCENDENT Detective toward other detectives with whom he comes in contact, is—doubtless because of the fierce light that beats upon his throne—one of complacent superiority.

Lecoq expresses himself thus, and Sherlock Holmes and his heirs and successors forever, voice similar sentiments:

"That will do," interrupted M Lecoq. "If I choose to lend you a helping hand, it is because it suits my fancy to do so. It pleases me to be the head, and to let you be the hand. Unassisted, with your preconceived ideas, you never would have found the culprit; if we two together don't find him, my name is not Lecoq."

And again:

"M. Lecoq shrugged his shoulders. 'You are an ass!' exclaimed he. 'Why, don't you know that on the very day you were sent for with the commissary to verify the fact of the robbery, you held—I do not say certainly, but very probably held—in your great stupid hands the means of knowing which key had been used when the money was stolen.'"

"How is that?"

"You want to know, do you? I will tell you. Do you remember the scratch you discovered on the safe? You were so struck by it, that you could not refrain from calling out directly you saw it. You carefully examined it, and were convinced that it was a fresh scratch, only a few hours old. You thought too, and rightly too, that this scratch was made at the time of the theft. Now, with what was it made? Evidently with a key. That being the case, you should have asked for the keys both of the banker and the cashier. One of them would have probably had some particles of the hard green paint sticking to it."

Fanferlot listened with open mouth to this explanation. At the last words, he violently slapped his forehead with his hand and cried out: "Idiot! Idiot!"

"You have correctly named yourself," said M. Lecoq. "Idiot! This proof stares you right in the face, and you don't see it! This scratch is the only clue there is to follow, and you must like a fool neglect it. If I find the guilty party, it will be by means of this scratch; and I am determined that I will find him."

Sherlock Holmes thus delivers himself:

"What do you think of it, sir?" they both asked.

"It would be robbing you of the credit of the case if I was to presume to help you," remarked my friend. "You are doing so well now that it would be a pity for anyone to interfere." There was a world of sarcasm in his voice, as he spoke.

And again:

"I am afraid, my dear Watson, that most of your conclusions were erroneous. When I said that you stimulated me I meant, to be frank, that in noting your fallacies I was occasionally guided towards the truth. Not that you are entirely wrong in this instance. The man is certainly a country practitioner. And he walks a good deal."

In "The Moonstone" the superiority of Sergeant Cuff to the Police officer is thus cleverly remarked:

Why Superintendent Seegrave should have appeared to be several sizes smaller than life, on being presented to Sergeant Cuff, I can't undertake to explain. I can only state the fact. They retired together; and remained a weary long time shut up from all mortal intrusion. When they came out Mr. Superintendent was excited and Mr. Sergeant was yawning.

"The Sergeant wishes to see Miss Verinder's sitting room," says Mr. Seegrave, addressing me with great pomp and eagerness. "The Sergeant may have some questions to ask. Attend the Sergeant, if you please!"

While I was being ordered about in this way, I looked at the great Cuff. The great Cuff, on his side, looked at Superintendent Seegrave in that quietly expecting way which I have already noticed. I can't affirm that he was on the watch for his brother officer's speedy appearance in the character of an ass—I can only say that I strongly suspected it.

Mr. Edmund Clarence Stedman tells us that, "Poe could teach Continental writers very little in the art of perfecting their own romance. His analytic tales made a great impression. Their ratiocination, applied to the solution of criminal mysteries, captured the Parisian fancy more readily than the quality of his other prose writings. Since then, detective stories of high and low degree have been written in France, England, and America; but no amateur, with a genius approximating to that of 'Monsieur C. Auguste Dupin,' has appeared, and had his exploits recounted, in our own or foreign literature."

3. The Real Sherlock Holmes

CONAN DOYLE HIMSELF, OR RATHER a friend of his, one Doctor Harold Emery Jones, denies Sherlock Holmes' dependence on any fictional detective. Thus Doctor Jones on the subject:

"The writer was a fellow-student of Conan Doyle. Together they attended the surgical demonstrations of Joseph Bell, at the Edinburgh Royal Infirmary. This man exhibited incredibly acute and sure deductive powers in diagnosis and in guessing the vocation of patients from external signs. Sir Henry Littlejohn, another medical lecturer, heard by the two students, was remarkable for his sagacious expert testimony, leading to the conviction of many a criminal. Thus is the character of Sherlock Holmes easily and naturally accounted for, and the absurd fiction that Conan Doyle drew upon Poe for his ideas is silenced forever."

In further account of Joseph Bell, Doctor Jones continues:

"He is the original Sherlock Holmes—the Edinburgh medical students' ideal—who could tell patients their habits, their occupations, nationality, and often their names, and who rarely, if ever, made a mistake. Oftentimes he would call upon one of the students to diagnose the cases for him. Telling the House Surgeon to usher in a new patient, he delighted in putting the deductive powers of the student to the test, with results generally amusing, except to the poor student victim himself."

Bell was as full of dry humor and satire, and he was as jealous of his reputation, as the detective Sherlock Holmes ever thought of being.

One day, in the lecture theatre, he gave the students a long talk on the necessity for the members of the medical profession cultivating their senses—sight, smell, taste, and hearing. Before him on a table stood a large tumbler filled with a dark, amber-colored liquid.

"This, gentlemen," announced the Professor, "contains a very potent drug. To the taste it is intensely bitter. It is most offensive to the sense of smell. Yet, as far as the sense of sight is concerned—that is, in color— it is no different from dozens of other liquids."

"Now I want to see how many of you gentlemen have educated your powers of perception. Of course, we might easily analyze this chemically, and find out what it is. But I want you to test it by smell and taste; and, as I don't ask anything of my students which I wouldn't be willing to do myself, I will taste it before passing it round."

Here he dipped his finger in the liquid, and placed it in his mouth. The tumbler was passed round. With wry and sour faces the students followed the Professor's lead. One after another tasted the vile decoction; varied and amusing were the grimaces made. The tumbler, having gone the round, was returned to the Professor.

"Gentlemen," said he, with a laugh, "I am deeply grieved to find that not one of you has developed this power of perception, which I so often speak about; for if you had watched me closely, you would have found that while I placed my forefinger in the medicine, it was the middle finger which found its way into my mouth."

These methods of Bell impressed Doyle greatly at the time. The impression made was a lasting one.

Regarding this matter Conan Doyle thus writes:

"Sherlock Holmes is the literary embodiment, if I may so express it, of my memory of a professor of medicine at Edinburgh University, who would sit in the patients' waiting-room with a face like a red Indian, and diagnose the people as they came in before even they had opened their mouths. He would tell them their symptoms, he would give them details of their lives, and he would hardly ever make a mistake." This professor was Dr. Joseph Bell, and that the resemblance to Sherlock Holmes was not merely intellectual, but strikingly physical as well, may be seen from the accompanying portrait. There are the same sharp, piercing eyes, the eagle nose, and the hawk-like features. Like Sherlock Holmes, Dr. Bell was in the habit of sitting in his chair with his fingers pressed together when engaged in solving a problem. Twenty-seven years ago Conan Doyle came in contact with him when he was finishing his medical studies.

"Gentlemen," Professor Bell would say to the students standing around, "I am not quite sure whether this man is a cork-cutter or a slater. I observe a slight callous, or hardening, on one side of his forefinger, and a little thickening on the outside of his thumb, and that is a sure sign he is either one or the other."

Dr. Bell, as well as Sherlock Holmes, was often inclined to be highly dramatic in the exposition of his singular faculties. A patient would enter his consulting-room. "Ah," the Professor would say, "I perceive that you are a soldier, a non-commissioned officer, and that you have served in Bermuda." The man would acknowledge the correctness of the indictment, and the students would express their surprise. "How did I know that, gentlemen? The matter is simplicity itself. He came into the room without taking his hat off, as he would go into an orderly's room. He was a soldier. A slight authoritative air, combined with his age, shows that he was a non-commissioned officer. A slight rash on the forehead tells me that he was in Bermuda, and subject to a certain rash known only there."

Then Conan Doyle began building up a scientific system by which everything might be logically reasoned out. Along purely intellectual lines Poe had done that before with M. Dupin. Sherlock Holmes was practical and systematic, and where he differed from Dupin was that in consequence of his previous scientific education he possessed a vast fund of exact knowledge from which to draw.

When he had written twenty-six stories about Sherlock Holmes, Conan Doyle determined that it would be bad policy to continue and decided to put an end to his hero. He feared that Holmes was becoming tiresome to others as well as to himself. Above all, he was afraid that the public would come to think that he had only one idea and could write only one kind of story. Dr. Doyle was in Switzerland at the time. One day, while on a walking tour through the country, he came to a waterfall, and immediately saw in it a romantic spot for anyone who wished to meet a spectacular death. Then and there he mentally mapped out "The Final Problem," in which Holmes and Moriarty settled accounts. But Holmes's death, instead of being welcomed, roused indignant protest. One lady wrote a letter to the author which began "You beast."

The Rationale of Ratiocination

In one of Doyle's stories, Sherlock Holmes himself states definitely his principles of deduction in what purports to be a magazine article written by himself. The opening paragraph, however, is in the words of the faithful Dr. Watson.

1. Sherlock Holmes' Method

Its somewhat ambitious title was "The Book of Life," and it attempted to show how much an observant man might learn by an accurate and systematic examination of all that came in his way. It struck me as being a remarkable mixture of shrewdness and absurdity. The reasoning was close and intense, but the deductions appeared to me to be far-fetched and exaggerated. The writer claimed by a momentary expression, a twitch of a muscle, or a glance of an eye, to fathom a man's inmost thoughts. Deceit, according to him, was an impossibility in the case of one trained to observation and analysis. His conclusions were as infallible as so many propositions of Euclid. So startling would his results appear to the uninitiated that, until they learned the processes by which he had arrived at them, they might well consider him a necromancer.

"From a drop of water," said the writer, "a logician could infer the possibility of an Atlantic or a Niagara without having seen or heard of one or the other. So all life is a great chain the nature of which is known whenever we are shown a single link of it. Like all other arts, the Science of Deduction and Analysis is one which can only be acquired by long and patient study, nor is life long enough to allow any mortal to attain the highest possible perfection of it. Before turning to those moral and mental aspects of the matter which present the greatest difficulties, let the inquirer begin by mastering more elementary problems. Let him, on meeting a fellow mortal, learn at a glance to distinguish the history of the man, and the trade or profession to which he belongs. Puerile as such an exercise may seem, it sharpens the faculties of observation and teaches one where to look and what to look for. By a man's finger-nails, by his coat-sleeve, by his boot, by his trouser-knees, by the callosities of his forefinger and thumb, by his expression, by his shirt cuffs—by each of these things a man's calling is plainly revealed. That all united should fail to enlighten the competent inquirer in any case is almost inconceivable."

It is the sentence last quoted that proclaims the Transcendent Detective, and it is this element of omniscience that gives him such popularity and homage as is received by any other worker in magic.

As an example of this sort of deduction let us examine definitely some of Sherlock Holmes' work.

Typical in every respect, are his deductions from an old hat as here given:

I took the tattered object in my hands and turned it over rather ruefully. It was a very ordinary black hat of the usual round shape, hard, and much the worse for wear. The lining had been of red silk, but was a good deal discolored. There was no maker's name; but, as Holmes had remarked, the initials "H.B." were scrawled upon one side. It was pierced in the brim for a hat-securer, but the elastic was missing. For the rest, it was cracked, exceedingly dusty, and spotted in several places, although there seemed to have been some attempt to hide the discolored patches by smearing them with ink.

"I can see nothing," said I, handing it back to my friend.

"On the contrary, Watson, you can see everything. You fail to reason from what you see. You are too timid in drawing your inferences."

"Then, pray tell me what it is that you can infer from this hat?"

He picked it up and gazed at it in the peculiar introspective fashion which was characteristic of him. "It is perhaps less suggestive than it might have been," he remarked, "and yet there are a few inferences which are very distinct, and a few others which represent at least a strong balance of probability. That the man was highly intellectual is of course obvious upon the face of it, and also that he was fairly well-to-do within the last three years, although he has now fallen upon evil days. He had foresight, but has less now than formerly, pointing to a moral retrogression, which, when taken with the decline of his fortunes, seems to indicate some evil influence, probably drink, at work upon him. This may account also for the obvious fact that his wife has ceased to love him."

"My dear Holmes!"

"He has, however, retained some degree of self-respect," he continued, disregarding my remonstrances. "He is a man who leads a sedentary life, goes out little, is out of training entirely, is middle-aged, has grizzled hair which he has had cut within the last few days, and which he anoints with lime-cream. These are the more potent facts which are to be deduced from his hat. Also, by-the-way, that it is extremely improbable that he has gas laid on in his house."

"You are certainly joking, Holmes."

"Not in the least. Is it possible that even now, when I give you these results, you are unable to see how they are attained?"

"I have no doubt that I am very stupid; but I must confess that I am unable to follow you. For example, how did you deduce that this man was intellectual?"

For answer Holmes clapped the hat upon his head. It came right over the forehead and settled upon the bridge of his nose. "It is a question of cubic capacity," said he; "a man with so large a brain must have something in it."

"The decline of his fortunes, then?"

"This hat is three years old. These flat brims curled at the edge came in then. It is a hat of the very best quality. Look at the band of ribbed silk and the excellent lining. If this man could afford to buy so expensive a hat three years ago, and has had no hat since, then he has assuredly gone down in the world."

"Well, that is clear enough, certainly. But how about the foresight and the moral retrogression?"

Sherlock Holmes laughed. "Here is the foresight," said he, putting his finger upon the little disk and loop of the hat securer. "They are never sold upon hats. If this man ordered one, it is a sign of a certain amount of foresight, since he went out of his way to take this precaution against the wind. But since we see he had broken the elastic, and has not troubled to replace it, it is obvious that he has less foresight now than formerly, which is a distinct proof of a weakening nature. On the other hand, he has endeavored to conceal some of these stains upon the felt by daubing them with ink, which is a sign that he has not entirely lost his self-respect."

"Your reasoning is certainly plausible."

"The further points, that he is middle-aged, that his hair is grizzled, that it has been recently cut, and that he uses lime-cream, are all to be gathered from a close examination of the lower part of the lining. The lens discloses a large number of hair-ends, clean cut by the scissors of the barber. They all appear to be adhesive and there is a distinct odor of lime-cream. The dust, you will observe, is not the gritty, gray dust of the street, but the fluffy brown dust of the house, showing that it has been hung up indoors most of the time; while the marks of moisture upon the inside are proof positive that the wearer perspired very freely, and could, therefore, hardly be in the best of training."

"But his wife—you said that she had ceased to love him."

"This hat has not been brushed for weeks. When I see you, my dear Watson, with a week's accumulation of dust upon your hat, and when your wife allows you to go out in such a state, I shall fear that you also have been unfortunate enough to lose your wife's affection."

"But he might be a bachelor."

"Nay, he was bringing home the goose as a peace-offering to his wife. Remember the card upon the bird's leg."

"You have an answer to everything. But how on earth do you deduce that the gas is not laid on in his house?"

"One tallow stain, or even two, might come by chance; but when I see no less than five, I think that there can be little doubt that the individual must be brought into frequent contact with burning tallow; walks upstairs at night, probably with his hat in one hand and a guttering candle in the other. Anyhow, he never got tallow-stains from a gas-jet. Are you satisfied?"

And we will follow this with a similar example:

"I think, Watson, that you have put on seven and a half pounds since I saw you."

"Seven!" I answered.

"Indeed, I should have thought a little more. Just a trifle more, I fancy, Watson. And in practice again, I observe. You did not tell me that you intended to go into harness."

"Then, how do you know?"

"I see it, I deduce it. How do I know that you have been getting yourself very wet lately, and that you have a most clumsy and careless servant girl?"

"My dear Holmes," said I, "this is too much. You would certainly have been burned, had you lived a few centuries ago. It is true that I had a country walk on Thursday and came home in a dreadful mess; but, as I have changed my clothes, I can't imagine how you deduce it. As to Mary Jane, she is incorrigible, and my wife has given her notice; but there, again, I fail to see how you work it out."

He chuckled to himself and rubbed his long, nervous hands together.

"It is simplicity itself," said he; "my eyes tell me that on the inside of your left shoe, just where the firelight strikes it, the leather is scored by six almost parallel cuts. Obviously they have been caused by someone who has very carelessly scraped round the edges of the sole in order to remove crusted mud from it. Hence, you see, my double deduction that you had been out in vile weather, and that you had a particularly malignant boot-slitting specimen of the London slavey. As to your practice, if a gentleman walks into my rooms smelling of iodoform, with a black mark of nitrate of silver upon his right forefinger, and a bulge on the side of his top-hat to show where he has secreted his stethoscope, I must be dull, indeed, if I do not pronounce him to be an active member of the medical profession."

In his early acquaintance Watson doubted Holmes ability at this sort of deduction, and said to him, by way of test:

"I have heard you say that it is difficult for a man to have any object in daily use without leaving the impress of his individuality upon it in such a way that a trained observer might read it. Now, I have here a watch which has recently come into my possession. Would you have the kindness to let me have an opinion upon the character or habits of the late owner?"

"Though unsatisfactory, my research has not been entirely barren," Holmes observed, staring up at the ceiling with dreamy, lack lustre eyes. "Subject to your correction, I should judge that the watch belonged to your elder brother, who inherited it from your father."

"That you gather, no doubt, from the H.W. upon the back?"

"Quite so. The W. suggests your own name. The date of the watch is nearly fifty years back, and the initials are as old as the watch: So it was made for the last generation. Jewellery usually descends to the eldest son, and he is most likely to have the same name as his father. Your father has, if I remember right, been dead many years. It has, therefore, been in the hands of your eldest brother."

"Right, so far," said I. "Anything else?"

"He was a man of untidy habits—very untidy and careless. He was left with good prospects, but he threw away his chances, lived for sometime in poverty with occasional short intervals of prosperity, and finally taking to drink, he died. That is all I can gather."

I sprang from my chair and limped impatiently about the room with considerable bitterness in my heart.

"This is unworthy of you, Holmes," I said. "I could not have believed that you would have descended to this. You have made inquiries into the history of my unhappy brother, and you now pretend to deduce this knowledge in some fanciful way. You cannot expect me to believe that you have read all this from his old watch! It is unkind, and to speak plainly, has a touch of charlatanism in it."

"My dear doctor," said he kindly, "pray accept my apologies. Viewing the matter as an abstract problem, I had forgotten how personal and painful a thing it might be to you. I assure you, however, that I never even knew that you had a brother until you handed me the watch."

"Then how in the name of all that is wonderful did you get these facts? They are absolutely correct in every particular."

"What seems strange to you is only so because you do not follow my train of thought or observe the small facts upon which large inferences may depend. For example, I began by stating that your brother was careless. When you observe the lower part of that watch-case you notice that it is not only dinted in two places, but it is cut and marked all over from the habit of keeping other hard objects, such as coins or keys, in the same pocket. Surely it is no great feat to assume that a man who treats a fifty-guinea watch so cavalierly must be a careless man. Neither is it a very far-fetched inference that a man who inherits one article of such value is pretty well provided for in other respects."

I nodded, to show that I followed his reasoning.

"It is very customary for pawnbrokers in England, when they take a watch, to scratch the number of the ticket with a pin-point upon the inside of the case. It is more handy than a label, as there is no risk of the number being lost or transposed. There are no less than four such numbers visible to my lens on the inside of this case. Inference that your brother was often at low water. Secondary inference—that he had occasional bursts of prosperity, or he could not have redeemed the pledge. Finally, I ask you to look at the inner plate, which contains the keyhole. Look at the thousand of scratches all round the hole—marks where the key has slipped. What sober man's key could have scored those grooves? But you will never see a drunkard's watch without them. He winds it at night, and he leaves these traces of his unsteady hand. Where is the mystery in all this?"

"It is as clear as daylight," I answered.

I could not help laughing at the ease with which he explained his process of deduction. "When I hear you give your reasons," I remarked, "the thing always appears to me to be so ridiculously simple that I could easily do it myself, though at each successive instance of your reasoning I am baffled, until you explain your process. And yet I believe that my eyes are as good as yours."

"Quite so," he answered, lighting a cigarette, and throwing himself down into an arm-chair. "You see, but you do not observe. The distinction is clear. For example you have frequently seen the steps which lead up from the hall to this room."

"Frequently."

"How often?"

"Well, some hundreds of times."

"Then how many are there?"

"How many? I don't know."

"Quite so! You have not observed. And yet you have seen. That is just my point. Now, I know that there are seventeen steps, because I have both seen and observed."

2. Lecoq's Method

LECOQ ANNOUNCES HIS DEDUCTIONS WITH rather more dramatic circumlocution. With nothing to deduce from but footprints in the snow, he at last cries triumphantly:

"Now I know everything."

"Oh, dear, that is a big word to say."

"When I say everything, I mean everything that has reference to the drama played at the Widow Chupin's which has culminated in bloodshed. This deserted piece of land covered with snow is like a vast white page of a book, and the persons whom we are hunting have written upon it, not only their movements and their proceedings, but also the secret doubts, hopes, and fears which are agitating their souls. What do these fleeting footprints teach you, old man? Nothing; well, to me they are as full of life as the people who have left them behind; they breathe, they speak, and they denounce!"

His conclusions being received somewhat dubiously he proceeds more definitely.

"Listen, then," continued Lecoq, "to the writing as I read it. While the murderer was taking the two women to the Poivriere, his companion or his accomplice, as I think I may call him, waited for him here. He was a middle-aged man, rather tall, wore a soft hat and a brown woolly great-coat; he was probably married, as he wore a wedding-ring on the little finger of his right hand."

After the usual, "this is too much!" he continues his recital:

"We have come, old fellow, to the moment when the accomplice had mounted guard here, and the time seemed to him rather long. To make the time pass, he walked backward and forward the length of the beam, and every now and then stopped to listen, so as to break the monotony of his promenade. As he heard nothing he stamped his feet, doubtless saying to himself, 'What the deuce is the other fellow doing down there?' He had walked up and down thirty times, for I have counted them, when a dull sound broke the silence—the two women were coming."

3. Other Methods

ALL OF THIS IS PURELY and simply the reasoning of Zadig and the early Orientals. On the whole this sort of "spurious profundity" is not difficult in detective fiction, however often it might fail to prove in real life.

The Present Writer, moved to attempt it, wrote the following scene in a story, the characters being a Transcendant Detective and an Admiring Friend.

I met him, accidentally one morning, when we both chanced to go into a basement of the Metropolis Hotel to have our shoes shined.

While waiting our turn to get a chair, we stood talking, and, seeing a pair of shoes standing on a table, evidently there to be cleaned, I said banteringly:

"Now, I suppose, Stone, from looking at those shoes, you can deduce all there is to know about the owner of them."

With a mild twinkle in his eye, but with a perfectly grave face, he said slowly:

"Those shoes belong to a young man, five feet eight inches high. He does not live in New York, but is here to visit his sweetheart. She lives in Brooklyn, is five feet nine inches tall, and is deaf in her left ear. They went to the theatre last night, and neither was in evening dress."

I stared at him incredulously, as I always did when confronted by his astonishing "deductions," and simply said:

"Tell this little Missourian all about it."

"It did sound well, reeled off like that, didn't it?" he observed, chuckling more at my air of eager curiosity than at his own achievement. "But it's absurdly easy, after all. He is a young man because his shoes are in the very latest, extreme, not exclusive style. He is five feet eight, because the size of his foot goes with that height of man, which, by the way, is the height of nine out of ten men, anyway. He doesn't live in New York or he wouldn't be stopping at a hotel. Besides, he would be down-town at this hour, attending to business."

"Unless he has freak business hours, as you and I do," I put in.

"Yes, that might be. But I still hold that he doesn't live in New York, or he couldn't be staying at this Broadway hotel overnight, and sending his shoes down to be shined at half-past nine in the morning. His sweetheart is five feet nine, for that is the height of a tall girl. I know she is tall, for she wears a long skirt. Short girls wear short skirts, which make them look shorter still, and tall girls wear very long skirts, which make them look taller."

"Why do they do that?" I inquired, greatly interested.

"I don't know. You'll have to ask that of someone wiser than I. But I know it's a fact. A girl wouldn't be considered really tall if less than five feet nine. So I know that's her height. She is his sweetheart, for no man would go from New York to Brooklyn and bring a lady over here to the theatre, and then take her home, and return to New York in the early hours of morning, if he were not in love with her. I know she lives in Brooklyn, for the paper says there was a heavy shower there last night, while I know no rain fell in New York. I know that they were out in that rain, for her long skirt became muddy, and in turn muddied the whole upper of his left shoe. The fact that only the left shoe is so soiled proves that he walked only at her right side, showing that she must be deaf in her left ear, or he would have walked part of the time on that side. I know that they went to the theatre in New York, because he is still sleeping at this hour, and has sent his boots down to be cleaned, instead of coming down with them on his feet to be shined here. If he had been merely calling on the girl in Brooklyn, he would have been home early, for they do not sit up late in that borough. I know they went to the theatre, instead of to the opera or a ball, for they did not go in a cab, otherwise her skirt would not have become muddied. This, too, shows that she wore a cloth skirt, and as his shoes are not patent leathers, it is clear that neither was in evening dress."

I didn't try to get a verification of Fleming Stone's assertions; I didn't want any. Scores of times I had known him to make similar deductions, and in cases where we afterward learned the facts, he was invariably correct. So, though we didn't follow up this matter, I was sure he was right, and, even if he hadn't been, it would not have weighed heavily against his large proportion of proved successes.

As it turned out, being fiction, these astute deductions were correct in every particular, and led ultimately to the conviction of the criminal!

4. Holmes' Method Evaluated

A SIDE LIGHT ON SHERLOCK HOLMES' character is shown by his attitude regarding the explanation of his own deduction. Doctor Watson thus expresses it:

"Like all Holmes' reasoning the thing seemed simplicity itself when it was once explained. He read the thought upon my features, and his smile had a tinge of bitterness.

"I am afraid that I rather give myself away when I explain," said he. "Results without causes are much more impressive."

Of course this is all part of the author's art, for it grasps the reader's sympathy and understanding, and forestalls his own slight feeling of disappointment at the exposed simplicity.

Not all of Sherlock Holmes' deductions are quite as marvelous as Watson asserts. For instance, a strong point is made by Holmes, in "The Hound of the Baskervilles," after reading a message concocted by means of pasting on paper words cut from a newspaper, and declaring at once that the words were cut from the London Times. Ability to distinguish the type of one great newspaper from another is not at all uncommon among newspaper readers. As a matter of fact, a large portion of the reading public could tell at once from what newspaper words were cut. It is the photographic memory rather than the analytic mind which performs this feat.

Again, not all of Holmes' deductions are true in every detail. A pair of gold rimmed eye-glasses leads him to declare their owner "a person of refinement and well-dressed," for, he says "it is inconceivable that anyone who wore such glasses could be slatternly in other respects." And yet, such conditions have often been known. But in the story, of course the lady proved to be refined and well-dressed, and thus the Transendent Detective's deductions were verified.

It is, of course, the spectacular deductions, the plays to the grand stand, that make for popularity. And no one could better combine the rational commonplace and the marvelous 'spurious profundity' than Doctor Doyle has done in the character of Sherlock Holmes.

But much of this profound reasoning is far from spurious. In a moment of a serious dissertation on his own art, we learn this about it:

Sherlock Holmes closed his eyes and placed his elbows upon the arms of his chair, with his finger-tips together.

"The ideal reasoner," he remarked, "would, when he had once been shown a single fact in all its bearings, deduce from it not only all the chain of events which led up to it, but also all the results which would follow from it. As Cuvier could correctly describe a whole animal by the contemplation of a single bone, so the observer who has thoroughly understood one link in a series of incidents, should be able to accurately state all the other ones, both before and after. We have not yet grasped the results which the reason alone can attain to. Problems may be solved in the study which have baffled all those who have sought a solution by the aid of their senses. To carry the art, however, to its highest pitch, it is necessary that the reasoner should be able to utilize all the facts which have come to his knowledge; and this in itself implies, as you will readily see, a possession of all knowledge, which, even in these days of free education and encyclopaedias, is a somewhat rare accomplishment. It is not so impossible, however, that a man should possess all knowledge which is likely to be useful to him in his work, and this I have endeavored in my case to do."

5. The Inductive and the Deductive Methods

IT IS NOT EASY FOR the untutored reader or writer of detective stories always to differentiate between inductive and deductive reasoning. Perhaps some light may be thrown on this abstruse subject by reading carefully this extract from a book by Arlo Bates, entitled "Talks on Writing English."

"It is proper and perhaps even important that the student shall learn the distinction which is made by logicians between reasoning which is inductive and that which is deductive. As a matter of practical work in the writing of arguments, the distinction is of less importance than might seem from the formality with which these terms are treated; but as Induction and Deduction are words which the true logician cannot mention without at least a seeming impulse to cross himself, it is well to know what the difference is.

"Induction, then, is reasoning from the particular to the general; the establishment of an hypothesis by showing that the facts agree with it. It is preeminently the scientific method. By observing natural phenomena, the scientist conceives what the law which governs them must be. This idea of the general principle is then the hypothesis which he attempts to prove; and his method is to examine the facts under all conditions possible, establishing his proposition by showing that the facts are in accord with it.

"Deduction is the converse of this, and consists in drawing out particular truths from general ones. A universal proposition may be regarded as a bundle in which are bound together many individual ones. It is the work of deduction to take these out,—to separate anyone of them from the rest. The general truth, 'All metals are elements,' includes in it the especial truths, 'Iron is an element,' 'Gold is an Element,' and so on for each metal which could be named. Deduction is the process of separating one of these from the whole. Speaking broadly, scientific reasoning is more likely to be inductive, while other reasoning is more likely to be deductive."

6. Two Striking Examples

A FAVORITE EXPLOIT OF THE Transcendent Detective, is to follow silently another's train of thought; and then suddenly and seemingly with clairvoyance, announce what the other's thoughts are.

This is done first by Poe:

We were strolling one night down a long dirty street, in the vicinity of the Palais Royal. Being both, apparently, occupied with thought, neither of us had spoken a syllable for fifteen minutes at least. All at once Dupin broke forth with these words.

"He is a very little fellow, that's true, and would do better for the Théatre des Variétés."

"There can be no doubt of that," I replied unwittingly, and not at first observing (so much had I been absorbed in reflection) the extraordinary manner in which the speaker had chimed in with my meditations. In an instant afterward I recollected myself, and my astonishment was profound.

"Dupin," said I gravely, "this is beyond my comprehension. I do not hesitate to say that I am amazed, and can scarcely credit my senses. How was it possible that you should know I was thinking of—?" Here I paused, to ascertain beyond a doubt whether he really knew of whom I thought.—"of Chantilly," said he, "why do you pause? You were remarking to yourself that his diminutive figure unfitted him for tragedy."

This was precisely what had formed the subject of my reflections. Chantilly was a quondam cobbler of the Rue St. Denis, who, becoming stage-mad, had attempted the role of Xerxes, in Crebillon's tragedy so-called, and been notoriously pasquinaded for his pains.

"Tell me, for Heaven's sake," I exclaimed, "the method—if method there is—by which you have been enabled to fathom my soul in this matter." In fact, I was even more startled than I would have been willing to express.

"It was the fruiterer," replied my friend, "who brought you to the conclusion that the mender of soles was not of sufficient height for Xerxes et id genus omne."

"The fruiterer!—you astonish me—I know no fruiterer whomsoever."

"The man who ran up against you as we entered the street—it may have been fifteen minutes ago."

I now remembered that, in fact, a fruiterer, carrying upon his head a large basket of apples, had nearly thrown me down, by accident, as we passed from the Rue C——into the thoroughfare where we stood; but what had this to do with Chantilly I could not possibly understand.

There was not a particle of charlatanerie about Dupin. "I will explain," he said, "and, that you may comprehend all clearly, we will first retrace the course of your meditations, from the moment in which I spoke to you until that of the rencontre with the fruiterer in question. The larger links of the chain run thus—Chantilly, Orion, Dr. Nichols, Epicurus, Stereotomy, the street stones, the fruiterer."

There are few persons who have not, at some period of their lives, amused themselves in retracing the steps by which particular conclusions of their own minds have been attained. The occupation is often full of interest; and he who attempts it for the first time is astonished by the apparently illimitable distance and incoherence between the starting-point and the goal. What, then, must have been my amazement when I heard the Frenchman speak what he had just spoken, and when I could not help acknowledging that he had spoken the truth. He continued:

"We had been talking of horses, if I remember right, just before leaving the Rue C—. This was the last subject that we discussed. As we crossed into this street, a fruiterer, with a large basket upon his head, brushing quickly past us, thrust you upon a pile of paving-stones collected at a spot where the causeway is undergoing repair. You stepped upon one of the loose fragments, slipped, slightly strained your ankle, appeared vexed or sulky, muttered a few words, turned to look at the pile, and then proceeded in silence. I was not particularly attentive to what you did; but observation has become with me, of late, a species of necessity.

"You kept your eyes upon the ground—glancing, with a petulant expression, at the holes and ruts in the pavement (so that I saw you were still thinking of the stones), until we reached the little alley called Lamartine, which has been paved, by way of experiment with the overlapping and riveted blocks. Here your countenance brightened up, and, perceiving your lips move, I could not doubt that you murmured the word 'stereotomy,' a term very affectedly applied to this species of pavement. I knew that you could not say to yourself 'stereotomy' without being brought to think of atomies, and thus of the theories of Epicurus; and since, when we discussed this subject not very long ago I mentioned to you how singularly, yet with how little notice the vague guesses of that noble Greek had met with confirmation in the late nebular cosmogony, I felt that you could not avoid casting your eyes upward to the great nebula in Orion, and I certainly expected that you would do so. You did look up; and I was now assured that I had correctly followed your steps. But in that bitter tirade upon Chantilly, which appeared in yesterday's Musée, the satirists, making some disgraceful allusions to the cobbler's change of name upon assuming the buskin, quoted a Latin line about which we have often conversed. I mean the line

'Perdidit antiquum litera prima sonum.'

"I had told you that this was in reference to Orion, formerly written Urion; and, from certain pungencies connected with the explanation, I was aware that you could not have forgotten it. It was clear, therefore, that you would not fail to combine the two ideas of Orion and Chantilly. That you did combine them I saw by the character of the smile which passed over your lips. You thought of the poor Cobbler's immolation. So far, you had been stooping in your gait; but now I saw you draw yourself up to your full height. I was then sure that you reflected upon the diminutive figure of Chantilly. At this point I interrupted your meditations to remark that as, in fact, he was a very little fellow—that Chantilly—he would do better at the Théatre des Variétés."

This feat is paralleled in the Sherlock Holmes story entitled "The Resident Patient":

"Finding that Holmes was too absorbed for conversation, I had tossed aside the barren paper, and leaning back in my chair, I fell into a brown study. Suddenly my companion's voice broke in upon my thoughts.

"You are right, Watson," said he. "It does seem a very preposterous way of settling a dispute."

"Most preposterous!" I exclaimed, and then, suddenly realizing how he had echoed the inmost thought of my soul, I sat up in my chair and stared at him in blank amazement.

"What is this, Holmes?" I cried. "This is beyond anything which I could have imagined."

He laughed heartily at my perplexity.

"You remember," said he, "that some little time ago, when I read you the passage in one of Poe's sketches, in which a close reasoner follows the unspoken thoughts of his companion, you were inclined to treat the matter as a mere tour de force of the author. On my remarking that I was constantly in the habit of doing the same thing you expressed incredulity."

"Oh, no!"

"Perhaps not with your tongue, my dear Watson, but certainly with your eyebrows. So when I saw you throw down your paper and enter upon a train of thought, I was very happy to have the opportunity of reading it off, and eventually of breaking into it, as a proof that I had been in rapport with you."

But I was still far from satisfied. "In the example which you read to me," said I, "the reasoner drew his conclusions from the actions of the man whom he observed. If I remember right, he stumbled over a heap of stones, looked up at the stars, and so on. But I have been seated quietly in my chair, and what clews can I have given you?"

"You do yourself an injustice. The features are given to man as the means by which he shall express his emotions, and yours are faithful servants."

"Do you mean to say that you read my train of thoughts from my features?"

"Your features, and especially your eyes. Perhaps you cannot yourself recall how your reverie commenced?"

"No, I cannot."

"Then I will tell you. After throwing down your paper, which was the action which drew my attention to you, you sat for half a minute with a vacant expression. Then your eyes fixed themselves upon your newly-framed picture of General Gordon, and I saw by the alteration in your face that a train of thought had been started. But it did not lead very far. Your eyes turned across to the unframed portrait of Henry Ward Beecher which stands upon the top of your books. You then glanced up at the wall, and of course your meaning was obvious. You were thinking that if the portrait were framed it would just cover that bare space and correspond with Gordon's picture over there."

"You have followed me wonderfully!" I exclaimed.

"So far I could hardly have gone astray. But now your thoughts went back to Beecher, and you looked hard across as if you were studying the character in his features. Then your eyes ceased to pucker, but you continued to look across, and your face was thoughtful. You were recalling the incidents of Beecher's career. I was well aware that you could not do this without thinking of the mission which he undertook on behalf of the North at the time of the Civil War, for I remember you expressing your passionate indignation at the way in which he was received by the more turbulent of our people. You felt so strongly about it that I knew you could not think of Beecher without thinking of that also. When a moment later I saw your eyes wander away from the picture, I suspected that your mind had now turned to the Civil War, and when I observed that your lips set, your eyes sparkled, and your hands clinched, I was positive that you were indeed thinking of the gallantry which was shown by both sides in that desperate struggle. But then, again, your face grew sadder; you shook your head. You were dwelling upon the sadness and horror and useless waste of life. Your hand stole towards your own old wound, and a smile quivered on your lips, which showed me that the ridiculous side of this method of settling international questions had forced itself upon your mind. At this point I agreed with you that it was preposterous, and was glad to find that all my deductions had been correct."

"Absolutely!" said I. "And now that you have explained it, I confess that I am as amazed as before."

"It was very superficial, my dear Watson, I assure you. I should not have intruded it upon your attention had you not shown some incredulity the other day. But the evening has brought a breeze with it. What do you say to a ramble through London?"

XI

Close Observation

Close observation is one of the high cards of the fiction detective's game. Dupin is often described as scrutinizing with great minuteness of attention everything in the vicinity of the scene of the crime. We subjoin an account of the search for "The Purloined Letter," as an example of what a thorough search really means to the Transcendent Detective.

"Suppose you detail," said I, "the particulars of your search."

"Why, the fact is, we took our time, and we searched everywhere. I have had long experience in these affairs. I took the entire building, room by room; devoting the nights of a whole week to each. We examined first, the furniture of each apartment, we opened every possible drawer; and I presume that you know that, to a properly trained police agent, such a thing as a secret drawer is impossible. Any man is a dolt who permits a 'secret' drawer to escape him in a search of this kind. The thing is so plain. There is a certain amount of bulk—of space—to be accounted for in every cabinet. Then we have accurate rules. The fiftieth part of a line could not escape us. After the cabinets we took the chairs. The cushions we probed with the fine long needles you have seen me employ. From the tables we removed the tops."

"Why so?"

"Sometimes the top of a table, or other similarly arranged piece of furniture, is removed by the person wishing to conceal an article; then the leg is excavated, the article deposited within the cavity, and the top replaced. The bottoms and tops of bedposts are employed in the same way."

"But could not the cavity be detected by sounding?" I asked.

"By no means, if, when the article is deposited, a sufficient wadding of cotton be placed around it. Besides, in our case, we were obliged to proceed without noise."

"But you could not have removed—you could not have taken to pieces all articles of furniture in which it would have been possible to make a deposit in the manner you mention. A letter may be compressed into a thin spiral roll, not differing much in shape or bulk from a large knitting-needle, and in this form it might be inserted into the rung of a chair, for example. You did not take to pieces all the chairs?"

"Certainly not; but we did better—we examined the rungs of every chair in the Hotel, and, indeed, the jointings of every description of furniture, by the aid of a most powerful microscope. Had there been any traces of recent disturbance we should not have failed to detect it instantly. A single grain of gimlet-dust, for example, would have been as obvious as an apple. Any disorder in the gluing—any unusual gaping in the joints—would have sufficed to insure detection."

"I presume you looked to the mirrors, between the boards and the plates, and you probed the beds and the bed-clothes, as well as the curtains and carpets."

"That, of course; and when we had absolutely completed every particle of the furniture in this way, then we examined the house itself. We divided its entire surface into compartments, which we numbered, so that none might be missed; then we scrutinized each individual square inch throughout the premises, including the two houses immediately adjoining, with the microscope, as before."

"The two houses adjoining!" I exclaimed; "you must have had a great deal of trouble."

"We had; but the reward offered is prodigious."

"You include the grounds about the houses?"

"All the grounds are paved with brick. They gave us comparatively little trouble. We examined the moss between the bricks, and found it undisturbed."

"You looked among D—'s papers, of course, and into the books of the library?"

"Certainly; we opened every package and parcel; we not only opened every book, but we turned over every leaf in each volume, not contenting ourselves with a mere shake, according to the fashion of some of our police officers. We also measured the thickness of every book cover, with the most accurate admeasurement, and applied to each the most jealous scrutiny of the microscope. Had any of the bindings been recently meddled with, it would have been utterly impossible that the fact should have escaped observation. Some five or six volumes, just from the hands of the binder, we carefully probed, longitudinally, with the needles."

"You explored the floors beneath the carpets?"

"Beyond doubt. We removed every carpet, and examined the boards with the microscope."

"And the paper on the walls?"

"Yes."

"You looked into the cellars?"

"We did."

"Then," I said, "you have been making a miscalculation, and the letter is not upon the premises, as you suppose."

"I fear you are right there," said the Prefect. "And now, Dupin, what would you advise me to do?"

"To make a thorough re-search of the premises."

Lecoq pursues the same methods of close scrutiny, and we find him in Gaboriau's "The Crime of Orcival."

" . . . lifting the fallen furniture, studying its fractures, examining the smallest bits of wood or stuff to see if they might betray the truth. Now and then he took out an instrument case, from which he produced a shank, with which he unlocked various drawers. Finding a towel hanging over a rack, he carefully put it on one side, as if he deemed it of importance. He went to and fro between the bedroom and the count's study, without losing a word of what was being said—making indeed a mental note both of the remarks themselves and of the tone in which they were exchanged."

As to Sherlock Holmes, it is not necessary to refer to his microscopic examinations. In fact, so addicted is he to the use of the lens, that it has become a by-word in connection with his methods.

But this close observation must have something to observe; the magnifying glass must have something to magnify; and these things must be of vital importance as evidence.

1. The Search for Clues

THIS COULD RARELY BE COMPASSED in real life, but it is, of course, easy for the author to provide the tiny clues necessary to his hero's microscope work.

And tiny clues are a favorite device of the detective story writer. There is a fascination about the solving of a big murder mystery by a bit of a broken cuff-link; or the tracing of a professional burglar by a speck of cigarette ash. Of course, the philosophy is that these dues are so small as to be unnoticed by the criminal who so conveniently leaves them behind him. Also they are unnoticed by the amateur or the Central Office sleuth, and so redound to the glory of the Transcendent Detective.

But most of all their use is to impress and astound the reader by a picturesque application of the truth that great oaks from little acorns grow. It is the dramatic contrast of the tiny indication that points the way to the enormous result of discovering the perpetrator of an atrocious crime.

But here again we have the great gulf fixed between the Real Detective and the Fiction Detective. Take the vital point in "File No. 113." Now really there is not one chance in a thousand that the particle of green paint would have been found adhering to that key, had the key been found. Green paint will adhere most annoyingly to clothing, or hands, or even keys when it is not desired, but if needed as criminal evidence it will in all probability be found wanting.

But the field of fiction is as a salted mine. What is searched for is found, and the detective triumphantly ferrets out the infinitesimal clues that have been most carefully put in place by the author.

When Sherlock Holmes looked for a burnt match in "Silver Blaze," he found it, though the really careful inspector had carefully overlooked it. This is the account of the scene:

"My dear Inspector, you surpass yourself!" Holmes took the bag, and, descending into the hollow, he pushed the matting into a more central position. Then stretching himself upon his face and leaning his chin upon his hands, he made a careful study of the trampled mud in front of him. "Hullo!" said he, suddenly. "What's this?" It was a wax vesta half burned, which was so coated with mud that it looked at first like a little chip of wood.

"I cannot think how I came to overlook it," said the Inspector, with an expression of annoyance.

"It was invisible, buried in the mud. I only saw it because I was looking for it."

"What! you expected to find it?"

"I thought it not unlikely."

This is a fine instance of spectacular detective work. And this is what is demanded for the true technique of the Mystery Story. It is not real life; it is a stage, set with the furnishings and properties of the dramatic plot. The dropped handkerchiefs, the shreds of cloth or torn bits of paper, are carefully placed, and the detective has only to step along and pick them up.

Wilkie Collins' creation, Sergeant Cuff, sanctions it emphatically:

"I made a private inquiry last week, Mr. Superintendent," he said. "At one end of the inquiry there was a murder, and at the other end there was a spot of ink on a table-cloth that nobody could account for. In all my experience along the dirtiest ways of this dirty little world I have never met with such a thing as a trifle yet."

A case in point, is this bit from "The Whispering Man":

"I turned to go. Just as I did so, my eye caught a glint from the carpet, of what I took to be a bent pin. Quite automatically—for by nature I am an orderly and methodical person—I stooped and picked it up. It was not a pin after all, but the broken end of a curved needle. It made no particular impression on my mind, and I was on the point of dropping it into the waste-paper basket when something stopped me. It was no very definite idea, probably just a reminiscence from detective stories I had read, of the immense importance of the most trivial things."

It was this that Lowell had in mind, when he said that Poe "combined in a very remarkable manner two faculties which are seldom found united,—a power of influencing the mind of the reader by the impalpable shadows of mystery, and a minuteness of detail which does not leave a pin or a button unnoticed. Both are, in truth, the natural results of the predominating quality of his mind, to which we have before alluded,—analysis." And the same principle is approved of in real life by Mr. Arthur C. Train's assertion: "The discovery and proper proof of minute facts which tend to demonstrate the guilt of an accused are the joy of the natural prosecutor, and he may in his enthusiasm spend many thousands of dollars on what seems, and often is, an immaterial matter."

2. The Bizarre in Crime

A DEEP CONVICTION OF THE Transcendent Detective is that a crime containing unusual or even bizarre characteristics is more easy of solution than a commonplace one. This is a somewhat disingenuous proposition; for the real reason that the bizarre crime is preferable, is because it offers greater dramatic and spectacular opportunities. But of course the author is not admitting this. No, he puts into the mouth of his detective such theories as these.

Thus Dupin speaks:

"It appears to me that this mystery is considered insoluble, for the very reason which should cause it to be regarded as easy of solution—I mean, for the outré character of its features. The police are confounded by seeming absence of motive; not for the murder itself, but for the atrocity of the murder. They are puzzled, too, by the seeming impossibility of reconciling the voices heard in contention, with the facts that no one was discovered upstairs but the assassinated Mademoiselle L'Espanaye, and that there were no means of egress without the notice of the party ascending. The wild disorder of the room; the corpse thrust, with the head downward, up the chimney; the frightful mutilation of the body of the old lady; these considerations, with those just mentioned, and others which I need not mention, have sufficed to paralyze the powers, by putting completely at fault the boasted acumen of the government agents. They have fallen into the gross but common error of confounding the unusual with the abstruse. But it is by these deviations from the plane of the ordinary that reason feels its way, if at all in its search for the true. In investigations such as we are now pursuing, it should not be so much asked 'what has occurred,' as 'what has occurred that has never occurred before.' In fact, the facility with which I shall arrive, or have arrived, at the solution of this mystery, is in the direct ratio of its apparent insolubility in the eyes of the police."

And again:

"This is a far more intricate case than that of the Rue Morgue from which it differs in one important respect. This is an ordinary although an atrocious instance of crime. There is nothing peculiarly outré about it. You will observe that, for this reason, the mystery has been considered easy, when, for this reason, it should have been considered difficult of solution."

Sherlock Holmes remarks on this matter thus:

"As a rule," said Holmes, "the more bizarre a thing is the less mysterious it proves to be. It is your commonplace, featureless crimes which are really puzzling, just as a commonplace face is the most difficult to identify. But I must be prompt over this matter.—It seems, from what I gather, to be one of those simple cases which are so extremely difficult."

"That sounds a little paradoxical."

"But it is profoundly true. Singularity is almost invariably a clew. The more featureless and commonplace a crime is, the more difficult is it to bring it home."

Indeed, so fond is Sherlock Holmes of the bizarre that he prefers that characteristic to the more culpable forms of crime. In one of his stories he observes:

"Amid the action and reaction of so dense a swarm of humanity, every possible combination of events may be expected to take place, and many a little problem will be presented which may be striking and bizarre without being criminal. We have already had experience of such."

"So much so," I remarked, "that of the last six cases which I have added to my notes, three have been entirely free of any legal crime."

3. The Value of the Trivial

BUT IN THE FOLLOWING EXTRACT, perhaps because he is in a disputatious mood, he acknowledges a liking for trivial and lowly manifestations of his art:

"To the man who loves art for its own sake," remarked Sherlock Holmes, tossing aside the advertisement sheet of the Daily Telegraph, "it is frequently in its least important and lowliest manifestations that the keenest pleasure is to be derived. It is pleasant to me to observe, Watson, that you have so far grasped this truth that in these little records of our cases which you have been good enough to draw up, and I am bound to say, occasionally to embellish, you have given prominence not so much to the many causes célèbres and sensational trials in which I have figured, but rather to those incidents which may have been trivial in themselves, but which have given room for those faculties of deduction and of logical synthesis which I have made my special province."

"And yet," said I, smiling "I cannot quite hold myself absolved from the charge of sensationalism which has been urged against my records."

"You have erred, perhaps," he observed, taking up a glowing cinder with the tongs, and lighting with it the long cherrywood pipe which was wont to replace his clay when he was in a disputatious rather than a meditative mood—"you have erred perhaps in attempting to put color and life into each of your statements, instead of confining yourself to the task of placing upon record that severe reasoning from cause to effect which is really the only notable feature about the thing."

"It seems to me that I have done you full justice in the matter," I remarked, with some coldness, for I was repelled by the egotism which I had more than once observed to be a strong factor in my friend's singular character.

"No, it is not selfishness or conceit," said he, answering, as was his wont, my thoughts rather than my words. "If I claim full justice for my art, it is because it is an impersonal thing—a thing beyond myself. Crime is common. Logic is rare. Therefore it is upon the logic rather than upon the crime that you should dwell. You have degraded what should have been a course of lectures into a series of tales."

But Watson himself confesses to the dangers of this literary Scylla and Charybdis with which Conan Doyle has seen fit to disturb him:

"In glancing over the somewhat incoherent series of Memoirs with which I have endeavored to illustrate a few of the mental peculiarities of my friend Mr. Sherlock Holmes, I have been struck by the difficulty which I have experienced in picking out examples which shall in every way answer my purpose. For in those cases in which Holmes has performed some tour de force of analytical reasoning, and has demonstrated the value of his peculiar methods of investigation, the facts themselves have often been so slight or so commonplace that I could not feel justified in laying them before the public. On the other hand, it has frequently happened that he has been concerned in some research where the facts have been of the most remarkable and dramatic character, but where the share which he has himself taken in determining their causes has been less pronounced than I, as his biographer, could wish. The small matter which I have chronicled under the heading of 'A Study in Scarlet,' and that other later one connected with the loss of the Gloria Scott, may serve as examples of this Scylla and Charybdis which are forever threatening the historian. It may be that in the business of which I am now about to write the part which my friend played is not sufficiently accentuated; and yet the whole train of circumstances is so remarkable that I cannot bring myself to omit it entirely from this series."

4. The Tricks of Imitation

THESE TRICKS OF THE TRADE are of course faithfully copied by the imitators and successors of these great authors. An example in point is this from Jacques Futrelle's "The Thinking Machine";

"Now, Mr. Hatch," said The Thinking Machine in his perpetually crabbed voice, "we have a most remarkable riddle. It gains this remarkable aspect from its very simplicity. It is not, however, necessary to go into that now. I will make it clear to you when we know the motives."

The following paragraph of philosophy has proved of immense use as a model:

"All this seems strange to you," continued Holmes, "because you failed at the beginning of the inquiry to grasp the importance of the single real clew which was presented to you. I had the good fortune to seize upon that, and everything which has occurred since then has served to confirm my original supposition, and, indeed, was the logical sequence of it. Hence things which have perplexed you and made the case more obscure have served to enlighten me and to strengthen my conclusions. It is a mistake to confound strangeness with mystery. The most commonplace crime is often the most mysterious because it presents no new or special features from which deductions may be drawn. This murder would have been infinitely more difficult to unravel had the body of the victim been simply found lying in the roadway without any of those outré and sensational accompaniments which have rendered it remarkable. These strange details, far from making the case more difficult, have really had the effect of making it less so."

Its principles are embodied in this quotation from Gordon Holmes' "A Mysterious Disappearance":

"The greater the apparent mystery," he communed, "the less it is in reality. We now have two tracks to follow. They are both hidden, it is true, but when we find one, it will probably intersect the other.

"You are not to blame, White," he said, "for having failed to note many things which I have now told you. You are the slave of a system. Your method works admirably for the detection of commonplace crime, but as soon as the higher region of romance is reached it is as much out of place as a steam-roller in a lady's boudoir. Look at the remarkable series of crimes the English police have failed to solve of late, merely because some bizarre element had intruded itself at the outset. Have you ever read any of the works of Edgar Allan Poe?"

The detective answered in the affirmative. "The Murders in the Rue Morgue" and "The Mystery of Marie Roget" were familiar to him.

"Well," went on Bruce, "there you have the accurate samples of my meaning. Poe would not have been puzzled for an hour by the vagaries of Jack the Ripper. He would have said at once—most certainly after the third or fourth in the series of murders—'This is the work of an athletic lunatic, with a morbid love of anatomy and a morbid hatred of a certain class of women. Seek for him among young men who have pestered doctors with outrageous theories, and who possess weak-minded or imbecile relatives.' Then, again, take the murder on the South-Western Railway. Do you think Poe would have gone questioning bartenders or inquiring into abortive love affairs? Not he! Jealous swains do not carry pistols about with them to slay their sweethearts, nor do they choose a four-minutes' interval between suburban stations for frenzied avowals of their passion. Here you have the clear trail of a clever lunatic, dropping from the skies, as it were, and disappearing in the same erratic manner."

In "The Master of Mysteries," Mr. Gelett Burgess puts this principle into the mouth of his psychic detective, Astro:

"It will probably be easy and interesting," he remarked to his assistant, Valeska, who had been present at the interview with McGraw. "It is these cases which are apparently so extraordinary that are most easily solved. Given any remarkable variation in the aspect of a crime, and you know immediately where to begin. This will be only play, I fancy."

XII

OTHER DETECTIVES OF FICTION

Some Original Traits
Two Unique Detectives
The detective of modern fiction is a combination of the stock
  principles already noticed with such further and varying
  characteristics as the author may invent. In so far as the personal
  traits of the detective can differ from Sherlock Holmes, the
  author is so far less liable to the charge of plagiarism.

1. Some Original Traits

A GOOD EXAMPLE OF HOW one of the later writers has invested
his detective with fresh qualities may be noted in this extract from
"Midnight at Mears House," by Harrison J. Holt:

At the time of his coming to Mears House, Garth looked very much
as he does today—a short, slight man of about my own age, well-built
and energetic, but of a nervous rather than a muscular type of energy.
He has grown a trifle stouter since, to be sure, but otherwise I can see
little change in him. He was as bald then as he is now, and had the same
trick of carrying his head a little to one side, as though the weight of it
were too much for his neck to support. I have never seen a head more
beautifully shaped than his, with a wide, high forehead, dark eyes far
apart and rather prominent—it was hard to believe them blind—the nose
and chin of an old Roman Emperor, and a somewhat small but finely
modelled mouth.

His ears, however, were the most remarkable of his features—not
that they were unusual in shape or size, but because they were so low
as to appear almost misplaced, and on account of their extraordinary
quality. I doubt if anyone was ever gifted with a more wonderful sense
of hearing. Certainly I have never met anybody, even among those
born blind, who could distinguish and interpret sound with such
unerring, almost uncanny skill. Without this power—which he had
developed to an altogether incredible degree—he could never have
achieved the results he did: he has told me so many times. The tiniest

noises, unremarked or meaningless to most people, were packed with significance to him. Each registered its own distinct, unequivocal impression, producing an emotion or resulting in a co-ordination of ideas which often enabled him to arrive instantly at the most momentous conclusions.

Especially was this the case in regard to the tones, inflection, and timbre of the human voice. From these he was able to deduct an astonishingly large number of facts concerning the person speaking—such as his age, nationality, occupation, physical and mental state of health, disposition, and character. This, as I am well aware, may strike the reader as fanciful and even preposterous. It seemed so to me at first, and yet I learned later that to a lesser degree this power of divination was no uncommon thing among the blind, though I have heard of very few instances in which it proved so uniformly infallible.

I should not forget to mention as well a veritable sixth sense which he possessed—a sort of clairvoyance which made up in great measure for his lost sight. And yet clairvoyance is hardly the right word to describe it. It was rather as if he had some strange invisible organ of sensibility, some occult medium, by means of which he became aware of things seemingly beyond his apprehension. Doubtless a psychologist could state it far more intelligibly; I can only repeat that he had some such way of sensitizing himself, as it were, so as to receive impressions not communicable through the ordinary channels of the senses.

Just how much this faculty, combined with his marvellously developed hearing, has aided him in his work, it would be hard to say. Personally I think he overestimates its value to him, and underrates the part his brain has played in the mastering of these abstruse problems. Without a very high degree of mental acuteness, the clearest and soundest of reasoning powers, and what—for want of a better word—I must call a sympathetic imagination, his unusual psychical and auditory perceptions would, I feel sure, have been of little help to him. It is, in my opinion, far more to the brilliant qualities of his mind, his marked analytical and synthetical abilities, and his unrivalled skill as a constructive logician, that he chiefly owes his success.

Again, some authors try to give their detectives prominence by using methods exactly opposite to those of Sherlock Holmes. LeDroit Conners, in Samuel Gardenhire's book, "The Long Arm," thus asserts his confidence in himself:

"You cannot understand how strongly such matters appeal to me. It is a faculty with me almost to know the solution of a crime when the leading circumstances connected with it are revealed. I form my conclusion first, and, confident of its correctness, hunt for evidence to sustain it. I do this because I am never wrong. It is not magic, telepathy, nor any form of mental science; it is a moral consciousness of the meaning of related facts, impressed upon my mind with unerring certainty."

"I do not understand you," I said.

"When I am given certain figures," he replied, "the process of addition is instantaneous and sure. So, when I know of established incidents relating to a matter, they group themselves in my mind in such a manner as to reveal to me their meaning."

"You say a gift developed; perhaps. Rather an instinct, as the faculty of scent to the blood-hound and the acute ear to the hare, an unfailing sight to the hawk and a sense of touch to the serpent. Deductive knowledge depends on reason, but inspiration is an exalted—no, perhaps I should say an acute sense of something else. The beasts, unclothed except by nature and unfed except by season and conquest, must make existence out of an absolute impression of certainty that is neither analytical nor deductive. I fear I am in that category, my dear fellow. I know things because I know them—that is, somethings."

This is decidedly in contrast to Holmes' statement,

"Now I make a point of never having any prejudices, and of following docilely wherever fact may lead me."

The foregoing is in line with this bit of Poe's wisdom:

"The mass of the people regard as profound only him who suggests pungent contradictions of the general idea. In ratiocination, not less than in literature, it is the epigram which is the most immediately and the most universally appreciated. In both, it is of the lowest order of merit.

"What I mean to say is, that it is the mingled epigram and melodrama of the idea that Marie Roget still lives, rather than any true plausibility in this idea, which have suggested it to L'Etoile."

Burton E. Stevenson works on this principle when his detective in "The Holladay Case" says:

"I think we're too apt to overlook the simple explanations, which are, after all, nearly always the true ones. It's only in books that we meet the reverse. You remember it's Gaboriau who advises one always to distrust the probable?"

"Yes. I don't agree with him."

"Nor I."

But it is a dangerous experiment for inexperienced authors to put forward views heterodox to the accepted laws of Detective Fiction, and it must be done with skill and judgment.

In Luther Trant's work, his scientific apparatus enables him to dispense with the more usual methods.

"No, thank you," he said, refusing the proffer of the paper. "I read from the marks made upon minds by a crime, not from scrawls and thumbprints upon paper. And my means of reading those marks are fortunately in my possession this morning. No, I do not mean that I have other evidence upon this case than that you have just given me, Mr. Eldredge," Trant explained. "I refer to my psychological apparatus which, the express company notified me, arrived from New York this morning. If you will let me have my appliance delivered direct to your house it will save much time."

2. Two Unique Detectives

Rouletabille appreciated the dramatic value of what Poe called the pungent contradiction of the general idea. In "The Mystery of the Yellow Room," by Gaston Leroux, the following conversation occurs:

"Have you any idea as to the murderer's station in life?"

"Yes," he replied; "I think if he isn't a man in society, he is, at least, a man belonging to the upper class. But that, again, is only an impression."

"What has led you to form it?"

"Well,—the greasy cap, the common handkerchief, and the marks of the rough boots on the floor," he replied.

"I understand," I said; "murderers don't leave traces behind them which tell the truth."

"We shall make something out of you yet, my dear Sainclair," concluded Rouletabille.

Like Lecoq, this young man was not infallible; but his author made him this way for the same reason. Because he figures in a novel, and the infallible detective must do his work in a short-story.

Rouletabille's strong card is pure reason.

"How did you come to suspect Larsan?" asked the President.

"My pure reason pointed to him. But I did not foresee the drugging. He is very cunning. Yes, my pure reason pointed to him."

"What do you mean by your pure reason?"

"That power of one's mind which admits of no disturbing elements to a conclusion. The day following the incident of 'the inexplicable gallery,' I felt myself losing control of it. I had allowed myself to be diverted by fallacious evidence; but I recovered and again took hold of the right end."

Again, he says:

"M. Sainclair, you ought to know that I never suspect any person or anything without previously having satisfied myself upon the 'ground of pure reason.' That is a solid staff which has never yet failed me on the road and on which I invite you all to lean with me."

His pure reason is of the subtlest variety, and his fine work throughout the book commands always the admiration of the connoisseur. In a seemingly inexplicable situation he exclaims:

"Let us reason it out!"

And he returned on the instant to that argument which had already served us and which he repeated again and again to himself (in order that, he said, he should not be lured away by the outer appearance of things): "Do not look for Larsan in that place where he reveals himself; seek for him everywhere else where he hides himself."

This he followed up with the supplementary argument:

"He never shows himself where he seems to be except to prevent us from seeing him where he really is."

And he resumed:

"Ah! the outer appearance of things! Look here, Sainclair! There are moments when, for the sake of reasoning clearly, I want to get rid of my eyes! Let us get rid of our eyes, Sainclair, for five minutes—just five minutes, and, perhaps, we shall see more clearly."

Rouletabille's subtlety of reasoning rose almost to clairvoyance. In his desperate endeavors to discover the identity of Larsan, he relates his experience thus:

"And why did all the others sit so silent and so motionless behind their dark glasses? All at once, I turned my head and looked behind me. Then I understood, more by instinct than anything else, that I was the object of a common physical attraction. Someone was looking at me. Two eyes were fixed upon me—weighing upon me. I could not see the eyes and I did not know from where the glance fixed upon me came, but it was there. I knew it—and it was his glance. But there was no one behind me, nor at the right, nor the left, nor in front, except the people who were seated at the table, motionless, behind their dark glasses. And then—then I knew that Larsan's eyes were glaring at me from behind a pair of those glasses and—ah! the dark glasses,—the dark glasses behind which were hidden Larsan's eyes. If I mention this incident here, it is for the purpose of showing to how great an extent I was haunted by the image of Larsan, hiding under some new form, and lurking unknown among us. Dear Heaven! Larsan had so often proved his talent—I may even say his genius—in this respect, that I felt that he was quite capable of defying us now, and of mingling with us while we thought that he was a stranger—or, perhaps, even a friend."

So fearful is he that one of the seemingly well-known people about him may be Larsan in disguise, that he says to Sainclair:

"Hold your left hand in your right for five minutes and then ask yourself: 'Is it you, Larsan?' And when you have replied to yourself, do not feel too sure, for he may, perhaps, have lied to you, and he may be in your own skin without your knowing it."

There is nothing imitative about this young detective. His methods are unique. His pure reasoning is most subtle; and though the farthest possible remove from realism it presents a semblance of reality that is entirely convincing.

In "The Whispering Man" Mr. Henry Kitchell Webster employs a very different principle for the use of his detective. It may be called the principle of The Inspired Guess, and though improbable, perhaps not more so than the laws of detective fiction permit. The Whispering Man thus describes it himself:

"I had happened to tell him once that I believed that I always knew a criminal when I saw one, without knowing how or why—by just looking at him. He didn't scout that theory as you would if I were to give you a chance."

"And you believed all the while," I repeated, incredulously, "that McWilliams was the man?"

"Not believed; knew. Oh, I don't know how. That's the whole point. That's what I've been preaching all the evening. The only certain knowledge is the inspired guess."

One of the most remarkable Detectives of Fiction is Mr. Zangwill's Grodman, who in "Big Bow Mystery," thus discourses:

"It grew daily clearer to me that criminals were more fools than rogues. Every crime I had traced, however cleverly perpetrated, was from the point of view of penetrability a weak failure. Traces and trails were left on all sides—ragged edges, rough-hewn corners; in short, the job was botched, artistic completeness unattained. To the vulgar, my feats might seem marvelous—the average man is mystified to grasp how you detect the letter 'e' in a simple cryptogram—to myself they were as commonplace as the crimes they unveiled. To me now, with my lifelong study of the science of evidence, it seemed possible to commit not merely one, but a thousand crimes that should be absolutely undiscoverable. And yet criminals would go on sinning, and giving themselves away, in the same old grooves—no originality, no dash, no individual insight, no fresh conception! One would imagine there were an Academy of crime with forty thousand armchairs. And gradually, as I pondered and brooded over the thought, there came upon me the desire to commit a crime that should baffle detection. I could invent hundreds of such crimes, and please myself by imagining them done but would they really work out in practice? Evidently the sole performer of my experiment must be myself; the subject whom or what? Accident should determine. I itched to commence with murder—to tackle the stiffest problems first, and I burned to startle and baffle the world—especially the world of which I had ceased to be. Outwardly I was calm, and spoke to the people about me as usual. Inwardly I was on fire with a consuming scientific passion. I sported with my pet theories, and fitted them mentally on everyone I met. Every friend or acquaintance I sat and gossiped with, I was plotting how to murder without leaving a clue. There is not one of my friends or acquaintances I have not done away with in thought. There is no public man—have no fear, my dear Home Secretary—I have not planned to assassinate secretly, mysteriously, unintelligibly, undiscoverably. Ah, how I could give the stock criminals points with their second-hand motives, their conventional conceptions, their commonplace details, their lack of artistic feeling and restraint."

And in the same book, we get this description of the contrasting official detective:

Wimp was at his greatest in collecting circumstantial evidence; in putting two and two together to make five. He would collect together a number of dark and disconnected data and flash across them the electric light of some unifying hypothesis in a way which would have done credit to a Darwin or a Faraday. An intellect which might have served to unveil the secret workings of nature was subverted to the protection of a capitalistic civilization.

XIII

Portraits

The appearance of the detective is always of interest and each author in turn endeavors to make his marvelous-minded creature look as physically unlike other fiction detectives as possible. And especially does he aim to have him totally different in his effects from the popular conception of the conventional detective. In fact the average detective of fiction is always declared to look absolutely unlike the average detective of fiction.

1. Some Early Detective Portraits

M. Dupin is not described physically, as Poe's marvelous economy of attention made him omit every possible bit of material extraneous to his actual story. But, beginning let us say, with Lecoq, all seem to be diametrically opposed to the conventional detective.

To quote from "The Crime of Orcival":

M. Lecoq, whom none of them had ever met before, in no wise resembled the conventional French detective. The latter is commonly depicted as a tall fellow, with heavy moustaches and "imperial," wearing a military stock collar, a greasy silk hat, and a threadbare frock-coat buttoned up to the throat so as to conceal either the complete absence of linen or at all events the extreme dirtiness of a calico shirt. Such an individual will have immense feet incased in heavy Wellingtons and will carry in his right hand a powerful sword-stick or bludgeon. Now M. Lecoq, as he appeared in the dining-room at Valfeuillu, had nothing whatever in common with this familiar type. It is true, however, that he can assume whatever air he pleases. Although his friends declare that he has features of his own which he retains at home when sitting by his own fire-side, with his slippers on, this is by no means certain. At all events, his mobile face lends itself to strange transformations, and he modifies his features according to his will just as the sculptor moulds his modelling clay. He changes everything, even the expression of his eyes. On this occasion M. Lecoq had assumed a handsome wig of lank hair, neither fair nor dark, but rather pretentiously parted on one side. Whiskers of the same vague colour puffed out with bad pomade, encircled his pallid face. His eyelids were very red; his eyes seemed weak and watery, and an open smile rested on his thick lips, which, in parting, disclosed a range of long yellow teeth. Timidity, self-sufficiency, and contentment were equally blended in the expression of his features. No one would ever have credited the possessor of such a head with even average intelligence. He looked the picture of some dull-minded, money-grubbing haberdasher, who after cheating his customers for thirty years, had retired on a large income. His coat was like all other coats, his trousers like all other trousers. A hair-chain, of the same colour as his whiskers, spanned his stomach, and a large silver watch could be seen bulging out of his left waistcoat pocket. While he spoke he fumbled with a horn box full of tiny square lozenges, and adorned on the cover with the portrait of a homely well-dressed woman, "the dear defunct," no doubt. As the conversation proceeded, according as he was satisfied or disturbed, M. Lecoq munched one of these lozenges or gave the portrait a glance which was quite a poem in itself.

To be sure, this was Lecoq in disguise. But the natural man, though seldom seen, was also unlike the regulation French detective. At his very first appearance on Gaboriau's pages he is described thus:

. . . he was about twenty-five years old, with a pale face, red lips and an abundance of curly black hair, but with scarcely a sign of beard or mustache. He was short but well-made, and his whole manner denoted energy of extraordinary character. With the exception of his eyes, there was nothing very remarkable in his appearance, but these either shone brilliantly or else grew dull, according to the disposition of the moment. His nose, which was rather wide, possessed an amount of flexibility that was extraordinary.

Nor is old Father Tabaret, except on close inspection, apparently possessed of detective insight. Here is his picture:

In a large, heavily curtained bed, covered up almost to the nose, lay the oracle of the Rue de Jerusalem. It was almost impossible to believe that such great intelligence could exist in that figure, the face of which showed nothing but the appearance of the greatest stupidity; a retreating forehead, huge ears, a little snub nose, small eyes, and thick lips, made M. Tabaret look more like a half-witted citizen than the sagacious citizen that he was. It is true that when he was closely examined there was something in him resembling a sleuth-hound, the habits and instincts of which he possessed to such a great extent. In the street the impudent young urchins would shout after him, "Oh! what a guy," but he laughed at all this, and even took a pleasure in putting on an extra appearance of folly and simplicity.

Vidocq, though not declared to be uncommon in his appearance, is sufficiently so to give him the necessary prestige. We are told that "he was a strong, well-built man with square shoulders and shambling gait. He had gray hair, a thick nose, blue eyes, a smooth face and a perpetual smile."

Although Vidocq really lived, yet his "Memoirs" are believed to be largely fiction, and so we may class him, in part at least, among our story-book friends.

Wilkie Collins deliberately draws his picture of the official detective thus:

For a family in our situation, the Superintendent of the Frizinghall police was the most comforting officer you could wish to see. Mr. Seegrave was tall and portly, and military in his manners. He had a fine, commanding voice, and a mighty resolute eye, and a grand frock coat which buttoned beautifully up to his leather stock. "I'm the man you want," was written all over his face; and he ordered his two inferior policemen about with a severity which convinced us all that there was no trifling with him.

And then, in every respect a vivid contrast, he gives us a picture of the engaging Sergeant Cuff, for after all, the beauty of a detective is largely in the eye of the beholder.

When the time came for the Sergeant's arrival I went down to the gate to look out for him.

A fly from the railway drove up as I reached the lodge; and out got a grizzled, elderly man, so miserably lean that he looked as if he had not got an ounce of flesh on his bones in any part of him. He was dressed all in decent black, with a white cravat round his neck.

His face was as sharp as a hatchet, and the skin of it was as yellow and dry and withered as an autumn leaf. His eyes, of a steely light gray, had a disconcerting trick, when they encountered your eyes, of looking as if they expected something more from you than you were aware of yourself. His walk was soft; his voice was melancholy; his long, lanky fingers were hooked like claws. He might have been a parson, or an undertaker, or anything else you like, except what he really was. A more complete opposite to Superintendent Seegrave than Sergeant Cuff, and a less comforting officer to look at for a family in distress, I defy you to discover, search where you may.

2. Some More Modern Portraits

SHERLOCK HOLMES IS TOO WELL known to the reading public to require description here, but a brief account of his appearance, as detailed by Watson, proves his unlikeness to those we have previously looked at:

His very person and appearance were such as to strike the attention of the most casual observer. In height he was rather over six feet, and so exceedingly lean that he seemed to be considerably taller. His eyes were sharp and piercing, save during those intervals of torpor to which I have alluded; and his thin, hawk-like nose gave his whole expression an air of alertness and decision. His chin, too, had the prominence and squareness which mark the man of determination. His hands were invariably blotted with ink and stained with chemicals, yet he was possessed of extraordinary delicacy of touch, as I frequently had occasion to observe when I watched him manipulating his fragile philosophical instruments.

In almost ludicrous contrast to Holmes is a young detective who never achieved Sherlock's popularity, but whose wonderful instinct for pure reasoning puts him at the head of his own class.

This is Rouletabille, who figures in "The Mystery of the Yellow Room," by Gaston Leroux.

His friend Sainclair, who is his Watsonian chronicler, says:

I first knew Joseph Rouletabille when he was a young reporter. At that time I was a beginner at the Bar and often met him in the corridors of examining magistrates, when I had gone to get a "permit to communicate" for the prison of Mazas, or for Saint-Lazare. He had, as they say, "a good nut." He seemed to have taken his head—round as a bullet—out of a box of marbles, and it is from that, I think, that his comrades of the press—all determined billiard-players—had given him that nickname, which was to stick to him and be made illustrious by him. He was always as red as a tomato, now gay as a lark, now grave as a judge. How, while still so young—he was only sixteen and a half years old when I saw him for the first time—had he already won his way on the press? That was what everybody who came into contact with him might have asked, if they had not known his history.

Practically, however, Rouletabille was not nominally the great detective of the book—that honor was given to Frederick Larsan—who seemed to show a few of Sherlock Holmes' physical characteristics. This is Larsan:

He might be about fifty years of age. He had a fine head, his hair turning grey; a colourless complexion, and a firm profile. His forehead was prominent, his chin and cheeks clean shaven. His upper lip, without moustache, was finely chiselled. His eyes were rather small and round, with a look in them that was at once searching and disquieting. He was of middle height and well built, with a general bearing elegant and gentlemanly. There was nothing about him of the vulgar policeman. In his way, he was an artist, and one felt that he had a high opinion of himself. The sceptical tone of his conversation was that of a man who had been taught by experience. His strange profession had brought him into contact with so many crimes and villainies that it would have been remarkable if his nature had not been a little hardened.

An interesting-looking detective is "The Thinking Machine" of Jacques Futrelle. His description is written with Mr. Futrelle's individual touch, and Professor Van Dusen possesses the squint which Mr. Train regards as a detective's birthright:

Practically all those letters remaining in the alphabet after Augustus S.F.X. Van Dusen was named, were afterward acquired by that gentleman in the course of a brilliant scientific career, and, being honorably acquired, were tacked on to the other end. His name, therefore, taken with all that belonged to it, was a wonderfully imposing structure. He was a Ph.D., an LL.D., an F.R.S. an M.D., and an M.D.S. He was also someother things—just what, he himself couldn't say—through recognition of his ability by various foreign educational and scientific institutions.

In appearance he was no less striking than in nomenclature. He was slender, with the droop of the student in his thin shoulders and the pallor of a close, sedentary life on his clean-shaven face. His eyes wore a perpetual, forbidding squint—the squint of a man who studies little things—and when they could be seen at all through his thick spectacles, were mere slits of watery blue. But above his eyes was his most striking feature. This was a tall, broad brow, almost abnormal in height and width, crowned by a heavy shock of bushy, yellow hair. All these things conspired to give him a peculiar, almost grotesque personality.

Anna Katharine Green is one of the very best constructors of a detective story. The first introduction of her Mr. Gryce begins:

And here let me say that Mr. Gryce, the detective, was not the thin, wiry individual with the piercing eye you are doubtless expecting to see. On the contrary, Mr. Gryce was a portly, comfortable personage with an eye that never pierced, that did not even rest on you. If it rested anywhere, it was always on some insignificant object in the vicinity, some vase, inkstand, book, or button. These things he would seem to take into his confidence, make the repositories of his conclusions; but as for you—you might as well be the steeple on Trinity Church, for all connection you ever appeared to have with him or his thoughts. At present, then, Mr. Gryce was, as I have already suggested, on intimate terms with the door-knob.

And in a later book she again insists upon this unlikeness to what may be expected:

I was therefore moving reluctantly away, when I felt a slight but peremptory touch on the arm, and turning, saw the detective at my side, still studying his piece of china.

He was, as I have said, of portly build and benevolent aspect; a fatherly-looking man, and not at all the person one would be likely to associate with the police. Yet he could take the lead very naturally, and when he spoke, I felt bound to answer him.

Grodman, in "Big Bow Mystery," is briefly described by Mr. Zangwill:

After an age seven minutes by any honest clock—Grodman made his appearance, looking as dressed as usual, but with unkempt hair and with disconsolate side-whisker yet, for it had only recently come within the margin of cultivation. In active service Grodman had been clean-shaven, like all members of the profession—for surely your detective is the most versatile of actors.

And this is the picture of Wimp the official detective in the same book.

Wimp was young and fresh-colored. He had a Roman nose, and was smartly dressed. He had beaten Grodman by discovering the wife Heaven meant for him. He had a bouncing boy, who stole jam out of the pantry without anyone being the wiser. Wimp did what work he could do at home in a secluded study at the top of the house. Outside his chamber of horrors he was the ordinary husband of commerce. He adored his wife, who thought poorly of his intellect, but highly of his heart. In domestic difficulties Wimp was helpless. He could not even tell whether the servant's "character" was forged or genuine. Probably he could not level himself to such petty problems. He was like the senior wrangler who has forgotten how to do quadratics, and has to solve equations of the second degree by the calculus.

The reference to Wimp's wife is thus explained:

In a moment the first floor window was raised—the little house was of the same pattern as her own—and Grodman's full, fleshy face loomed through the fog in sleepy irritation from under a nightcap. Despite its scowl the detective's face dawned upon her like the sun upon an occupant of the haunted chamber.

"What in the devil's the matter?" he growled. Grodman was not an early bird, now that he had no worms to catch. He could afford to despise proverbs now, for the house in which he lived was his, and he lived in it because several other houses in the street were also his and it is well for the landlord to be about his own estate in Bow where poachers often shoot the moon. Perhaps the desire to enjoy his greatness among his early cronies counted for something, too, for he had been born and bred at Bow, receiving when a youth his first engagement from the local police quarters, whence he drew a few shillings a week as an amateur detective in his leisure hours.

Grodman was still a bachelor. In the celestial matrimonial bureau a partner might have been selected for him, but he had never been able to discover her. It was his one failure as a detective. He was a self-sufficing person, who preferred a gas stove to a domestic; but in deference to Glover Street opinion he admitted a female factotum between ten A.M. and ten P.M., and, equally in deference to Glover Street opinion, excluded her between ten P.M. and ten A.M.

3. Some Less Known Portraits

GORDON HOLMES INCLINES TO WILKIE COLLINS' plan of contrasting the appearance of the real detective and the fictional at once. In "A Mysterious Disappearance" he presents these opposite physical effects:

Inspector White, of Scotland Yard, was announced, and a short, thick-set man entered. He was absolutely round in every part. His sturdy, rotund frame was supported on stout, well-moulded legs. His bullet head, with close-cropped hair, gave a suggestion of strength to his rounded face, and a pair of small bright eyes looked suspiciously on the world from beneath well-arched eyebrows.

Two personalities more dissimilar than those of Claude Bruce and Inspector White could hardly be brought together in the same room. People who are fond of tracing resemblances to animals in human beings would liken the one to a gray-hound, the other to a bull-dog.

Yet they were both masters in the art of detecting crime—the barrister subtle, analytic, introspective; the policeman direct, pertinacious, self-confident. Bruce lost all interest in a case when the hidden trail was laid bare. Mr. White regarded investigation as so many hours on duty until his man was transported or hanged.

In "The Whispering Man," an astonishing detective story by Henry Kitchell Webster, we have this description of the detective:

He was the sort of a man who never would be spoken of as old, if it were not for his attempts to look young. He was actually, I should judge, somewhere in the middle forties, a tall, graceful, and commanding figure, with a strikingly handsome face. There was nothing weak about it. The features were big and boldly, though finely, modeled, and the deep-set eyes singularly expressive. The only fault one could find with him was that he carried everything just a little too far. He was too aggressively well dressed; too painfully clean-shaven; his manner a little too dignified; his voice and features a little too expressive. It came upon me all at once what he must be—an actor. That was it. Everything about him was heightened just enough to carry itself over the footlights. He was in evening dress, wore an overcoat and gloves, and carried a walking stick, as well as an irreproachable silk hat, in his hand.

In "The Scales of Justice," an exceptionally clever surprise story by George L. Knapp, the Hero Detective is not a professional one, but a young newspaper reporter. He is therefore allowed the characteristics of our best newspaper men, but in all probability he inherits his sardonic humor from his predecessor Holmes.

Kern tossed the shears into a drawer, and stood up. He was as tall as the other man, and as straight; and both had that alert look of expectancy, quite unmixed with either wonder or nervousness, which marks our best newspaper men. There the resemblance ended. Jennings was about thirty-five, smooth-shaven, smiling brown of hair and blue of eye; with humorous little wrinkles around the eyes to testify of the many funny things he had seen. Kern was twenty-eight or twenty-nine; and his coal-black hair and bronze-black Vandyke beard made him look more like an Austrian surgeon than an American reporter. His humor was apt to be sardonic; and a certain element of moodiness was seldom absent from his face. "Kern is really a secret sufferer from the artistic temperament," said the managing editor once, "but so long as he's trying to live it down, I won't give him away."

"Average Jones," the creation of Samuel Hopkins Adams, achieves a distinction by being inconspicuous:

He was, so to speak, a composite photograph of any thousand well-conditioned, clean living Americans between the ages of twenty-five and thirty. Happily, his otherwise commonplace face was relieved by the one unfailing characteristic of composite photographs, large, deep-set and thoughtful eyes. Otherwise he would have passed in any crowd, and nobody would have noticed him pass. Now, at twenty-seven, he looked back over the five years since his graduation from college and wondered what he had done with them; and at the four previous years of undergraduate life and wondered how he had done so well with those, and why he had not in some manner justified the parting words of his favorite professor: "You have one rare faculty, Jones. You can, when you choose, sharpen the pencil of your mind to a very fine point. Specialize, my boy, specialize."

A little like "The Thinking Machine" is "The Man in the Corner," described thus by the Baroness Orczy:

The appearance of the man was sufficient to tickle the most ultramorose fancy. Polly thought to herself that she had never seen anyone so pale, so thin, with such funny light-coloured hair, brushed very smoothly across the top of a very dubiously bald crown. He looked so timid and nervous as he fidgeted incessantly with a piece of string; his long, lean, and trembling fingers tying and untying it into knots of wonderful and complicated proportions.

Astro, the hero of Gelett Burgess's book of Mystery Stories, is perhaps the farthest possible remove from a conventional detective in appearance. Though not described categorically, we are given various word pictures of him in his "psychic studio." There he lounges among oriental divans and draperies, wearing a jewelled turban, flowing silken robes, and other characteristic apparel, as he indulges in the enjoyment of his silver-mounted water-pipe or his pet white lizard. He has sufficiently unusual eccentricities to put him in the list of correctly made up fiction detectives, and though blasé, he is original and interesting.

4. Idiosyncrasies of Fictional Detectives

MOST FICTIONAL DETECTIVES HAVE PECULIAR and individual tricks of personality which are doubtless intended for the reader to remember them by.

Dupin had the most pronouncedly queer traits of all. Perhaps none of his successors ever achieved anything so freakish as this described below; and which, had he lived today, would have given him a claim to the title of "Sun Dodger."

It was a freak of fancy in my friend (for what else shall I call it?) to be enamoured of the night for her own sake, and into this bizarrerie, as into all his others, I quietly fell; giving myself up to his wild whims with a perfect abandon. The sable divinity would not herself dwell with us always; but we could counterfeit her presence. At the first dawn of the morning we closed all the messy shutters of our old building; lighted a couple of tapers, which, strongly perfumed, threw out only the ghastliest and feeblest of rays. By the aid of these we then busied our souls in dreams—reading, writing, or conversing, until warned by the clock of the advent of the true darkness. Then we sallied forth into the streets, arm and arm, continuing the topics of the day, or roaming far and wide until a late hour, seeking, amid the wild lights and shadows of the populous city, that infinity of mental excitement which quiet observation can afford.

Sherlock Holmes' idiosyncrasies are too well known to need recapitulation. His morphine habit, his musical taste and his sardonic moods are familiar to all. Holmes also had a habit of listening to his clients' recitals with his eyes shut. Though to be sure this was less radical than the proceeding of Dupin who "sat in his accustomed armchair, the embodiment of respectful attention" but he wore green spectacles which allowed him to "sleep not the less soundly, though silently" throughout the long account of the case by the Prefect.

Holmes' odd habits are here referred to:

An anomaly which often struck me in the character of my friend Sherlock Holmes was that, although in his methods of thought he was the neatest and most methodical of mankind, and although also he affected a certain quiet primness of dress, he was none the less in his personal habits one of the most untidy men that ever drove a fellow-lodger to distraction. Not that I am in the least conventional in that respect myself. The rough-and-tumble work in Afghanistan, coming on the top of a natural Bohemianism of disposition, has made me rather more lax than befits a medical man. But with me there is a limit, and when I find a man who keeps his cigars in the coal-scuttle, his tobacco in the toe end of a Persian slipper, and his unanswered correspondence transfixed by a jack-knife into the very centre of his wooden mantelpiece, then I begin to give myself virtuous airs. I have always held, too, that pistol practice should be distinctly an open-air pastime; and when Holmes, in one of his queer humors would sit in an arm-chair with his hair-trigger and a hundred Boxer cartridges, and proceed to adorn the opposite wall with a patriotic V.R. done in bullet-pocks, I felt strongly that neither the atmosphere nor the appearance of our room was improved by it.

These are, we must admit, unusual habits, but still Dr. Watson assures us that:

Holmes was certainly not a difficult man to live with. He was quiet in his ways and his habits were regular. It was rare for him to be up after ten at night, and he had invariably breakfasted and gone out before I rose in the morning. Sometimes he spent his day at the chemical laboratory, sometimes in the dissecting-rooms, and occasionally in long walks, which appeared to take him into the lowest portions of the city. Nothing could exceed his energy when the working fit was upon him; but now and again a reaction would seize him, and for days on end he would lie upon the sofa in the sitting-room, hardly uttering a word or moving a muscle from morning to night. On these occasions I have noticed such a dreamy, vacant expression in his eyes, that I might have suspected him of being addicted to the use of some narcotic, had not the temperance and cleanliness of his whole life forbidden such a notion.

Later, Dr. Watson's suspicions were confirmed.

Lecoq's eccentricity was his habit of silent communion with a portrait of his wife which he carried with him:

M. Lecoq had recourse to the portrait on the lozenge-box. His look was more than a glance, it was a confidence. He was evidently saying something to the dear defunct, which he dared not utter aloud.

This habit is also noted in Mr. Gryce. This delightful old gentleman had a way of addressing himself to any small inanimate object in his neighborhood. It might be an inkstand or a doorknob, but he treated it, to all appearance, as his guide, philosopher and friend. On one occasion he became very chummy with a statue at the foot of a staircase:

Whereupon I repeated my words, this time very quietly but clearly, while Mr. Gryce continued to frown at the bronze figure he had taken into his confidence. When I had finished, Mr. Van Burnam's countenance had changed, so had his manner. He held himself as erect as before, but not with as much bravado. He showed haste and impatience also, but not the same kind of haste and not quite the same kind of impatience. The corners of Mr. Gryce's mouth betrayed that he noted this change, but he did not turn away from the newel-post.

And, upon occasion, Mr. Gryce is unable to take active interest in the evidence being deposed by a witness because of his intense absorption in a "close and confidential confab with his own finger-tips."

Sergeant Cuff, however, has a very sane and pleasant fad of his own, but he puts it to its proper use when he employs it to evade impertinent or unwelcome queries. Instead of dashing madly into his "investigations" the celebrated detective goes off on a side track thus:

"Ah, you've got the right exposure here to the south and sou'west," says the Sergeant, with a wag of his grizzled head, and a streak of pleasure in his melancholy voice. "This is the shape for a rosery—nothing like a circle set in a square. Yes, yes; with walks between all the beds. But they oughtn't to be gravel-walks like these. Grass, Mr. Gardener—grass-walks between your roses; gravel's too hard for them. That's a sweet pretty bed of white roses and blush roses. They always mix well together, don't they? Here's the white musk-rose, Mr. Betteredge—our old English rose holding up his head along with the best and newest of them. Pretty dear!" says the Sergeant, fondling the musk-rose with his lanky fingers, and speaking to it as if he were speaking to a child.

This was a nice sort of a man to recover Miss Rachel's Diamond, and to find out the thief who stole it!

"You seem to be fond of roses, Sergeant?" I remarked.

"I haven't much time to be fond of anything," says Sergeant Cuff. "But, when I have a moment's fondness to bestow, most times, Mr. Betteredge, the roses get it. I began my life among them in my father's nursery garden, and I shall end my life among them if I can. Yes. One of these days (please God) I shall retire from catching thieves, and try my hand at growing roses. There will be grass-walks, Mr. Gardener, between my beds," says the Sergeant, on whose mind the gravel-paths of a rosery seemed to dwell unpleasantly.

"It seems an odd taste, sir," I ventured to say, "for a man in your line of life."

"If you will look about you (which most people won't do)," says Sergeant Cuff, "you will see that the nature of a man's tastes is, most times, as opposite as possible to the nature of a man's business. Show me any two things more opposite one from the other than a rose and a thief, and I'll correct my tastes accordingly—if it isn't too late at my time of life. You find the damask-rose a goodish stock for most of the tender sorts, don't you, Mr. Gardener? Ah! I thought so. Here's a lady coming. Is it Lady Verinder?"

The peculiarity of "The Whispering Man," and what gives him his title, is a curious vocal defect which at times prevents his audible speech.

5. Favorite Phrases of Detectives

"THE THINKING MACHINE," ASIDE FROM his petulance and impatience, continually repeats two or three favorite phrases that annoy the reader quite as much as the clients annoy this astute detective. One of them is, "Don't say it is impossible! that annoys me exceedingly! Nothing is impossible to the human mind!" This assertion, innocent enough in itself, is so frequently repeated as to become intolerable. Another phrase of which Professor Van Dusen is inordinately fond, is, "Two and two make four, not sometimes, but all the time." This also is repeated so often as to become tiresome. To quote the Professor:

"Two and two make four, not sometimes, but all the time," he began, at last as if disputing some previous assertion. "As the figure two, wholly disconnected from any other, gives small indication of a result, so is an isolated fact of little consequence. Yet that fact added to another, and the resulting fact added to a third, and so on, will give a final result. That result, if every fact is considered must be correct. Thus any problem may be solved by logic; logic is inevitable."

Indeed, variations on a theme of two and two making four are hackneyed in detective fiction.

As a figure of speech, the proposition that two and two make four except in unusual cases, is fair enough. It is paraphrased thus: in "A Mysterious Disappearance":

"I can't s'y as I know anythink about it, sir, but by puttin' two and two together it makes four sometimes—not always."

"Quite right. You're a philosopher. Let me hear the two two's. We'll see about the addition afterwards."

And it is humorously referred to in "The Circular Staircase," by Mary Roberts Rinehart:

At this point in my story, Halsey always says:

"Trust a woman to add two and two together, and make six." To which I retort that if two and two plus X make six, then to discover the unknown quantity is the simplest thing in the world. That a houseful of detectives missed it entirely was because they were busy trying to prove that two and two make four.

The same proposition is quoted as the keynote of a detective's method in "The Holladay Case" where, in praise of the detective, it is remarked, "Your work convinced us that you know how to put two and two together, which is more than can be said for the ordinary mortal."

And in "The House Opposite" the detective declares that to succeed in his profession requires, "accurate and most minute powers of observation, unlimited patience, and a capacity for putting two and two together."

Sherlock Holmes shows a grasp of the principle, when he says, "If you were asked to prove that two and two make four, you might find some difficulty, and yet you are quite sure of the fact."

Poe disdained the simple reference to two plus two, but embodied a similar idea in this subtle manner:

"In short, I never yet encountered the mere mathematician who could be trusted out of equal roots, or one who did not clandestinely hold it as a point of his faith that X squared plus px was absolutely and unconditionally equal to q. Say to one of these gentlemen, by way of experiment, if you please, that you believe occasions may occur where X squared plus px is not altogether equal to q, and, having made him understand what you mean, get out of his reach as speedily as convenient, for, beyond doubt, he will endeavor to knock you down."

The aspiring author, then, will do well to omit further references to the adding of two and two as an illuminating point in his story. Eccentricities or freakish habits on the part of his detective are permissible if not harped upon too continuously. But let them be of a pleasant or at least of an unobjectionable nature, and not like a habit attributed to a detective in a series of stories now current, who pulled at the lobe of his ear, until a fastidious reader was fain to close the book in disgust. Let the habits of your hero be whimsical, mysterious, or erratic, if you choose; but let them be agreeable and not too frequently reiterated.

XIV

Devious Devices

Snow and Rain
Some Particularly Hackneyed Devices
Devices Which Are Not Plausible

O f the many devices introduced by detective writers to arrest and hold the readers' attention, some are admittedly legitimate and used by best authors. Others are unfair; and still others were permissible but have become so hackneyed as to be taboo.

1. Snow and Rain

IN "MONSIEUR LECOQ" MUCH DEPENDS on the footprints in the snow. Thereafter in the first chapter of nearly every detective story we are informed that "a light snow had fallen the evening before." Then witnesses are brought to prove the exact hour the snow began to fall, and the moment it stopped. This fixes the time of the murder, and the footprints in the snow lead to or from the criminal as the author may decree.

Later this light snow was varied by "a gentle rain, the first for two weeks," that left paths and flower-beds soft for the indicative footprints.

In "A Study in Scarlet" there is a torrential downpour. This is in order to soften the clay of the garden path sufficiently to take footmarks; but it is a little overdone, for the torrents pour down all night, and would have obliterated any footprints save those made by a fictive criminal for the benefit of a fictive detective.

This same rain is treated a little better by Miss Mary E. Wilkins in her story "The Long Arm," for she relates "There had been heavy rain in the morning of the 17th, and the soil is a sticky clay. I examined it at daybreak on the morning of the 18th and, as it had not rained during the night the footprints were as fresh as if they had just been made."

This is the same accurately scheduled, time-lock rain, but it is a little more logical than the cloudburst variety.

If possible, then, get along without the light snow or the gentle rain or even the torrents. They seem almost indispensable, but endeavor for once to construct a crime without them.

2. Some Particularly Hackneyed Devices

FOG, THOUGH NOT SO MUCH of a factor here, is incessantly used in English detective stories. It is so obviously a convenient device for concealing crime, that it is the foundation of Richard Harding Davis's "In the Fog" and also of "A Mysterious Disappearance," "Big Bow Mystery," "The Masquerader," and scores of others.

Another hackneyed device is the secret panel in the wall, which slides open by pressing a hidden spring. This was overdone in sensational fiction, before Detective Stories began, but was seized upon as a valuable device for Mystery tales. But it is easily suspected, and is unsatisfactory in modern settings.

Avoid too, if you can, the packet of valuable papers that disclose secret plans of enormous political importance. This has been overdone, and the plot of Conan Doyle's "The Naval Treaty" has been paraphrased and parodied until it has become tiresome.

Another trite incident is the finding of a pistol engraved with initials, near the body of the victim. The youngest reader nowadays, knows better than to suspect the owner of those initials.

To quote from a personal letter of Mr. Burton E. Stevenson: "If I were to find a murdered man,—which the Lord forbid!—and should also discover beside the body a pistol with a name on it or a visiting card or a monogrammed watch charm, or anything else of a clearly identifying character, I should conclude at once that the person thus identified was not guilty. This is a weakness which often annoys me in the modern detective story. When the hero's cane is found in the bushes near the body, and everyone concludes that the hero is therefore guilty, I put the book down with a sigh of disappointment."

A fine example of this mistaken device is in "The Villa Mystery," by Herbert Flowerdew:

The old man was staring at him stupidly. Now suddenly his face became alive again.

"You think that I shot the master?" he whispered incredulously. "I wish to God it was me. Do you know this, Mr. Esmond?"

He was taking from his pocket a dainty lace-edged handkerchief, and as he passed it across to the young man, Esmond recognized the subtle perfume it carried, even before his eyes fell on the embroidered initial, and his face paled.

"Well?" he said hoarsely.

Mason glanced apprehensively at the door, although it was locked, and dropped his voice to an even lower whisper.

"It was lying by the side of the master when I found him. That is why I did not send for the police. I wanted to give her time to get away."

The veriest ignoramus in the tricks of Detective Fiction would know better than to suspect the owner of that handkerchief! Again, we find this scene in "The Circular Staircase":

In one of the tulip beds back of the house an early blackbird was pecking viciously at something that glittered in the light. I picked my way gingerly over through the dew and stooped down: almost buried in the soft ground was a revolver! I scraped the earth off it with the tip of my shoe, and, picking it up, slipped it into my pocket. Not until I had got into my bedroom and double-locked the door did I venture to take it out and examine it. One look was all I needed. It was Halsey's revolver! I had unpacked it the day before and put it on his shaving stand, and there could be no mistake. His name was on a small silver plate on the handle.

I seemed to see a network closing around my boy, innocent as I knew he was. The revolver—I am afraid of them, but anxiety gave me courage to look through the barrel—the revolver had still two bullets in it. I could only breathe a prayer of thankfulness that I had found the revolver before any sharp-eyed detective had come around.

I decided to keep what clues I had, the cuff-link, the golf-stick and the revolver, in a secure place until I could see some reason for displaying them. The cuff-link had been dropped into a little filigree box on my toilet table. I opened the box and felt around for it. The box was empty—the cuff-link had disappeared!

Cuff-links, or other small articles kept for clues, invariably disappear in Detective Stories, and many authors seek to mislead by such devices, but the trained reader is not to be fooled by them.

Omit the use of a magpie, raven or parrot as an instrument for stealing jewels. A bird of this sort made an effective criminal when "The Jackdaw of Rheims" was written; but, though still a plausible one, the poor bird has been overworked and deserves a rest.

And oh, young writer, avoid, as you would the plague, the introduction of shreds or threads of wearing apparel as incriminating evidence! Probably this began with Lecoq's discovery of a few threads of brown wool, which were torn off by splinters, as a man wiped snow from a beam with his coat sleeve. This was credible and even plausible, and as it was the first time such a device had appeared in detective fiction it was acceptable. But how that poor detail has been abused and tortured ever since!

3. Devices Which Are Not Plausible

In "The Accomplice," an unusually good court-room story, by Frederick Trevor Hill, we have this sort of evidence reduced almost to an absurdity. To quote from page 13:

"The first error consisted in leaving the drippings of candle-grease on the veranda roof, and the second was in kneeling on those drippings before they were quite dry. As though it had been a hand gripping the skirt of the criminal, that wax held in its clutch, half a dozen threads of a hairy cloth, blue in color, and of a texture known to the trade as dress goods. When you have found the wearer of the cloth from which those threads were torn, gentlemen, you will have found the murderer of Mr. Gregory Shaw."

At the end of the book it was revealed that sure enough the criminal, who, however, was a man instead of the young woman at first suspected, had knelt in the candle drippings, and had left there bits of blue wool shreds from his trouser knees.

We can scarcely imagine a candle-dripping sufficiently tenacious to grasp in its clutch and hold for evidence a portion of material necessarily drawn tightly over the bent knees of the criminal. Even granting the especially hairy cloth from which the murderer obligingly had his costume made for the occasion, candle-grease of any sort does not possess such strongly adherent, not to say bull-dog, qualities as would allow it to clutch and keep pieces of that cloth.

Mr. Jacques Futrelle uses the thread clue with a little more plausibility, though still slightly forced:

The Thinking Machine opened his pocketbook and took from it the scarlet thread which he had picked from the rope of the flagpole.

"Here, I believe, is the real clue to the problem," he explained to Hatch. "What does it seem to be?"

Hatch examined it closely.

"I should say a strand from a Turkish bath robe," was his final judgment.

"Possibly. Ask some cloth expert what he makes of it, then if it sounds promising look into it. Find out if by any possibility it can be any part of any garment worn by any person in the apartment house."

"But, it's so slight—" Hatch began.

"I know," the other interrupted, tartly. "It's slight, but I believe it is a part of the wearing apparel of the person, man or woman, who has four times attempted to kill Mr. Henley and who did kill the girl. Therefore it is important."

Of course this thread led to the capture of the criminal, and as it was found caught in a rope near the scene of the crime it was a fairly good clue; but as a matter of fact, the threads of Turkish toweling are of fairly stout calibre, and are not likely to be broken off as they trail across a rope. So much depends on the plausibility of these clues, that not only care but common sense must be exercised in their selection. In the Thinking Machine story, another scarlet thread from the same bath-robe attached itself importantly and conspicuously to a metal corner of a trunk, and so by the trail of red threads the criminal was hunted down. Here again we see the beautiful workings of the salted mine. In real life those tell-tale threads would have stayed stubbornly in their own warp or woof; or if they did leave their rightful abiding place they would creep behind the bureau or somehow get into the dustbin undiscovered.

In Samuel Gardenhire's story, "The Abduction of Mary Ellis," the discovery of the criminal hinges on a piece of brown wrapping-paper, on which the kidnappers wrote an advertisement asking for ransom. This paper, after passing through several hands, was examined microscopically by the Transcendent Detective, and he discovered wax and a strand or two of floss doll's hair. Now, think of the thousands of dolls that are bought and never leave a hair of their heads fastened by a bit of their own wax face to their wrapping paper! and then think of this doll intelligently leaving these traces at the critical juncture, where such a clue was necessary, and then judge for yourself the relationship between truth and fiction.

This habit of using shredded evidence is not confined to writers in our own language. An exceedingly good detective story is by a Russian, Anton Chekhov, and is called the "Safety Match." There was a bushy burdock growing under the window, which was greatly trampled. On its upper branches, Detective Dukovski succeeded in finding some fine hairs of dark blue wool. Now, had the bushy burdock pulled out a jagged piece of woolen cloth we might have forgiven it, but to catch and hold up for inspection a few fine hairs is drawing too long a bow. However, they cut off these twigs of burdock and carefully wrapped them in paper in true conventional style. These few fine hairs lead directly to the trousers of the murderer and the naive author quite calmly acknowledges his debt to an illustrious predecessor: "See what a fellow who has read Gaboriau can do!" he exclaimed, which is not too self-depreciatory, for even in the same story he has adapted to his own use many more of Lecoq's devices.

The most logical and plausible instance of detection by the means of tiny threads for clues is found in Mary E. Wilkins's "The Long Arm."

"I began today at the bottom—that is, with the room least likely to contain any clue, the parlour. I took a chalk-line and a yard-stick, and divided the floor into square yards, and everyone of these squares I examined on my hands and knees. I found in this way literally nothing on the carpet but dust, lint, two common white pins, and three inches of blue sewing silk."

"At last I got the dustpan and brush, and yard by yard swept the floor. I took the sweepings in a white pasteboard box out into the yard in the strong sunlight, and examined them. There was nothing but dust and lint and five inches of brown woollen thread—evidently a ravelling of some dress material. The blue silk and the brown thread are the only possible clues which I found today and they are hardly possible. Rufus's wife can probably account for them."

These two threads were very naturally dropped from the clothing of a dressmaker, who has a perfect right to shed her snippings and ravelings wherever she may list.

It is wise to be careful in the use of shreds and threads that the author may not bring a smile to the face of the "gentle reader." Think of the absurdity of this statement, quoted from a modern English story:

It all began with the murder of Mr. Andrew Carrthwaite, at Palermo.

He had been found dead in the garden of his villa just outside the town, with a stiletto between his shoulder blades and a piece of rough Irish tweed, obviously torn from his assailant's coat, clutched tightly in his hand.

It would be interesting to see a hand that could tear a piece out of a coat of rough Irish tweed! The strength of such a clutch would put to blush the feats of the Murderer of the Rue Morgue.

XV

Footprints and Fingerprints

The Omnipresence of Footprints
Other Miraculous Discoveries
Remarkable Deductions from Footprints
Fingerprints and Teeth-marks

1. The Omnipresence of Footprints

WITHOUT A DOUBT THE MOST woefully overdone and mix-done evidence is that of footprints.

Perhaps with the exception of that one found by Robinson Crusoe, no footprints in fiction,—not even those left on the sands of time for that hypothetical forlorn and shipwrecked brother,—have been either plausible or, in their evidence, credible.

The trouble began with Gaboriau and M. Lecoq, for Poe never descended to the low level of footprints. But in "Monsieur Lecoq," the stage is set on the very first page by the phrase, "It had snowed heavily for the past few days and the thaw had now begun."

But the obliging thaw by no means obliterates the footprints on which the story stands. As Lecoq remarks, "The fellow had a neat pair of boots. What an impression, eh! clear and distinct. Why, you may count every nail."

Such an impression in thawing snow is remarkable of itself, but is as nothing compared to the further details that they learn. Indeed, for twenty-four pages the revelations and declarations of those footprints hold us spellbound. They are dramatically eloquent and show what seems to be even more than human intelligence. No quotation can do them justice. The aspiring author will do well to read, mark and inwardly digest those footprints.

Especially interesting is the detailed description of how Lecoq made plaster of Paris casts of these footprints, undeterred by the fact that the weather had grown much milder and a warm rain had begun to fall. But the thoughtful and considerate rain merely drizzled until the plaster casts were all done, and then, we are told, "it immediately began to come down in earnest."

But the plaster casts were safe, and ready to corroborate all M. Lecoq's deductions, and lead the reader through the devious mazes of Gaboriau's genius.

Now we must agree that a great responsibility was put upon those thoughtlessly made footprints. But it is a no more elaborate affair of the sort than that described in Doyle's "A Study in Scarlet."

To begin with: "No rain had fallen for a week before the evening of the murder." The clayey soil thus being very dry required a great deal of moisture to fit it for footprints, and so, as we are told, "It rained in torrents." This left everything very wet and sloppy for Holmes' investigation. But notwithstanding this and notwithstanding that the pathway was so trampled that Holmes said, "If a herd of buffaloes had passed along there, there could not be a greater mess," our Transcendent Detective had no trouble whatever in reading the footnotes of the case.

Nor was there any difficulty in reading further footprints made in the dust inside the house, where one man had stood still and one had "walked up and down, growing more and more excited." It was no matter that their shoes were soaking wet and muddy; it was no matter that they themselves were dripping with the torrential rain; they left clear and legible footprints in the dust. Then another man came, tramped along the buffalo walk and went into the room, walked around, knelt down, and cut various capers, but though soaking wet, he too, left neat prints that any running detective might read!

In the story of "The Resident Patient," it had "rained hard that very afternoon" and the suspected man rather untidily left several muddy footprints on the light stair carpet. The hero of the story came in directly afterwards, and went both up and down the same stairs, leaving no footprints! But this paradox presents no difficulties to the footprint expert.

"My dear fellow," said he, "it is one of the first solutions that occurred to me, but I was soon able to corroborate the doctor's tale. This young man has left prints upon the stair-carpet which made it quite superfluous for me to ask to see those which he had made in the room. When I tell you that his toes were square-toed instead of being pointed like Blessington's, and were quite an inch and a third longer than the doctor's, you will acknowledge that there can be no doubt as to his individuality."

These square-toed prints, since they showed that they were an inch and a third longer than the doctor's, lead us to think that the man who made them went upstairs sidewise like a crab, or else he could scarcely have made the complete footprint visible. Truly the footprints in detective stories are fearfully and wonderfully made!

One time, however, even Sherlock Holmes confesses his powers at fault. In "The Hound of the Baskervilles" there is a fearful quagmire, so quivering and undulating that "its tenacious grip plucked at our heels as we walked, and when we sank into it, it was as if some malignant hand was tugging us down. Holmes sank to his waist as he stepped from the path, and had we not been there to drag him out he could never have stepped his foot upon firm land again."

Of this peculiar land formation we are told, "there was no chance of finding footsteps in the mire, for the rising mud oozed swiftly in upon them." True, one would hardly expect footprints in that morass, but you never can tell!

2. Other Miraculous Discoveries

SHERLOCK HOLMES, HAVING DECLARED HIMSELF Past Grand Master in the art of reading footprints, it is not surprising to hear him discourse thus:

"Roof quite out of reach. Yet a man has mounted by the window. It rained a little last night. Here is a print of a foot in mould upon the sill. And here is a circular muddy mark, and here again upon the floor, and here again by the table. See here, Watson! This is really a very pretty demonstration."

I looked at the round, well-defined muddy discs.

"That is not a footmark," said I.

"It is something much more valuable to us. It is the impression of a wooden stump. You see here on the sill is the boot-mark, a heavy boot with a broad metal heel, and beside it is the mark of the timber toe."

"It is the wooden-legged man."

"Quite so."

In another story, a subordinate tells Holmes that "the garden path was saturated with recent rain, and ought to show footprints," but he could discern none.

"One moment," said Holmes. "Where does this path lead to?"

"To the road."

"How long is it?"

"A hundred yards or so."

"At the point where the path passes through the gate, you could surely pick up the tracks?"

"Unfortunately, the path was tiled at that point."

"Well, on the road itself?"

"No, it was all trodden into mire."

"Tut-tut! Well, then, these tracks upon the grass, were they coming or going?"

"It was impossible to say. There was never any outline."

"A large foot or a small?"

"You could not distinguish."

Holmes gave an exclamation of impatience.

"It has been pouring rain and blowing a hurricane ever since," said he. "It will be harder to read now than that palimpsest. Well, well, it can't be helped. What did you do, Hopkins after you had made certain that you had made certain of nothing?"

But, although harder than palimpsest reading, Mr. Holmes went to the grass border in question, and had no difficulty in reading it glibly. Here is the scene:

"This is the garden path of which I spoke, Mr. Holmes. I'll pledge my word there was no mark on it yesterday."

"On which side were the marks on the grass?"

"This side, sir. This narrow margin of grass between the path and the flower-bed. I can't see the traces now, but they were clear to me then."

"Yes, yes; someone has passed along," said Holmes, stooping over the grass border. "Our lady must have picked her steps carefully must she not, since on the one side she would leave a track on the path, and on the other an even clearer one on the soft bed?"

To discern these carefully-picked steps on grass, though it had been "pouring rain and blowing a hurricane" ever since they were made, is indeed good work of its sort! One of Ottolengui's best stories, "A Conflict of Evidence," has its third chapter called "Footprints in the Snow."

"I see," said the detective, "what we may be most grateful for, and that is fresh snow. We must extend our investigation presently, and search for footprints."

This they proceeded to do, and the reader is invited to participate by means of a full-page map of house and grounds, with so many and such complicated trails of footprints all over it, that it looks like a Fashion Paper Supplement of patterns.

"We found four sets of tracks," said the detective, exultantly, "besides the dog's, which latter may prove of value. Two of these we think were made by women, and two by men. For convenience, I have numbered them 1, 2, 3 and 4."

So astute are the deductions from these interlaced trails that a small portion of them reads as follows:

"The same as you selected, but for this reason. Notice that here the direction is towards the summer-house, as you just now said; whilst on this side, the point of the toe shows that the owner of the foot returned to her starting point. Unless we find another trail, leading from the house, we have here proof conclusive that this party has remained indoors."

"How so? I don't see that."

"Yet it is simple. Notice that the steps away from the house are very indistinct, whilst those coming toward us are, on the contrary, clear, and sharply defined. The woman left this spot whilst it was yet snowing, so the snow filled up the tracks somewhat. Wherever she went, and that we shall find out perhaps by following the trail, she did not start for home, or to be accurate, she did not reach here, till the snow had ceased falling, as the clear marks testify."

A kind-hearted though uneducated neighbor helps them out with the usual testimony as to weather observations:

"Well, as I said before, I went ter bed airly, seven o'clock in fact; 't was snowin' hard then, an' I 'lowed 't would keep up all night; I slept purty sound but was waked up by the noise my girls made comin' in from a visit ter a neighbor's. You know how 't is when a man's woke up? He's kinder crusty an' more 'an all, can't tell whether he's slept ten hours or ten minutes. So as the girls went by my door, I growled out: 'An't you purty late gittin' home?' 'No pop, it's just nine o'clock,' come the answer. Seein' as how I had a goodnight's rest before me, I felt a leetle mite pleasanter an' in a' easier tone I said: 'I s'pose the snow's purty deep, an't it?' 'Not very,' says one on 'em, 'it stopped awhile ago, an' the moon's out now!' That's all was said. But you see that shows it didn't snow after nine, tho' ef you want it nearer, mebbe I kin find out from the girls."

3. Remarkable Deductions from Footprints

In "The Quests of Paul Beck," by M. McDonnell Bodkin, we find this exceedingly clever deduction from footprints:

Bending low he scrutinized the edge of the pathway closely as he walked. Twice he found a break in the clean-cut edge, examined it carefully and went on. The third time he found the mark of one of the new-fashioned rubber heels in the turf. The ground had been soft when the mark was made—it was hard now. The segment of the circular heel was cut deep and clear.

"Mr. Rutherford wore rubber heels," he said to the other, rather as one who makes a statement than one who asks a question.

Strangely nodded. Mr. Beck was on his knees on the grass sward with a magnifying glass close to the ground. He put the grass softly aside as a surgeon parts the hair to examine a scalp wound.

"Was Mr. Rutherford a heavy man?"

Mr. Strangely did not hear him at first, and he repeated the question. "Well, no, he was rather light and wiry, but he had big feet if that's what you mean."

"Right," said Mr. Beck, "here is a full footmark." He got up from his knees and walked on briskly, picking up the trail as if it were the "scent" of a paper-chase, though Strangely's eyes could find only a few vague marks amongst the grass. The track skirted the woods and led them to the banks of a deep, dumb river that ran slowly, level with its brim. Along the banks of the river the track led them for about a mile, tending always away from the house.

Under the shelter of a clump of beech, Mr. Beck stopped short and began to cast about like a sporting dog that makes a dead set, weakens on it when he finds the bird has just left, and begins beating cautiously again. He examined every mark about the place with scrupulous care, went on about twenty yards to where the river was crossed by a new iron bridge, and walked a little with bent head on the further side.

Mr. Strangely watched him curiously all the time, till he came back at last to the place where he had first pointed his game, and looked fixedly at the water.

Then very quietly he said to Mr. Strangely:

"Mr. Rutherford's body is out there, under the water."

For reading from footprints on grass, that is doing fairly well!

He repeats his success in this instance:

Early next morning Mr. Beck was on the scene of the murder—not the stolid Mr. Beck of the day before, but active, eager, every sense keenly alert.

There was a curious suggestion about him of a well-trained setter dog when it is close upon the game—every nerve and muscle vibrant with suppressed excitement.

Like a setter he beat round the spot, searching the ground with his eyes. There had been much rain of late, and the ground was still soft enough to take and hold footprints. He found three or four prints, small and sharp, of the heel of a girl's shoe. He could even trace where Dick Ackland's foot had slipped and torn the sod as he stopped and turned on his way to the brook when he heard the second revolver shot.

The Vicar's footprints were faint and hard to follow (the lame foot lighter than the other) as he ran for the doctor. At first Mr. Beck could only find a mere trace at intervals through the grass, but after a bit he reached the bottom of stiff clay that took the mould of the footprints like plaster of Paris.

Miss Mary E. Wilkins outdoes all competitors in her number of tabulated footprints. In her short detective story, "The Long Arm," we find this interesting report:

"I'll tell you what," he said, after a longish pause, "we'd trampled down the ground a good bit all round; we must have trampled out the murderer's footprints."

"It's just possible," I said, "but not likely that you shouldn't have left a square inch of shoeprint anywhere."

No, indeed, that would not be likely in a Detective Story! So the Sergeant went hunting for footprints, with this gratifying result:

Sergeant Edwardes' report on the footprints near the spot where the body of Miss Judson was found, at 9.35 p.m., on October 17, 189-:

"I have counted 43 distinct human footsteps and 64 partial imprints.

"Of the 43, 24 are made by the left foot and only 19 by the right.

"Of the 54 faint or partial impressions, I found 17 of the left foot and only 12 of the right, the rest are not distinctive enough to pronounce upon.

"Of the total number of the fainter footprints, 18 are deeply marked in the soft clay, the others are less strongly impressed. Of the 18 that are deeply marked, 11 are made by the left foot, 7 by the right.

"This accords with what I was told subsequently—that Mr. Jex's three labourers, and Mr. Jex himself, on finding Miss Judson's dead body, at once took it up in their arms and bore it to the house.

"Bearers of a heavy weight, such as a dead body, walking together, invariably bear heavily upon the left foot, both those who are supporting it on the left, and those who are supporting it on the right side.

"Distinguishing the Footprints by their length, breadth, and the pattern of the nail marks upon them, I find that they are the footprints of five separate persons, all of them men. I also found, clearly impressed, the footprints of the victim herself.

"There had been heavy rain in the morning of the 17th, and the soil is a sticky clay. I examined it at daybreak on the morning of the 18th and, as it had not rained during the night, the impressions were as fresh as if they had just been made. By my orders no one had been allowed to come near the spot where the body was found during the night. Just outside the gate of the orchard, the grass has been long trodden away by passersby, leaving the earth bare; and the patch of bare earth forms an area rather broader than the gate. On this area the body had fallen, and round about the spot where it had lain I found all the footprints on which I am reporting.

"I have compared the boots worn by the labourers with the impressions near the gate. They correspond in every particular.

"In the case of the footprints of the three labourers, a majority of the deeper impressions are made by the left boot.

"I therefore conclude that all three men came upon the spot only to carry away the body of the girl, and had no hand in her death.

"I argue the same from the footprints made by Mr. Jex. He also had borne more heavily with the left than with the right foot. He also, therefore, must have come on the spot only to bear off the body, and could have taken no part in the girl's murder.

"There are almost an exactly equal number of impressions, plain or faint, of the footprints of these four persons.

"There remain the footprints of a fifth person. They are the impressions of a man's foot, but the hobnailed boots that made them, though full sized, are of a rather lighter make than the others, and the nail marks are smaller, the boots are newer, for the sides of the impression have a cleaner cut, and, what is important, the impressions of the left foot are in no case deeper than those of the right."

But all this is only a beginning in each case. Such wonders as are discovered from the footprints we have referred to can only be appreciated by reading the books in question.

In "Midnight at Mears House," by Harrison J. Holt, one of the characters states in the first chapter, "someone must have carried him out of the house and thrown him over the cliff; in which case there should be footprints to prove it."

Quite right, of course there should be in a detective story. And there were.

"After the rain of the night before, the ground was still soft in places. We had gone but a few steps when we came upon a clear deep footprint."

And then they went on and followed the footprints to the very edge of the cliff, to "the exact spot, below which Arthur had found the body!"

Now there's a criminal for you! He knew his business, and he went to it, making his footprints in a neat, workmanlike manner.

A really good example of a logical and credible footprint is found in "The Whispering Man," by Henry Kitchell Webster.

"On the hardwood floor was the imprint of the heel of a man's rubber, showing the criss-cross marks that keep you from slipping—a new rubber, but it had been a little damp and a little dirty, and had left a mark."

Now that is an honest, truthful footprint, and the statement that it was a new rubber gives it the last touch of veracity.

But the best disquisition on footprints and their value is found in "The Mystery of the Yellow Room," by Gaston Leroux.

Rouletabille's unerring perspicacity realizes the absurdity of much of this footprint evidence. He remarks on it thus:

"I awaited the coming of daylight and then went down to the front of the chateau, and made a detour, examining every trace of footsteps coming towards it or going from it. These, however, were so mixed and confusing that I could make nothing of them. Here I may make a remark,—I am not accustomed to attach an exaggerated importance to exterior signs left in the track of a crime.

"The method which traces the criminal by means of the tracks of his footsteps is altogether primitive. So many footprints are identical. However, in the disturbed state of my mind, I did go into the deserted court and did look at all the footprints I could find there, seeking for some indication, as a basis for reasoning.

"If I could but find a right starting point! In despair I seated myself on a stone. For over an hour I busied myself with the common, ordinary work of a policeman. Like the least intelligent of detectives, I went on blindly over the traces of footprints which told me just no more than they could.

"I came to the conclusion that I was a fool, lower in the scale of intelligence than even the police of the modern romancer. Novelists build mountains of stupidity out of a footprint on the sand, or from an impression of a hand on the wall. That's the way innocent men are brought to prison. It might convince an examining magistrate or the head of a detective department, but it's not proof. You writers forget that what the senses furnish is not proof. If I am taking cognizance of what is offered me by my senses I do so but to bring the results within the circle of my reason. That circle may be the most circumscribed, but if it is, it has this advantage—it holds nothing but the truth! Yes, I swear that I have never used the evidence of the senses but as servants to my reason. I have never permitted them to become my master. They have not made of me that monstrous thing—worse than a blind man—a man who sees falsely. And that is why I can triumph over your error and your merely animal intelligence, Frederic Lársán!"

But the would-be author need not deem these footprint clues entirely unavailable for his use. They are a permissible part of the required mechanism, and utilized in moderation, add rather than detract from the usual plot. They are not truth, but they make interesting fiction, if worked up with a semblance of reality and with convincing circumstance.

4. Fingerprints and Teethmarks

MORE RECENT IS THE READING of thumb and fingerprints. The discovery of the individuality of fingerprints gave detectives a new field, both in fiction and in life.

In a book of stories, "Adventures of the World's Greatest Detectives," by George Barton, which are said by the author to be literally true, we have an astonishing coincidence. A detective found in a public house a drinking glass that had on it perfectly distinct marks of four fingers and a thumb. Following the trail, a cab was found, on the door of which were five distinct prints of four fingers and a thumb. After reproducing on sensitized paper, the two sets of imprints were found to be identical! This is a Scotland Yard story, but as the author confesses in his preface to "a few pardonable embellishments," we can't help thinking that pardon is desired in this case. However, fingermarks are undoubtedly used largely in real detection, and have not yet been overdone in fiction.

Indeed, our up-to-date criminals are said to wear rubber gloves so they will leave no prints. And in "The Silent Bullet," by Arthur B. Reeve, we are told of an ingenious miscreant who "painted his hands lightly with a liquid rubber which he had invented himself. It did all that rubber gloves would do, and yet left him the free use of his fingers with practically the same keenness of touch."

Another ingenious contrivance is described in a recent tale, where a very bad man gets a wax impression of another man's thumb and makes falsely incriminating prints in suspicious places.

Now all of these devices are legitimate, and if the alert author can contrive a new combination, or a new twist to an old one, he may produce a good situation.

Speaking of imprints, marks of teeth used in biting an apple, figure prominently in at least two modern stories.

One, in Arthur Morrison's "The Case of Mr. Foggatt" gives the detective an opportunity to air his knowledge of apples, which is as extraordinary as Sherlock Holmes's erudition regarding cigar ash. As it is of interest, we append his dissertation:

"First, now, the apple was white. A bitten apple, as you must have observed, turns of a reddish brown color if left to stand long. Different kinds of apples brown with different rapidities, and the browning always begins at the core. This is one of the twenty thousand tiny things that few people take the trouble to notice, but which it is useful for a man in my position to know. A russet will brown quite quickly. The apple on the sideboard was, as near as I could tell, a Newtown pippin or other apple of that kind, which will brown at the core in from twenty minutes to half an hour, and in other parts in a quarter of an hour more. When we saw it, it was white with barely a tinge of brown about the exposed core. Inference: somebody had been eating it fifteen or twenty minutes before, perhaps a little longer—an inference supported by the fact that it was only partly eaten.

"I examined that apple, and found it bore marks of very irregular teeth. While you were gone, I oiled it over, and, rushing down to my rooms, where I always have a little plaster of Paris handy for such work, took a mould of the part where the teeth had left the clearest marks. I then returned the apple to its place for the police to use if they thought fit. Looking at my mould, it was plain that the person who had bitten that apple had lost two teeth, one at top and one below, not exactly opposite, but nearly so. The other teeth, although they would appear to have been fairly sound, were irregular in size and line. Now, the dead man had, as I saw, a very excellent set of false teeth, regular and sharp, with none missing. Therefore, it was plain that somebody else had been eating that apple. Do I make myself clear?"

"Quite! Go on!"

"There were other inferences to be made—slighter, but all pointing the same way. For instance, a man of Foggatt's age does not, as a rule, munch an unpeeled apple like a school-boy. Inference a young man, and healthy."

By great good luck, the detective ran across the apple-biter again, took another cast and with the pair, which were identical, marched to success.

The other apple-biter is in "The Saintsbury Affair," by Roman Doubleday, and the details of the biting are much the same as in Mr. Morrison's story. This is an ingenious identification idea and any plan of such interesting nicety may be used in detective fiction. As Shakespeare's characters bite their thumbs when they choose, so may an all-wise author cause his puppets to bite apples at his own sweet will.

In the Fictive Detectives' Working Library, this Monograph on Apples and their Habits should stand beside Sherlock Holmes technical monographs.

XVI

MORE DEVICES

Tabulated Clues
Worn-out Devices
The Use of Disguise
Other "Properties"

1. Tabulated Clues

A GOOD DEVICE FOR THE use of the Detective Story Writer is a list or catalog of clues, evidences, or suspects. A distinct tabulation serves to lay the conditions of the story clearly before the reader, and arouses his curiosity as to their meaning and consequences. Of course, if need be, the clues may be misleading; but if done properly, that, too, is a legitimate device.

Wilkie Collins appreciated the use of this tabulation, and thus summed up the opening situation in "The Moonstone":

"Follow me carefully, Betteredge; and count me off on your fingers, if it will help you," says Mr. Franklin, with a certain pleasure in showing how clear-headed he could be, which reminded me wonderfully of old times when he was a boy. "Question the first: Was the Colonel's Diamond the object of a conspiracy in India? Question the second: Has the conspiracy followed the Colonel's Diamond to England? Question the third: Did the Colonel know the conspiracy followed the Diamond; and has he purposely left a legacy of trouble and danger to his sister, through the innocent medium of his sister's child?"

And much later in the story he again uses this device, purposely to mislead the reader:

"As to the person, or persons, by whom the crime was committed: It is known (1) that the Indians had an interest in possessing themselves of the Diamond. (2) It is at least probable that the man looking like an Indian, whom Octavius Guy saw at the window of the cab speaking to the man dressed like a mechanic, was one of the three Hindoo conspirators. (3) It is certain that this same man, dressed like a mechanic, was seen keeping Mr. Godfrey Ablewhite in view all through the evening of the twenty-sixth, and was found in the bedroom (before Mr. Ablewhite was shown into it) under circumstances which lead to the suspicion that he was examining the room. (4) A morsel of torn gold thread was picked up in the bedroom, which persons expert in such matters declared to be of Indian manufacture and to be a species of gold thread not known in England. (5) On the morning of the twenty-seventh, three men, answering to the description of the three Indians, were observed in lower Thames Street were traced to the Tower Wharf, and were seen to leave London by the steamer bound for Rotterdam.

"There is here moral, if not legal, evidence that the murder was committed by the Indians."

Notice how cleverly he makes it seem certain that the crime was committed by the Indians. In a long and somewhat rambling tale like "The Moonstone," a concise summary of evidence now and then is exceedingly effective.

Anna Katharine Green frequently makes use of listed statistics. In "That Affair Next Door," the heroine, who is doing detective work, makes a list, which is here given in part:

Having, as I thought, noticed some few facts in connection with it, from which conclusions might be drawn, I amused myself with jotting them down on the back of a disputed grocer's bill I happened to find in my pocket.

Valueless as explaining this tragedy, being founded upon insufficient evidence, they may be interesting as showing the workings of my mind even at this early stage of the matter. They were drawn up under three heads.

First, was the death of this young woman an accident?

Second, was it a suicide?

Third, was it a murder?

Under the first head I wrote:

My reasons for not thinking it an accident:

1. If it had been an accident and she had pulled the cabinet over upon herself, she would have been found with her feet pointing towards the wall where the cabinet had stood.

(But her feet were towards the door and her head under the cabinet.)

2. The decent, even precise, arrangement of the clothing about her feet, which precludes any theory involving accident.

Under the second:

Reason for not thinking it suicide:

She could not have been found in the position observed without having lain down on the floor while living and then pulled the shelves down upon herself.

(A theory obviously too improbable to be considered.)

Under the third:

Reason for not thinking it murder, etc., etc.

One of the principals in "The Circular Staircase," by Mary Roberts Rinehart, makes a similar list:

I made out a list of questions and possible answers, but I seemed only to be working around in a circle. I always ended where I began. The list was something like this:

Who had entered the house the night before the murder?

Thomas claimed it was Mr. Bailey, whom he had seen on the footpath, and who owned the pearl cuff-link.

Why did Arnold Armstrong come back after he had left the house the night he was killed?

No answer. Was it on the mission Louise had mentioned?

Who admitted him?

Gertrude said she had locked the east entry. There was no key on the dead man or in the door. He must have been admitted from within.

Who had been locked in the clothes chute?

Someone unfamiliar with the house, evidently. Only two people missing from the household, Rosie and Gertrude. Rosie had been at the lodge. Therefore—but was it Gertrude? Might it not have been the mysterious intruder again?

In "The Holladay Case," Mr. Burton E. Stevenson tells us that his detective "drew up a résumé of the case—to clear the atmosphere, as it were." It ran something like this:

March 13, Thursday—Holladay found murdered; daughter drives to Washington Square.

March 14, Friday—Coroner's inquest; Miss Holladay released; mysterious note received.

March 16, Sunday—Holladay buried.

March 18, Tuesday—Will opened and probated.

March 28, Friday—Miss Holladay returns from drive, bringing new maid with her and discharges old one.

March 29, Saturday—Gives orders to open summer house.

April 1, Tuesday—Asks for $100,000.

April 2, Wednesday—Gets it.

April 3, Thursday—Leaves home ostensibly for Belair, in company with new maid.

April 14, Monday—Butler reports her disappearance; Royce taken ill; I begin my search.

There I stopped. The last entry brought me up to date.

One of the cleverest lists, for the purpose of telling the story is one in "The Leavenworth Case," by Anna Katharine Green:

Taking a piece of paper, I jotted down the leading causes of suspicion as follows:

1. Her late disagreement with her uncle, and evident estrangement from him, as testified to by Mr. Harwell.

2. The mysterious disappearance of one of the servants of the house.

3. The forcible accusation made by her cousin—overheard, however, only by Mr. Gryce and myself.

4. Her equivocation in regard to the handkerchief found stained with pistol smut on the scene of the tragedy.

5. Her refusal to speak in regard to the paper which she was supposed to have taken from Mr. Leavenworth's table immediately upon the removal of the body.

6. The finding of the library key in her possession.

"A dark record," I involuntarily decided, as I looked it over; but even in doing so began jotting down on the other side of the sheet the following explanatory notes:

1. Disagreements and even estrangements between relatives are common. Cases where such disagreements and estrangements have led to crime, rare.

2. The disappearance of Hannah points no more certainly in one direction than another.

3. If Mary's private accusation of her cousin was forcible and convincing, her public declaration that she neither knew nor suspected who might be the author of this crime, was equally so. To be sure, the former possessed the advantage of being uttered spontaneously, but it was likewise true that it was spoken under momentary excitement, without foresight of the consequences, and possibly without due consideration of the facts.

4, 5. An innocent man or woman, under the influence of terror, will often equivocate in regard to matters that seem to criminate.

Here much of the problem is clearly stated in the first half of the list, and the working out of the solution is definitely indicated in the second part.

Listed suggestions are more useful in books than in short-stories; for in the former the complexities of the plot are more likely to need occasional rounding up and recalling to view.

2. Worn-out Devices

A TRITE AND GREATLY WORN device is the watch that stopped presumably when the crime was committed.

Here is a typical use of this incident quoted from R. Ottolengui's "The Crime of the Century":

"I found Mr. Mora's watch under the bed, where it must have been knocked from the dressing-table. The fall had caused it to stop, and the hands indicated seven minutes of two, agreeing with the time during which the watchman testifies that young Mora was at home."

"Yes," said Mr. Mitchel, "but do not go too fast. The watch may have run down. It is uncommon for a good watch to stop merely because it falls to the floor."

"Both of your points are good, in theory," replied the detective. "But neither applies in this instance. If a watch runs down, it cannot be started again without winding. By merely shaking this one I set it going, and to make assurance doubly sure, I let it run for an hour, when it was still keeping time. Next, though it be true that most watches would not be so easily stopped, this one, for some reason, is very sensitive to a blow. I tried the experiment of pushing it from the table to the floor, and at every attempt I found that it would cease its movement."

This idea of a stopped watch is so obvious that it led authors at once to the idea of purposely stopping a watch with the intent of leading the detective and the reader astray. In fact, this was done as long ago as in Gaboriau's "Crime of Orcival," where Lecoq, finding a clock which has been overturned in the struggle between the victim and his assassin, purposely turns the hands some four hours backward.

This device has been used so often that the astute reader now disregards the evidence of the stopped watch in fiction. But still the clock or watch may play an important part in the plot, if managed with any degree of originality. In "The Quests of Paul Beck" the device is well used:

Mr. Beck looked at the German with manifest admiration. "Forgive me for mentioning it. You would have made a first-class detective if you hadn't gone into another line of business. I should have told you that the evidence of the watch had been faked."

"Faked?" queried the other, with a blank look on his face.

"Oh! I see. Being a German, of course you don't understand our slang phrases. I examined the watch, and found that though the glass had been violently broken, the dial was not even scratched. The spring had been snapped, not by the blow but by overwinding. It was pretty plain to me the murderer had done the trick. He first put the hands on to half-past eight and then broke the spring, and so made his alibi. He got the watch to perjure itself. Neat, wasn't it?"

The German merely grunted. He was plainly impressed by the devilish ingenuity of the murderer.

In "The Whispering Man," by Henry Kitchell Webster, a large office clock seen in a mirror, makes twenty minutes before twelve appear to be twenty minutes after twelve, which leads to worth-while complications, and proves a clever device.

In Brander Matthews' story, "The Twinkling of an Eye," a clock is used to conceal and manipulate a camera for the purposes of detection.

Any such original application of commonplace material is worth-while in detective fiction.

Another maneuvre that has lost its grip on the attention of the trained reader, is the clumsily-upset table.

In "The Reigate Puzzle," Dr. Watson tells us; "Near the foot of the bed stood a dish of oranges and a carafe of water. As we passed it, Holmes, to my unutterable astonishment, leaned over in front of me and deliberately knocked the whole thing over. The glass smashed into a thousand pieces and the fruit rolled about into every corner of the room. You've done it now, Watson," said he, coolly. "A pretty mess you've made of the carpet."

This incident was effective and of importance as Conan Doyle used it, but it has since been done so often as to have lost its power to surprise.

A hackneyed misleading device is that of high words between a victim and a suspect. In Chekhov's Russian story, "The Safety Match," the author thus tries to cast suspicion on the valet.

"The master's valet, your worship," answered Ephraim. "Who else could it be? He's a rascal, your worship! He's a drunkard and a blackguard, the like of which Heaven should not permit! He always took the master his vodka and put the master to bed. Who else could it be? And I also venture to point out to your worship, he once boasted at the public-house that he would kill the master!"

This idea was right enough when first used; but experience has taught the modern reader that the one who threatens, or boasts an intent to kill never does so. The man who is overheard quarrelling with the victim just before his death is never by any chance the criminal in Fiction.

Whispered words is a legitimate though slightly overworked way of preserving the secret. One character whispers to another something the reader is not allowed to overhear. This rouses the eavesdropping instinct latent in every human mind, and the reader scans the pages in endeavor to learn that whispered message.

But attentive reading of the best detective stories will soonest teach a writer what devices may be used effectively and what not. It is a matter of taste, originality and cleverness. Even a trite device may be used with a new turn or twist and prove of great value.

Perhaps the longest roll of hackneyed devices in one book is found in "That Mainwaring Affair," by A.M. Barbour. This is a most excellent and interesting story and of exceedingly good construction. The surprise is perfect and the plot original, but old and time-worn devices are repeatedly used. It includes the return of a long-lost brother, supposed to have been shipwrecked years before; stolen family jewels, a missing will; a twin brother; a birthmark identification; an illegitimate son of a designing housekeeper; a suspected private secretary; whispered words conveying the secret; a dragged lake; and innumerable disguises. All of these are justifiable, but a writer will do well to strike out on more original lines.

3. The Use of Disguise

Disguise is not so much employed now as in former years when Lecoq was young. And the general public is now more keen to see through false whiskers than in the old days when Vidocq made his fame. Both these celebrated detectives were experts in the art of disguise. To quote from Vidocq's Memoirs:

At last, by dint of much effort of memory, I recalled to mind one Germain, alias "the Captain," who had been an intimate acquaintance of Noel's, and although our similarity was very slight, yet I determined on personating him. Germain, as well as myself, had often escaped from the Bagnes, and that was the only point of resemblance between us; he was about my age, but a smaller-framed man, he had dark brown hair, mine was light; he was thin, and I tolerably stout; his complexion was sallow, and mine fair, with a very clear skin; besides, Germain had an excessively long nose, took a vast deal of snuff which, begriming his nostrils outside, and stuffing them up within, gave him a peculiarly nasal tone of voice. I had much to do in personating Germain; but the difficulty did not deter me; my hair, cut a la mode des Bagnes, was dyed black, as well as my beard, after it had attained a growth of eight days; to embrown my countenance I washed it with white walnut liquor; and to perfect the imitation, I garnished my upper lip thickly with a kind of coffee grounds, which I plastered on by means of gum-arabic, and thus became as nasal in my twang as Germain himself. My feet were doctored with equal care; I made blisters on them by rubbing in a certain composition, of which I had obtained the receipt at Brest. I also made the marks of the fetters; and when all my toilet was finished, dressed myself in the suitable garb. I had neglected nothing which could complete the metamorphosis,—neither the shoes nor the marks of those horrid letters G.A.L. The costume was perfect.

"If I were your lieutenant, and wanted to take Vidocq," replied I, "I would contrive that he should not escape me."

"You! Oh yes, you and everybody! He is always completely armed. You know they said that he fired twice at Delrue and Carpentier; and that is not all, for he can change himself into a bundle of hay whenever he likes."

"A bundle of hay!" cried I, surprised at the novel endowment assigned to me. "A bundle of hay! How?"

"Yes, sir; my father pursued him one day, and at the moment he laid his hand upon his collar, he found that he only held a handful of hay. He did not only say it, but all the brigade saw the bundle of hay, which was burnt in the barrackyard."

Lecoq also depends largely on disguises for his successes. He says himself:

"A detective who is worth his salt can give an actor any amount of lessons. Since last year I have been studying the art of disguising my face, and I can at my desire become short or tall, dark or fair a perfect gentleman, or the vilest scoundrel that hangs about the outskirts of the suburbs."

And in "File No. 113" we are told:

His amazement gave so singular an expression to his face that M. Lecoq could not restrain a smile. "Then it was you!" continued the bewildered detective; "you were the stout gentleman at whom I stared, so as to impress his appearance upon my mind, and I never recognized you! You would make a superb actor, my chief, if you would go on the stage; but I was disguised too—very well disguised."

"Very poorly disguised: it is only just to you that I should let you know what a failure it was, Fanferlot. Do you think that a huge beard and a blouse are a sufficient transformation? The eye is the thing to be changed—the eye! The art lies in being able to change the eye. That is the secret." This theory of disguise explained why the lynx-eyed Lecoq never appeared at the Prefecture of Police without his gold spectacles.

"You can't swear to that, because no one can boast of knowing the real face of M. Lecoq. It is one thing today, and another tomorrow; sometimes he is a dark man, sometimes a fair one, sometimes quite young, and then an octogenarian. Why, at times he even deceives me. I begin to talk to a stranger—bah! it turns out to be M. Lecoq! Anybody on the face of the earth might be he. If I were told that you were he, I should say 'Very likely it is so.' Ah! he can convert himself into any form he pleases. He is a wonderful man!"

Of modern fictive detectives, few use disguise to great extent, with the exception perhaps of Frederic Larsan in the books of Gaston Leroux. So punctilious was this French detective in the details of his disguise, that his young opponent himself admitted that Larsan's disguises were impenetrable.

"And Old Bob?" I asked.

"No, dear boy, no!" scoffed Rouletabille, almost angrily. "Not he, either. You have noticed that he wears a wig, I suppose. Well, I assure you that when Larsan wears a wig, it will fit him!"

And so perfectly did Larsan's wigs fit him, as well as all the other details of his disguise, that he assumed the personality of anyone at will, without fear of discovery.

Sherlock Holmes often assumed disguise, but Conan Doyle does not make a strong point of it, relying not so much on physical appearances as on acute mentality.

4. Other "Properties"

A pet device is the discovery of a torn bit of paper containing part of a written communication. The writing is usually readable, but incomprehensible for want of context.

This is very bunglingly done by Vidocq, who finds a torn scrap of an envelope with these words on it:

Monsieur Rao—

Marchand de vins, bar—

Roche

Cli

and after much effort, mental and otherwise, he thus solved the enigma:

The torn address was, in my estimation, an enigma, which must first be solved; and, to effect this, I racked my brains day and night and at last felt satisfied, that excepting the name (respecting which I had but few doubts) the perfect address would run thus:

A Monsieur—, Marchand de vins,

Barriere Rochechouart.

Chaussee de Clignancourt.

But, better managed, a torn bit of paper is helpful in rousing the reader's curiosity and there are few authors who have not utilized it.

Conan Doyle goes farther, in using what seems to be part of a woman's name, "Rache," but is really a whole word in German.

Anna Katharine Green gives an original twist to this old idea in her title, "One of My Sons." In truth, this phrase, found on a bit of paper and pointing directly to the criminal, was really part of the line, "None of my Sons." It may be seen at a glance how the intent and the evidence of this line are purposely contradictory. The detective story is essentially dramatic, and therefore picturesque incidents and sensational situations are not only permissible, but advisable. The trained reader has learned to expect them. But unless they can be novel or original, there must be a skillful handling of the old devices.

Likewise, there are certain stage properties with the use of which the author should be entirely familiar, and which he should be able to employ with grace and skill.

The Weapon, the Papers, the Jewels, the Safe, the Alibi, are all his rightful belongings. So, too, the Lens, the Desk Blotter, the Waste Basket, the Cabman, the Deserted Wing, the Inquest, and the Mistaken Identity,—all are his, to manipulate at his pleasure.

If he can afford to ignore such as these, and use The Monkey's Paw, or The Speckled Band, so much the better for his originality.

XVII

False Devices

S everal false notions which have been so often exploited as to command belief, the young writer should strive to correct.

1. The "Trace" Fallacy

ONE HACKNEYED STATEMENT, THOUGH OF great value to a fiction detective, is far from being true. This is the assertion that it is impossible for a human being to go into a room for any purpose and out again without leaving trace of his presence. Sherlock Holmes insists on this, and says, on one occasion:

"My good Hopkins, I have investigated many crimes, but I have never yet seen one which was committed by a flying creature. As long as the criminal remains upon two legs so long must there be some indentation, some abrasion, some trifling displacement which can be detected by the scientific searcher. It is incredible that this blood-bespattered room contained no trace which could have aided us. I understand, however, from the inquest that there were some objects which you failed to overlook?"

And Mary E. Wilkins in her fine detective story, "The Long Arm," makes the same impressive statement:

"I have a theory that it is impossible for any human being to enter any house, and commit in it a deed of this kind, and not leave behind traces which are the known quantities in an algebraic equation to those who can use them."

Ninety-nine times out of a hundred anyone can go into a room, stay for a time and come out again, and leave absolutely no trace of his presence there. A practical test, or a series of them will convince anyone of this. Let your criminal or your innocent suspect leave as many traces and clues as you will, but don't allow your detective to assert that this is inevitable.

2. The Destruction of Evidence

ANOTHER USEFUL BUT FALSE NOTION is the great difficulty that the criminal experiences in getting rid of his blood-stained garments or other incriminating impedimenta. If he endeavors to burn them, or throw them in the river or ashbarrel, they come back with feline certainty. Now it is not so difficult to destroy or conceal material successfully, and all that is necessary in this regard is to make the proceedings of your criminal natural and not forced. But let the destruction or concealment be done with common sense, and at least an elementary knowledge of your subject.

One of the most absurd incidents of destruction is the burning of large packets of papers. A case in point is found in "The Adventure of Milverton," where we are told:

With perfect coolness Holmes slipped across to the safe, filled his two arms with bundles of letters, and poured them all into the fire. Again and again he did it, until the safe was empty.

Someone turned the handle and beat upon the outside of the door. Holmes looked swiftly round. The letter which had been the messenger of death for Milverton lay, all mottled with his blood, upon the table. Holmes tossed it in among the blazing papers. Then he drew the key from the outer door, passed through after me, and locked it on the outside. "This way, Watson," said he, "we can scale the garden wall in this direction."

Although we are told that it was "a good fire" that was burning in the fireplace, nothing short of a crematory furnace could have continued to burn when these letters were thrown upon it. Remember that Holmes "filled his two arms with bundles of letters and poured them all into the fire." "Again and again he did this," until he must have had, by a conservative estimate, some hundreds of letters. Anyone who has tried to burn even three or four letters without unfolding their pages knows the result. As a matter of fact, when Holmes departed, leaving those letters lying on the fire, very few of them could have been greatly injured.

If papers must be burned, as is sometimes the case, let them be unfolded and each sheet crumpled a little, and then give sufficient time to the operation. If this is not possible, omit the incident. How often a will or a deed has been "tossed into the grate and reduced to ashes at once." A folded paper of four or five thicknesses obstinately refuses to burn, except around the edges, and these instantaneous holocausts rouse only amusement in the mind of the common-sense reader.

3. False Hypotheses

ANOTHER ENTIRELY FALSE NOTION IS that "Murder will out." As to the real fact of this matter, Arthur C. Train, in his admirable work, "Courts, Criminals and the Camorra," asserts that the prisoners tried for murder are only a mere fraction of those who commit the crime.

In the stories of Luther Trant, we are informed "that for ninety-three out of everyone hundred homicides no one is ever punished," and in "The Scales of Justice," George L. Knapp tells us, "If you'd cut out the proverbs and stick to the evidence, you'd find out that about one murder in six comes to light enough to get the murderer convicted." Then too, Samuel N. Gardenhire asserts that "thousands of murders are never found out. Given a doctor, a lack of motive and a good chance, and detection may be laughed at."

But though the authors quoted understand this, scores of other Detective Story writers persist in standing by the old adage.

Again the beliefs that "a murderer is involuntarily drawn back to the scene of his crime," and that "a murderer can't help talking of his crime to somebody," are the basis of many false situations. These hypotheses may be used as working arguments, if desired, but should not be quoted as universal laws.

Another false notion inherent in the average citizen is, that a bystander is forbidden by law to touch the body of a murdered man before the arrival of the coroner. There never was any such law, is not now, and probably never will be. The citizen who is of an inquiring turn of mind has a perfect right to examine dead bodies he runs across in the course of his travels, to move the remains and even search the pockets of the deceased, provided, of course, that his motives are honest. That is all that is necessary.

4. Errors of Fact and of Inference

ASIDE FROM THESE FALSE AND erroneous notions which are common, let the writer of detective fiction be careful to avoid absolute mistakes, paradoxes, or anachronisms. In this class of story, accuracy and logic are imperative, and nothing can excuse carelessness in descriptive details or sequential happenings.

Our greatest and best writers have been caught napping in this respect, and though we can forgive it when Homer nods, it is not excusable in a tyro.

To take one of the most flagrant errors, let us look at a page in Poe's "The Mystery of Marie Roget."

If the clothing and the condition of the clothing of the drowned girl had been hastily or superficially described, it would not be so surprising. But Poe, with his wonderful "minuteness of detail which does not leave a pin or a button unnoted," makes this absurd statement:

The clothing was much torn and otherwise disordered. In the outer garment, a slit, about a foot wide, had been torn upward from the bottom hem to the waist, but not torn off. It was wound three times around the waist, and secured by a sort of hitch in the back.

Assuming the young girl to have a waist measure, outside her clothing, of at least twenty inches, simple arithmetic allows us that that strip "torn upward," "wound three times around the waist," "and secured by a sort of hitch in the back" (said "hitch" being enough to serve as a loop or handle), must have been at least seventy-two inches long. Therefore, as Marie Roget's skirt from hem to waist measured six feet, the young lady herself must have been nearly nine feet tall!

Other details of this extraordinary young woman's costume are also absurd to a rational mind, but perhaps Poe's genius did not include millinery.

However, Poe was often careless, even in important matters. The idea that supports the story of "The Purloined Letter," is so very good that it is a pity to have such an absurd contradiction as this creep in:

"At length my eyes, in going the circuit of the room, fell upon a trumpery filigree card-rack of pasteboard, that hung dangling by a dirty blue ribbon from a little brass knob just beneath the middle of the mantel-piece. In this rack, which had three or four compartments, were five or six visiting cards and a solitary letter. This last was much soiled and crumpled. It was torn nearly in two, across the middle—as if a design, in the first instance, to tear it entirely up as worthless, had been altered, or stayed in the second. It had a large black seal, bearing the D——cipher very conspicuously, and was addressed, in a diminutive female hand, to D——, the Minister, himself. It was thrust carelessly, and even, as it seemed, contemptuously, into one of the upper divisions of the rack."

It is not probable that any eccentricity on the part of the writer of the missive resulted in having the seal and the address on the same side of the letter; it is more likely a slip of Poe's fertile pen.

The well-known impossible condition mentioned in "The Raven," where the lamp-light streams over the bird and casts his shadow on the floor, while the bird himself is sitting on a bust over the door, can perhaps be explained by a transom and a hall light. But one rarely places a bust in front of a transom, as it would mean decreased efficiency for both, and we prefer to think this another of Poe's slips of attention.

From Poe's "The Oblong Box," we quote this description:

The box in question was, as I say, oblong. It was about six feet in length by two and a half in breadth;—I observed it attentively, and like to be precise. Now this shape was peculiar; and no sooner had I seen it, than I took credit to myself for the accuracy of my guessing. I had reached the conclusion, it will be remembered, that the extra baggage of my friend, the artist, would prove to be pictures, or at least a picture; for I knew he had been for several weeks in conference with Nicolino; and now here was a box which, from its shape, could possibly contain nothing in the world but a copy of Leonardo's "Last Supper"; and a copy of this very "Last Supper" done by Rubini the younger, at Florence, I had known for sometime to be in the possession of Nicolino. This point, therefore, I considered as sufficiently settled. I chuckled excessively when I thought of my acumen.

As the box was really a coffin, containing a dead body, it seems scarcely possible that it could look like a flat picture! At any rate, a coffin could not be mistaken for a box, which from its shape, could possibly contain nothing but a copy of "The Last Supper." It would need several superimposed pictures to fill a box of that shape.

Sir Conan Doyle is exceedingly careful in the logic of his details; and, except for rapidly burning papers in bulk, he makes few definite slips. Occasionally, however, he forgets what he has previously said about Sherlock Holmes' mental characteristics. But perhaps the reason is that instead of stepping into the pages of "A Study in Scarlet" a fully rounded and developed figure, Sherlock Holmes, during the first four or five years of his career as a public character, was in a constant state of evolution. It would be no easy matter for his creator to explain away certain striking inconsistencies of statement. For example, in an early chapter of "A Study in Scarlet," Watson tries to fathom the intentions of his reticent roommate by making a list of Holmes' curious accomplishments and limitations. His knowledge of literature was put down as "nil." "Of contemporary literature, philosophy, and politics, he appeared to know next to nothing. Upon my quoting Thomas Carlyle, he inquired in the naivest way who he might be and what he had done." This is rather definite. Yet in "The Sign of the Four," the very next book, we are shown Sherlock Holmes advising Watson to read Winwood Reade's "The Martyrdom of Man," citing French aphorisms, quoting Goethe in the original German, referring to Jean Paul in reference to Carlyle, reverting once more to Winwood Reade, and finally winding up with another bit of Goethe. In "The Adventure of the Red-Headed League," he quoted from Gustave Flaubert's correspondence with George Sand and in "A Case of Identity" he makes use of a quotation from the Persian Hafiz, who, he asserts, has as much sense and as much knowledge of the world as the Latin Horace.

In "The House Opposite" by Elizabeth Kent, the heroine is greatly embarrassed for lack of funds, and makes the definite statement that she has not enough money to carry her from New York to Bar Harbor. But almost in the next paragraph she states that she has some shopping to do, and she finds this is a good opportunity.

These slips are unnecessary; and though not heinous offences, they cause the reader to lose confidence in his author.

Again, some statements, while barely possible, are too improbable for ready belief. In Gaboriau's "The Widow Lerouge," we read this:

Old Taberet examined with extreme care the dead woman's finger-nails; and, using infinite precaution, he even extracted from behind them several small particles of kid. The largest of these pieces was not above the twenty-fifth part of an inch in length; but all the same their color was easily distinguishable.

We can scarcely imagine human finger-nails scraping off sufficient lavender kid from an assailant's gloves to serve as evidence, and we doubt if it could be proved possible by practical experiment. Though original and picturesque clues are desirable, yet care should be taken to have them carry the weight of common sense.

5. The Use of Illustrative Plans

A VERY ANNOYING ERROR OFTEN met, is putting the plans in the book too late. By plans, we mean, the architectural sketch showing the rooms of the house or the arrangement of the grounds, with an X "where the body was found."

In general, it is wise not to have a plan necessary to the understanding of the story. But some plots cannot be clearly understood without a plan. In such a case, have the diagram well and simply drawn, with as few lines as possible, and no unnecessary details. Moreover, present the plan at the beginning of the story. It is a most frequent error to insert the plan long after the situation has been fully described and the reader has pictured the entire scene for himself in his own mind. Then comes the plan, and it not infrequently turns his mental picture topsy-turvy. In a short-story it is less absolutely necessary, but in a book it is important to introduce the plan at the very first.

In "Hand and Ring," by Anna Katharine Green, the intricacies of the plot necessitate two plans; one of the house where the crime is committed, and another of the neighboring town and country. The first of these plans appears on page 170 and the other on page 364. Both should have been given when the scenes they represent were first brought into the story.

In "The Leavenworth Case" by Anna Katharine Green, the plan of the house is given on page 8, and thereby allows the reader to start with a correct mental picture of the scene of the crime.

"The Mystery of the Yellow Room" and "The Perfume of the Lady in Black," both by Gaston Leroux, require definite and somewhat elaborate plans. These are beautifully drawn, and occur in the book exactly at the time they are needed.

6. The Locked and Barred Room

A SITUATION GREATLY BELOVED OF mystery-mongers is a crime committed in a room so locked and barred that there is apparently no possible ingress.

This was the case in Poe's "The Murders in the Rue Morgue," and the later explanation of how the intruder entered is simple, ingenious, and satisfactory. But since then, hundreds of stories have been written around a crime committed in a sealed room, with solutions of varying interest.

The plot is usually the same. The barred doors necessitate a forcible breaking in to discover the crime. Then, owing to the fact of the locks and bars, the dead man found in the room is adjudged a suicide. But, of course, later developments prove it to be murder and finally disclose how the murderer could get in and out and yet leave everything bolted on the inside.

Often a secret passage is the solution, but this is trite; and to invent a cleverer explanation is the aim of the ambitious author. Gaston Leroux succeeded perfectly, in his "Mystery of the Yellow Room," and few authors can touch the simple subtlety of his idea.

Zangwill went at the matter deliberately. To quote from the introduction to "Big Bow Mystery":

"For a long time before the book was written I said to myself that no mystery-monger had ever murdered a man in a room to which there was no possible access. The puzzle was scarcely propounded ere the solution flew up and the idea lay stored in my mind till years later."

This particular problem and its solution, in Zangwill's hands, is a masterpiece; and though incidentally in his book he tells of many suggested solutions, none compares with his own in simple though daring ingenuity.

A writer does well to use this always arrestive plot, if he have some new and interesting explanation to offer.

XVIII

Murder in General

I t cannot be denied that the greatest Detective Stories, short or long, have been written around a murder. Poe, Gaboriau, Conan Doyle, and Anna Katharine Green all look upon murder as the theme par excellence for a Detective Story, and other crimes are used by authors only as a relief from monotony.

Human nature thinks more lightly of robbery, or arson; but murder stirs up a spirit of righteous indignation and a desire for justice or revenge. "A life for a life" is the logical sequence of "an eye for an eye" and a murder mystery will hold a reader's interest when a lesser crime will pall.

1. Murder Considered in the Abstract

But, first of all, let us dissociate the real horror felt at a real murder, from a murder plot used as a peg on which to hang the absorbing puzzle meant to enthrall the intellect. People who say, "How can you enjoy reading about such a revolting subject as murder?" are unable to discern the difference between a realistic newspaper story and a carefully planned romance.

The reason for reading newspaper accounts of a real murder trial are absolutely separate and distinct from the reasons for reading a Detective Story. The latter is an absorbing mental occupation, with a setting of human interest that differentiates it from a mere mathematical problem. If the reader is thrilled, it is through the intellect, not through the emotions. Sympathy is not called for; pity is not kindled; every situation is viewed by the cold light of reasoning. The whole affair is entirely divested of the sentiment that would surround it in real life. As Charles Lamb says of dramatic art:

"We dare not dally with images, or names, of wrong. We bark like foolish dogs at shadows. We dread infection from the scenic representation of disorder; and fear a painted pustule. In our anxiety that our morality should not take cold, we wrap it up in a great blanket surtout of precaution against the breeze and sunshine.

"I confess for myself that I am glad for a season to take an airing beyond the diocese of the strict conscience, now and then, for a dreamwhile or so, to imagine a world with no meddling restrictions.

"I come back to my cage and my restraint the fresher and more healthy for it. I wear my shackles more contentedly for having respired the breath of an imaginary freedom.

"I am the gayer at least for it; and I could never connect those sports of a witty fancy in any shape with any result to be drawn from them to imitation in real life. They are a world of themselves almost as much as fairyland."

And of a criminal he says:

"In its own world do we feel the creature is so very bad? In their own sphere, they do not offend my moral sense; in fact, they do not appeal to it at all. They seem engaged in their proper element. They break through no laws, or conscientious restraints. They know of none. They have got out of Christendom into the land—what shall I call it? The Utopia of gallantry, where pleasure is duty, and the manners perfect freedom. It is altogether a speculative scene of things, which has no reference whatever to the world that is. No good person can be justly offended as a spectator, because no good person suffers.

"The whole is a passing pageant, where we should sit as unconcerned at the issues, for life or death, as at a battle of the frogs and mice. But like Don Quixote, we take part against the puppets, and quite as impertinently. We dare not contemplate an Atlantis, a scheme, out of which our coxcombial moral sense is for a little transitory ease excluded. We have not the courage to imagine a state of things for which there is neither reward nor punishment. We cling to the painful necessities of shame and blame. We would indict our dreams."

In a word, the reader is transported to a pleasant land of burglary and murder, which is acceptable—because it is not true.

One need not be of a murderous instinct to enjoy the story of "Murders in the Rue Morgue." How many happily married people read stories of divorce; how many just and upright citizens read tales of men who succumb to temptation; how many strictly conventional people enjoyed "Trilby."

No, the devotee of the Detective Story must be willing, for the time being, to look upon.

2. Murder as a Fine Art

THE EXACT POINT OF VIEW is perfectly set forth in De Quincey's essay with that title. I wish I might quote it all here the delicious satire that is yet sound philosophy, is marred by separation from its context.

But a few passages may be given:

"People begin to see that something more goes to the composition of a fine murder than two blockheads to kill and be killed—a knife—a purse—and a dark lane. Design, gentlemen, grouping, light and shade, poetry, sentiment, are now deemed indispensable to attempts of this nature. Mr. Williams has exalted the ideal of murder to all of us; and to me, therefore, in particular, has deepened the arduousness of my task. Like Aeschylus or Milton in poetry, like Michael Angelo in painting, he has carried his art to a point of colossal sublimity; and, as Mr. Wordsworth observes, has in a manner 'created the taste by which he is to be enjoyed.' To sketch the history of the art, and to examine its principles critically, now remains as a duty for the connoisseur, and for judges of quite another stamp from his Majesty's Judges of Assize."

This is the right spirit in which to read of a murder in Detective Fiction. De Quincey goes on to say:

"The murder was a sad thing, no doubt, very sad; but we can't mend it. Therefore, let us make the best of a bad matter; and, as it is impossible to hammer anything out of it for moral purposes, let us treat it aesthetically, and see if it will turn to account in that way. Such is the logic of a sensible man, and what follows? We dry up our tears, and have the satisfaction, perhaps, to discover that a transaction, which, morally considered, was shocking, and without a leg to stand upon, when tried by principles of Taste, turns out to be a very meritorious performance."

Still in his whimsical mood, De Quincey thus goes back to Ancient History:

"The first murder is familiar to you all. As the inventor of murder, and the father of the art, Cain must have been a man of first-rate genius. All the Cains were men of genius. Tubal Cain invented tubes, I think, or some such thing. But, whatever might be the originality and genius of the artist, every art was then in its infancy, and the works must be criticized with a recollection of that fact. Even Tubal's work would probably be little approved at this day in Sheffield; and therefore of Cain (Cain senior, I mean) it is no disparagement to say, that his performance was but so-so. Milton, however, is supposed to have thought differently. By his way of relating the case, it should seem to have been rather a pet murder with him, for he retouches it with an apparent anxiety for its picturesque effect:—

> 'Whereat he inly raged; and, as they talk'd,
> Smote him in the midriff with a stone
> That beat out life: he fell; and, deadly pale
> Groan'd out his soul with gushing blood effused.'

—Paradise Lost, Book XI

Following history's list, we learn that:

"The finest work of the seventeenth century is, unquestionably, the murder of Sir Edmondbury Godfrey, which has my entire approbation. In the grand feature of mystery, which in some shape or other ought to color every judicious attempt at murder, it is excellent."

And another excellent affair is mentioned:

"The King of Sweden's assassination, by-the-by, is doubted by many writers, Harte amongst others; but they are wrong. He was murdered; and I consider his murder unique in its excellence; for he was murdered at noon-day, and on the field of battle—a feature of original conception, which occurs in no other work of art that I remember. No unpracticed artist could have conceived so bold an idea as that of a noonday murder in the heart of a great city. It was no obscure baker, gentlemen, or anonymous chimney-sweeper, be assured, that executed this work.

"With respect to the Williams' murders, the sublimes" and most entire in their excellence that ever were committed, I shall not allow myself to speak incidentally. Nothing less than an entire lecture, or even an entire course of lectures, would suffice to expound their merits. Indeed, all of these assassinations may be studied with profit by the advanced connoisseur. They are all of them exemplaria, model murders, pattern murders of which one may say,—

"'Nocturnâ versate menu, versate diurna,' especially nocturnâ."

Continuing this remarkable essay, we come upon this:

"But it is now time that I should say a few words about the principles of murder, not with a view to regulate your practice, but your judgment: as to old women, and the mob of newspaper readers, they are pleased with anything, provided it is bloody enough, but the mind of sensibility requires something more. First, then let us speak of the kind of person who is adapted to the purpose of the murderer; secondly, of the place where; thirdly, of the time when, and other little circumstances.

"As to the person, I suppose that it is evident that he ought to be a good man; because, if he were not, he might himself, by possibility, be contemplating murder at the very time; and such 'diamond-cut-diamond' tussles, though pleasant enough where nothing better is stirring, are really not what a critic can allow himself to call murders. I could mention some people (I name no names) who have been murdered by other people in a dark lane; and so far all seemed correct enough but on looking farther into the matter, the public have become aware that the murdered party was himself, at the moment, planning to rob his murderer, at the least, and possibly to murder him, if he had been strong enough. Whenever that is the case, or may be thought to be the case, farewell to all the genuine effects of the art."

"THE SUBJECT CHOSEN OUGHT TO be in good health: for it is absolutely barbarous to murder a sick person, who is usually quite unable to bear it. On this principle, no tailor ought to be chosen who is above twenty-five, for after that age he is sure to be dyspeptic."

"SO MUCH FOR THE PERSON. As to the time, the place, the tools, I have many things to say, which at present I have no room for. The good sense of the practitioner has usually directed him to night and privacy. Yet there have not been wanting cases where this rule was departed from with excellent effect."

AS MIGHT BE SUPPOSED, THIS essay of De Quincey's brought forth various criticisms. To these he replies in another essay:

"A good many years age, the reader may remember that I came forward in the character of a dilettante in murder. Perhaps dilettante is too strong a word. Connoisseur is better suited to the scruples and infirmity of public taste. I suppose there is no harm in that, at least. A man is not bound to put his eyes, ears, and understanding into his breeches-pocket when he meets with a murder. If he is not in a downright comatose state, I suppose he must see that one murder is better or worse than another, in point of good taste. Murders have their little differences and shades of merit, as well as statues, pictures, oratorios, cameos, intaglios, or what not.

"I am for morality, and always shall be, and for virtue, and all that; and I do affirm and always shall (let what will come of it), that murder is an improper line of conduct, highly improper; and I do not stick to assert, that any man who deals in murder, must have very incorrect ways of thinking, and truly inaccurate principles; and so far from aiding and abetting him by pointing out his victim's hiding place, as a great moralist of Germany declared it to be every good man's duty to do, I would subscribe one shilling and sixpence to have him apprehended, which is more by eighteen pence than the most eminent moralists have hitherto subscribed for that purpose. But what then? Everything in this world has two handles, Murder, for instance, may be laid hold of by its moral handle (as it generally is in the pulpit, and at the Old Bailey); and that, I confess, is its weak side; or it may also be treated aesthetically, as the Germans call it—that is, in relation to good taste. Genius may do much, but long study of the art must always entitle a man to offer advice. So far I will go—general principles I will suggest. But as to any particular case, once for all I will have nothing to do with it. Never tell me of any special work of art you are meditating—I set my face against it in toto. For, if once a man indulges himself in murder, very soon he comes to think little of robbing; and from robbing he comes next to drinking and Sabbath-breaking, and from that to incivility and procrastination. Once begin upon this downward path, you never know where you are to stop. Many a man has dated his ruin from some murder or other that perhaps he thought little of at the time."

THOUGH WRITTEN IN A WHIMSICAL vein, these observations of De Quincey apply definitely to the Murder Fanciers of Detective Fiction.

Shakespeare's murders are calmly accepted on the stage, and our children are placidly told Who Killed Cock Robin because these killings are not true, but are merely the manufactures of art.

3. The Murder Theme

As A PROOF THAT MURDER, or apparent murder, or attempted murder, is the favorite theme with our best detective writers, we may note these statistics.

Of the two-score-odd Sherlock Holmes stories, more than twenty have murder as the crime; and this, in spite of his assertion in "The Adventure of the Blue Carbuncle" that "there are many interesting little problems for detectives which are striking and bizarre without being criminal." Yet in more than half of his stories, Conan Doyle uses a murder motive.

Of Poe's three Dupin stories, two are based on murder.

Jacques Futrelle in his clever "Thinking Machine" stories, employs murder as an interest in eight out of nineteen.

Of Samuel Gardenhire's eight stories in "The Long Arm," five are murder stories.

And so on, through all the books of short stories, each volume of which narrates the exploits of a Transcendent Detective, the average of the murder plot is more than one-half.

Novels of detective fiction almost invariably use a murder plot. "The Moonstone" is an exception; but nearly all of Gaboriau's, Du Boisgobey's, Anna Katharine Green's and Ottolengui's are murder mysteries.

4. The Robbery Theme

AFTER MURDER, ROBBERY IS NEXT in favor as a crime for detective fiction. It is not easy to create intense interest in a robbery.

To quote Sir Walter Besant on this subject:

"Consider—say, a diamond robbery. Very well; then first of all, it must be a robbery committed under exceptional any mysterious conditions, otherwise there will be no interest in it. Also, you will perceive that the robbery must be a big and important thing—no little shop-lifting business. Next, the person robbed must not be a mere diamond merchant, but a person whose loss will interest the reader, say, one to whom the robbery is all-important."

These conditions are all perfectly observed in "The Moonstone. Indeed, so well did Wilkie Collins know that the jewel must be of not only enormous but peculiar value, that he thus describes it, through the medium of the old House Steward:

"Lord bless us! It was a Diamond! As large, or nearly, as a plover's egg! The light that streamed from it was like the light of the harvest-moon. When you looked down into the stone, you looked into a yellow deep that drew your eyes into it so that they saw nothing else. It seemed unfathomable; this jewel, that you could hold between your finger and thumb, seemed unfathomable as the heavens themselves. We set it in the sun, and then shut the light out of the room, and it shone awfully out of the depths of its own brightness, with a moony gleam, in the dark. No wonder Miss Rachel was fascinated; no wonder her cousins screamed. The Diamond laid such a hold on me that I burst out with as large an 'O!' as the Bouncers themselves."

And even before this description, the Diamond had been given a value quite other than intrinsic. It was a historic gem famous in the native annals of India. It was the subject of tradition and superstition, and it had been having adventures since the eleventh century. It had been the reason for theft and bloodshed, and was the cause of a family feud. All this interest in addition to the setting of the story, the personality of the characters and the adroit art of Wilkie Collins, causes the mystery to be a worth-while one.

A later story of a jewel robbery is found in Robert Barr's book, called "The Triumphs of Eugene Valmont."

This story is built around a diamond necklace which a court jeweler made, hoping to sell to Marie Antoinette. It contained half a thousand marvelous stones and had been through desperate adventures for many years. After its thrilling history is narrated the necklace is thus introduced to the reader:

The jeweler who made the necklace met with financial ruin; the Queen for whom it was constructed was beheaded; that high-born prince, Louis René Edouard, Cardinal de Rohan, who purchased it, was flung into prison; the unfortunate countess, who said she acted as go-between until the transfer was concluded, clung for five awful minutes to a London window sill before dropping to her death to the flags below; and now, a hundred and eight years later, up comes this devil's display of fireworks to the light again!

These preliminaries, though so similar to those employed in "The Moonstone," are in no sense a plagiarism. They are the legitimate methods of whetting the reader's interest in a robbery.

Gaboriau's "File No. 113" hinges on a robbery. This, a bank robbery, is not a great one, the sum of $70,000 being stolen. But the popularity of the story is caused by the skill of the detective Lecoq and the contrasting inefficiency of a younger detective in unraveling the complicated web of circumstances. As is usual with Gaboriau, the story is spun out to a tiresome length; and the simple plot of the robbery, the clue of the scratch on the safe and the mixed-up social relations of the characters are presented as a novel, when they are barely enough material for a novelette.

Robberies other than of jewels or money are sometimes thefts of valuable papers. These papers are often of political import, and not infrequently are of such nature that their falling into wrong hands would precipitate dire and disastrous war among the greatest of the world's powers. Naval treatises, war maps, or specifications for astonishing new inventions in the way of explosives, are among the most used sorts, followed closely by wills, love letters, photographs, and, in one instance at least, college examination papers.

Poe's "Purloined Letter" is the first and best of these stories; but the value of that masterpiece is more in the work of the detective than in the actual situation.

Conan Doyle's "A Scandal in Bohemia" is a similar plot with an incriminating photograph for the booty.

Theft stories are built, too, around antiques or curios, idols, heirlooms, and, especially since the disappearance of the Mona Lisa, around valuable paintings. There was even a very clever and original story written about the theft of the Venus of Milo from the Louvre; and this some years before the abstraction of the Mona Lisa.

Any article will do for fiction robbery, provided it be of exceeding great value, either intrinsically or by association.

In the Sherlock Holmes stories, one-quarter hinge on robbery as against one-half on murder. Next in favor is mysterious disappearance, or abduction.

5. The Mysterious Disappearance

The kidnapping of children is unpopular, as it is difficult to eliminate personal feeling when a child is brought into the story.

Samuel N. Gardenhire thus refers to it in "The Abduction of Mary Ellis":

"The stealing of children," he said, reflectively, "is probably the most unpopular crime that can be committed in this country. It is not indigenous to the soil. It is an exotic—an imported offence, one that has best thriven in communities where the poor are oppressed by the rich and where the element of revenge is combined with the instinct of greed."

"The Millionaire Baby," by Anna Katharine Green, is perhaps a unique instance of a full-sized book with a kidnapping case for its theme. But treated by this skillful author it is in all respects a success.

Among the Luther Trant stories, a kidnapping mystery is well solved in "The Red Dress"; and in "The Master of Mysteries," Astro happily rescues a kidnapped child.

Sherlock Holmes' nearest approach to a child-stealing case is the tracing of a missing school-boy in "The Adventure of the Priory School."

The abduction of older girls, or young women, is more often narrated, "The Strange Disappearance of Eleanor Cuyler," and "A Mysterious Disappearance," by Anna Katharine Green, being among the best examples.

Mysterious disappearance, though not necessarily abduction, is always a useful theme. In "The Adventure of the Noble Bachelor," Sherlock Holmes remarks thus on the disappearance of a bride during her own wedding breakfast:

"Before the what?" asked Holmes with a start.

"The vanishing of the lady."

"When did she vanish, then?"

"At the wedding breakfast."

"Indeed. This is more interesting than it promised to be; quite dramatic in fact."

"Yes; it struck me as being a little out of the common."

"They often vanish before the ceremony, and occasionally during the honey-moon; but I cannot call to mind anything quite so prompt as this."

A man is abducted in "The Adventure of the Missing Three-Quarter," value being given to this particular man because he is a three-quarter in a celebrated football team.

Other authors average much the same as Conan Doyle; and, to sum up, we find that throughout Detective Fiction half of the stories are murder mysteries, one quarter are robberies, and the other quarter is divided among crimes more or less dramatic or picturesque. These include forgery, counterfeiting, blackmail, arson, dynamiting, body-snatching, and other rare and even unique crimes invented by a daring author for a jaded public.

XIX

Persons in the Story

The Victim
The Criminal
Faulty Portrayal of the Criminal
The Secondary Detective
The Suspects
The Heroine and the Element of Romance
The Police
The Supernumeraries

Admitting that, according to a consensus of opinion, a murder mystery makes the most interesting plot for a Detective Story, let us consider the characters that necessarily belong to such a plot.

1. The Victim

DE QUINCEY HAS POINTED OUT, in his entertaining essay, that the victim of the crime should be selected with great care. Let us then, in planning our story, first decide upon the victim. Shall we choose a man or a woman—old or young?

A favorite victim with the writers of Detective Fiction is an elderly man, perhaps a banker, or someother wealthy citizen of importance to the community. This is a reasonable choice, for the character has the regard and interest of his fellow townsmen, without too great sympathy on the part of the reader.

Again, a charming young woman may be chosen for this role, but in this case the reader must not be allowed to know and love her before the tragedy.

The point to be remembered by the author is that the victim must be of the greatest possible importance generally, yet not specifically in the sympathy of the reader. Indeed, the victim, if beautiful or worthy, must be almost or entirely a stranger to the reader. But if the victim be wicked or unattractive, it matters not how great the reader's acquaintance with him. In a word, the reader must be averse to or indifferent to the victim, in order that he-may be satisfied with the conditions of the story.

Undoubtedly Poe reached the height of perfection in his choice, when he selected a mother and a daughter for the victims of the "Rue Morgue." What could be more dramatic? And yet as the reader knew nothing and never learned anything of these two people except their names, casually named in a newspaper report, he could not feel a personal grief at their death.

We accept the deceased gentleman of Doyle's "The Hound of the Baskervilles" or the murdered bride of Green's "The Filigree Ball" or the brutally-assassinated "Widow Lerouge" by Gaboriau, because they are all strangers to us, and we know they are a necessary part, indeed, the very foundation of the machinery of the story.

So guard against introducing the victim too long before the murder, or allowing him or her to engage too deeply the reader's sympathy or admiration.

This is not so likely to be the case in a short-story as in a novel. There are few, if any, of Conan Doyle's victims for whom we have any personal feeling whatever. Indeed, they are usually dead when the story begins, unless the problem may be a matter of preventing the crime.

Select your victim for his or her intrinsic worth or prominence and the sympathetic interest he or she may have for the other characters of the story, but not for the reader.

In "The Leavenworth Case" and "Hand and Ring," these principles are strictly observed. In "The Big Bow Mystery," the horrible deed is committed on a man we know nothing of, and one who is quite as much a lay figure as is a tailor's dummy.

In "The Mystery of the Yellow Room," the victim is a beautiful young woman who has our entire sympathy and admiration, but the situation is saved because she is not really killed in the attempt at murder.

An occasional device is to have the victim apparently a good and kind old gentleman, most foully murdered. But later it transpires that the seemingly good and kind victim was in reality a very bad man, and was killed in justice and righteous indignation.

Conan Doyle as a rule makes his victim an inconspicuous and even uninteresting character—oftenest, perhaps, a bad old man. When, as in the case of "The Speckled Band," the intended victim is a young woman, the tragedy is whisked around and the villain proves to be the victim.

All this is entirely legitimate and advisable. The ideal victim is one in whom we have no personal interest, but whose importance we easily recognize.

2. The Criminal

THE NEXT CHARACTER TO BE chosen must be our criminal. Here again is one, who, if he is to be convicted, must not be too deeply in the reader's sympathy. And yet he must be a worth-while character; it is old-fashioned, now, to have the crime committed by the butler or the private secretary. The drawing of the criminal calls for fine shading and strong effects. He must be both intelligent and ingenious, in order to give the Transcendent Detective a foeman worthy of his steel. The reader must have no liking or pity for him. In his perfection he should be what Poe calls, "that monstrum horrendum, an unprincipled man of genius."

Moreover, he must be cleverly drawn in order to conceal his identity from the reader until the last. He must appear to be what he is not, and he must not appear to be what he is; and this calls for Machiavelian cunning on the part of both criminal and author. The identity of the criminal, disclosed at the last, must be the greatest surprise of the story.

This is marvellously well accomplished in "Hand and Ring" and "Big Bow Mystery." In both these books the reader cannot possibly guess the criminal, although he is inconspicuously in plain view from the very beginning. But so adroitly is his identity concealed and so definitely is he made to appear what he is not, that detection by the reader is not possible. To be sure, in neither book is the motive so much as hinted at until the final disclosures, and this is not quite in accordance with the unwritten law of the Detective Story. But it is forgivable in the books mentioned, because of their splendid workmanship and original plot.

In "The Leavenworth Case," written many years ago, we have one of the earliest and best examples of the private secretary criminal. Here, too, he is before our eyes from the very beginning, yet we suspect everyone else in the book before we think of him.

3. Faulty Portrayal of the Criminal

GABORIAU WAS AT FAULT IN this matter in the "Widow Lerouge." By the time we are half through the book and long before any hint of the true state of affairs is necessary, we are forced to the inevitable conclusion of the guilt of Noel, start ling as that theory seems on its face, simply because Noel is the only possible person who has consistently avoided being the object of suspicion. A still greater mistake is when during the course of a story every character is at sometime suspected and then cleared of suspicion, and at the end we learn that the crime is committed by a person of whom we have never heard.

Conan Doyle employs this hitherto unknown criminal frequently. Usually he is some old man who had known and quarreled with his old friend, the victim, many years before. For instance, in "The Adventure of Black Peter" and in "The Five Orange Pips," these are the circumstances. But Conan Doyle's motive is the exploitation of the powers of his Transcendent Detective in discovering the unheard-of criminal, and so in his case the end justified the means. But ordinarily, and especially in a book, it is bad workmanship to absent the criminal from the scene until the last.

Notwithstanding the criminal of the Rue Morgue murders, it is ill-advised to have a freakish or a superhuman agency. The imitators of Poe's masterpiece have not been successful, though many have impressed members of the Simian tribe into their service as criminals.

The ideal criminal is a sane, respectable and well-educated man, like Lawyer Orcutt, or Mr. Grodman. Such as these escape the reader's suspicion by seeming to belong among the reputable characters of the story.

4. The Secondary Detective

THE TRANSCENDENT DETECTIVE BEING OF such importance as to require a chapter to himself, we come next to the sub ordinate detective. He is usually a Central Office Man, or a young reporter, or a lawyer with a taste for detective work. He serves as a foil for the higher detective's glories. He makes mistakes for the other to correct. He starts false trails to lead the reader astray and to give the superior detective opportunity to scoff at him and to set him right. This character may not be a detective at all, but simply a "Greek Chorus," like Dr. Watson, or like Hutchinson Hatch in "The Thinking Machine," or Walter Jameson in the "Silent Bullet." But usually this character is a detective who variously hinders or assists, as Sweetwater with Mr. Gryce, or Mr. Barnes with Mr. Mitchel.

This secondary detective character is, at times and quite effectively, a woman. In "That Affair Next Door" this role is taken by Miss Amelia Butterworth, who is also the teller of the story. In "The Master of Mysteries," Astro is aided and abetted in his charlatanry by a beautiful young woman called Valeska. In a clever series of stories called "Tales from the Red Ledger," the Transcendent Detective is helped at times by a mysterious and vaguely-pictured woman known as "The Orchid."

But invariably it is a good device to have a major and a minor detective character, that by comparison or contrast their leads and misleads may further the author's ends.

5. The Suspects

THE SUSPECTS ARE HIGHLY IMPORTANT characters in our Detective Story. They appear one after another, few or many, according to the length of the story. As each suspect is brought forward, the reader must be made to feel certain that this is the criminal. Then a doubt is raised or positive innocence is shown, and the next suspect is brought forward.

In a tale of simple construction, the suspects will come forward, a, b, c, d. The first three are eventually proved innocent and D is the criminal.

A more complex plot would have D wrongly accused and proved innocent and show that, after all, C was the criminal. In this case the reader must be made to insist to himself that he knew it was C all the time, even though the case looked pretty black against D. Or, a clever dodge is to suspect the characters in order, and though A was exonerated long ago, prove at the last that he was the real criminal after all.

It is the variations of these plans that make for interest in a Detective Story, and the characterization of these suspects has much to do with the success of the plot. The breathless fear that the criminal may be the beautiful but headstrong young woman; the ever rising suspicion that the criminal is the handsome, manly hero; the lurking doubt of the nephew who inherits; the distrust of certain old family servants all these serve to keep interest alive and curiosity piqued.

The principal characteristics, then, of our criminal must be his own importance, his dramatic personality, and his successful concealment until the dénouement.

These rules are not inflexible for short-stories, where there is less room for characterization than in books. The criminals in Conan Doyle's stories, like the victims, have little personality, because the fierce light that beats upon Sherlock Holmes leaves most of the other characters in shadow. But in a full-sized novel, where characterization is an important factor of the workmanship, the criminal's make-up is of vital importance.

6. The Heroine and the Element of Romance

As to the advisability of a heroine, authorities differ. The true economy of the Detective Story forbids the introduction of romance, especially in short-stories. The purists hold that the single-minded artist in detective fiction must not introduce two kinds of interest, for they can seldom be so perfectly balanced that one or the other shall not surer. The mind of the reader does not wish to jump continually from the solution of the problem to a love interest, and back again.

On the other hand, some writers deem it necessary to introduce a charming young woman who has little to do with the story, and who invariably marries the subordinate detective. The truth is, the magazine editors are largely to blame for this use of romance. In their inexorable demand for "a happy ending," they insist upon those wedding bells at the end of the story, that their joyful peals may drown the sound of the sentence pronounced on the criminal.

But Poe and Conan Doyle and all their worth-while successors omit the element of romance, except where it is an inherent part of the plot. Otherwise, romance in a Detective Story is wasteful and ridiculous excess. The whole intent of the problem and its solution is to engage the attention of the reader to the very utmost, and if this be successfully done, the reader has no nook or corner of his attention vacant to accommodate this love interest.

But if, as in "A Scandal in Bohemia," the beautiful woman is an integral part of the story, then she may be introducer and expatiated upon at the pleasure of the author.

In the story just referred to, this point is marvelously well taken in these opening words:

To Sherlock Holmes she is always the woman. I have seldom heard him mention her under any other name. In his eyes she eclipses and predominates the whole of her sex. It was not that he felt any emotion akin to love for Irene Adler. All emotions, and that one particularly, were abhorrent to his cold, precise, but admirably balanced mind. He was, I take it, the most perfect reasoning and observing machine that the world has seen; but, as a lover, he would have placed himself in a false position. He never spoke of the softer passions, save with a gibe and a sneer. They were admirable things for the observer—excellent for drawing the veil from men's motives and actions. But for the trained reasoner to admit such intuitions into his own delicate and finely adjusted temperament was to introduce a distracting factor which might throw a doubt upon all his mental results. Grit in a sensitive instrument, or a crack in one of his own high-power lenses, would not be more disturbing than a strong emotion in a nature such as his. And yet there was but one woman to him and that woman was the late Irene Adler, of dubious and questionable memory.

Though expressing it strongly, it is true that extraneous romance in a Detective Story is like grit in a sensitive instrument, or a crack in a high-power lens. But, of course, in a novel or even a novelette the case is altered. Here we require a setting of picturesque complexity. And a love interest, properly managed, and woven into the mystery plot is almost a necessity.

But the introduction of the feminine element in a Detective Story is subject to certain and definite rules. A victim she may be, a suspect she may be, but only in rare cases and when exceptionally well done, should she be the criminal. As a suspect, a feminine character gives opportunity for sympathetic thrills, but the experienced reader of detective stories feels fairly sure that an attractive feminine suspect is not the real criminal.

7. The Police

MEMBERS OF THE POLICE FORCE are inevitable characters in Detective Fiction and have been presented in every possible light from a realistic picture of the actual Inspector to the ignorant and fanciful author's conception of the same. As these strong arms of the law must appear on our pages, let us endeavor to know whereof we speak, and learn a few simple and primitive facts about these people before we endeavor to portray them. It is amusing to read some of the absurd effects given to these clearly defined and easily recognized American citizens. Make them as picturesque as possible; give them dramatic, even humorous personality, but do not endow them with absurd responsibilities or official powers.

8. The Supernumeraries

As to the supernumerary characters, the author must exercise his own taste and judgment, and he has fine scope for both. Of less importance in a short-story, they require merely to be kept in the background; but in a novel, they have their exits and their entrances, and play many, though subordinate parts. Each of these characters must have a positive and definite reason for being, and, if at all prominent, must be an inherent part of the plot. They are not to be scamped or slurred over in workmanship, for they are as important a part of the whole as the setting of a jewel or the binding of a book. They are the pence of a Detective Story, and must be taken care of; though in this case it does not follow that the pounds will take care of themselves.

XX

The Handling of the Crime

The method of the murder is a point to be carefully chosen and this consideration of course includes the weapon.

Shooting is perhaps the means most often used, with stabbing as a close second. If a shooting, the weapon is usually a revolver, or occasionally a rifle. In this case, care must be taken that the scene is out of doors; or, if indoors, in an isolated apartment or so placed that the report shall be out of hearing of the other characters, unless immediate discovery is intended.

Various devices are used to keep the innocent characters from hearing the shooting. In one case only a half-charge of powder was put into a gun. In another, of recent date, a silent bullet was used.

A strong point is always made of the evidence of the weapon, if it be found. But, as we have before hinted, do not persist in having the revolver marked with the initials of a perfectly innocent person, for this has come to be looked upon as a tacit acquittal. It is hackneyed, also, to have the pistol one of a pair, and trace it by means of its duplicate still reposing in its case in the criminal's library. Learn to avoid these over-worked devices, as there are surely plenty of others. If a pistol is your chosen weapon, treat it either inconspicuously, or in some novel and original fashion that will interest the reader.

The advantage of a stabbing is principally that the weapon may be picked up at the moment, in a sudden impulse to kill; while a pistol usually implies a premeditated murder.

A weapon picked up on the spot has the advantage of not necessitating its concealment after use, for it incriminates no one in particular. Oftenest this weapon is a dagger used as a paper cutter, and so lying at hand on a table. Or a dagger or sword which is one of a decorative group on the wall of the room. Another weapon which has crept into use of late years is the hatpin. This, though popular among writers, is implausible and in many cases impossible; for the average hatpin bends but does not break. Yet one author after another kills his victim by stabbing him with a hatpin which breaks off and disappears in the wound.

One would-be clever author caused his victim to fall violently forward (with his mouth conveniently open), and allow a hatpin held by a near-by lady to strike through the roof of his mouth and pierce his brain. The obliging hatpin broke off at just the right place, and as the lady concealed the head end, the point end of the fatal weapon was never discovered. This related incident is practically impossible and should not have been used.

A Spanish story called "The Nail," by Pedro de Alarçon, practically reverses this method. A large nail was driven into the victim's skull and accomplished its purpose immediately. The head of the nail was concealed by the man's thick hair, and all unsuspecting of villainy, three medical experts declared the man's death due to apoplexy. Nor were they entirely to blame, as the physical effects brought about by the nail were precisely the same as the conditions of death by apoplexy.

The nail is a horrible suggestion, but whatever weapon brings about violent death is necessarily horrible. It is wise to dwell on the physical details as little as possible. Granted a murder, there must be a method, and if the exigencies of the story demand a horrible method, so be it; but remember Poe's injunction, and when painting the decayed cheeses make them look as little like decayed cheeses as possible.

Poison is a method giving the author a wider scope and necessitating somewhat less gruesome conditions. It is easier to administer poison than to shoot or stab. Poison may be given in food or drink, or introduced into medicine or administered in more ingenious and original ways.

If this method is used, the author should study up on poisons and their effects, and not run the risk of making absurd mistakes in his text. Abstruse scientific information is not necessary; enough can be learned from an encyclopaedia or a medical dictionary; but the plausibilities must be maintained.

A favorite poison with writers who know little of the subject, is "a curious Indian or Persian drug, which acts instantaneously and leaves no trace." This drug, with its various and unintelligible names, has been somewhat over-worked; but it is acceptable because of its mystery and it is useful because its description is so vague as to need no real knowledge of it on the part of the author.

The plot of a poison murder implies more complexities than a death by shooting or stabbing. The poisoner is a person of more ingenuity and is more anxious to escape discovery; and it also gives scope for treachery and deceit. Then, too, it has the advantage of allowing the detail of bloodshed to be omitted, thus making the scene less ghastly to sensitive minds.

Drowning and strangling and chloroforming eliminate also the necessity for bloodshed, and have the added advantage of requiring no especial weapon; though the presence of the weapon, or the absence of one known to have been used, is a valuable asset to the mystery writer.

Though the principal means of murder are enumerated above, the various manifestations of these means are innumerable.

The ambitious writer often strives to find some new and original way of committing a hackneyed crime. So far has this been carried, that the latest detective stories employ the use of cultures of typhoid or diphtheria to bring about the necessary demise.

Such means are perfectly legitimate in detective fiction, and if detailed with accurate and correct scientific knowledge are convincing, though not picturesque. Sherlock Holmes, with his fancy for the bizarre, rarely is satisfied with a plain shooting or stabbing. He uses such means as a blunt weapon, pushing into the water, a venomous snake, a harpoon, a poker, charcoal fumes, and a fall from a steep precipice.

One of Anna Katharine Green's best stories, "Hand and Ring," employs the homely weapon of a billet of fire-wood. We are told at the outset that:

Half the criminals are caught because they do make tracks and then resort to such extraordinary means to cover them up. The true secret of success in this line lies in striking your blow with a weapon picked up on the spot, and in choosing for the scene of your tragedy a thoroughfare where, in the natural course of events, other men will come and go and unconsciously tread out your traces, provided you have made any. This dissipates suspicion, or starts it in so many directions that justice is at once confused, if not ultimately baffled.

This is a sound principle of construction, and is the starting point of many of the best detective stories.

In "The Mystery of the Yellow Room," the author goes back to the primitive weapon of a mutton bone, and in the skillful hands of both author and criminal this weapon is truly dramatic.

An author's first plot almost invariably centers around a shooting or a stabbing affair. It is in his later efforts that he feels moved to vary his methods.

Regarding crimes other than murder, we find that more depends on the setting. A robbery, however great the booty, must be made interesting by unusual characters or conditions, and must implicate the hero or other important characters to the danger point. The discovery of the wrong-doer must mean disgrace and disaster of the strongest sort. For your detective story fancier is an extremist; and, owing to the predominance of murder stories and capital punishment, a short imprisonment for a robbery seems tame by contrast.

"The Moonstone" is a robbery story, but it combines all the elements that make for a dramatic setting, and though not the main motive, it includes a murder, and also a suicide, incidentally in the plot. It is one of the very few full-sized novels built upon a robbery, and it required the peculiar genius of a Wilkie Collins to hold the reader's attention through its five hundred pages.

Other crimes than those we have considered, such as forgery, arson, blackmail, etc., are used only by authors in search of a novelty. They fancy that these crimes will interest because they are not so hackneyed as murder and robbery. But unless worked up with great care as to atmosphere and technique, stories of these crimes often prove dull reading.

Some authors incline to such subjects as Nihilism and the workings of secret societies. These are not of such general interest as the ones we have been discussing, but they offer picturesque possibilities and scope for melodrama.

XXI

The Motive

Having decided upon our characters, our crime, and our weapon, let us consider next the motive for the crime. Of course in all crimes except murder, the motive is obvious; for who would commit a robbery except to obtain the booty? Who would commit arson except with the intent of destroying property?

But in a murder story the motive is one of the principal parts of the mystery. It has been said that there are only three motives for murder: money, love and revenge. While this is true in a general way, there are many other specific motives.

In Mr. Train's book, "Courts, Criminals and the Camorra," there is a most interesting chapter devoted to this question of motive. Though it is impossible to quote it all, we will refer to his published record compiled by a man who had been trying murder cases for ten years. Several pages tell the details of the record, but a concise summing up is also given. We are told, "Out of the sixty-two homicides recorded, there were seventeen cold-blooded murders, with deliberation and premeditation; three homicides due to negligence; five committed while perpetrating a felony; thirty-seven manslaughters, due in sixteen cases to quarrels, thirteen to drink, four to disputes over money, three to women, one to race antagonism."

A further classification is given, and the whole chapter, indeed, the whole book, should be read by every writer of detective fiction.

Only a small percentage, however, of recorded murders are adaptable to fiction plots. A study of the causes of real murders is useful, if one has discrimination in choice.

The motive in fiction must be picturesque if possible, and interesting in any case. We care little what ruffian murdered another in a back alley; but we are intensely curious to know who killed Mr. Leavenworth or the Widow Lerouge.

The most interesting motives are doubtless money, love and revenge; but the ramifications of these include hate, jealousy, greed, safety, ambition, inheritance and many others—in fact, the whole category of human emotions.

Occasionally there is what might be called a freakish motive, such as the homicidal mania of The Whispering Man; or the curious motive of the criminal in the "Big Bow Mystery."

But these are sporadic instances. The soundest motives are the best, and in most cases the soundest are the simplest. Murder is the result of one of the most primitive impulses in man; and though the working out of the plot may be subtle, it is wise, so far as is possible, to have the motive simple, straightforward and strong.

If consistent with the plot, let the motive be of recent date. It is annoying to discover at the end of the book that the motive is retaliation for a wrong done thirty or forty years ago, as in "A Study in Scarlet" or "Hand and Ring." These, otherwise perfect and really great detective stories, finally reveal motives which could not possibly be discovered by the reader, however much he might guess at them.

Let the motive be as carefully concealed as you like, but offer adroit hints and veiled allusions that the astute reader may catch if he can, and when at last the motive is revealed, let it be a logical and sound one, and, above all, let it be adequate.

XXII

Evidence

1. The Coroner

IN CASE OF A MURDER, the Inquest should follow, as the night the day.

"The Scales of Justice" is a book which, aside from its very clever pages, has most interesting and enlightening aphorisms at the head of its chapters. One of these tells us "When evolution has produced a perfect thing, it stops working. Crowner's quest law has not changed in three centuries."

This is by way of a fleer at the Coroner's Inquest.

Another current authority says, "Mr. Coroner has been losing his importance so rapidly that not long ago it was seriously proposed to do away with him and his utterly useless performances. However, he is still in power, but it is a very much shorn power nowadays."

Mr. Arthur C. Train refers to this subject in stronger terms. "The coroner," says he, "is at best no more than an appendix to the legal anatomy, and frequently he is a disease. The spectacle of a medical man of small learning and less English trying to preside over a court of first instance is enough to make the accused himself chuckle for joy."

This argues a good sense of humor on the part of the accused, but Mr. Train must know whereof he speaks. But be that as it may, the Coroner has not yet been ousted from his position in detective fiction, and is too picturesque a figure to fear imminent dethronement. On the contrary, this official gives opportunity for what is known as a character sketch, and is often described as if with the author's keen relish for satire.

For instance this description is quoted from "The Scales of Justice," by George L. Knapp:

Coroner Lutgers was the sort of doctor who gets a political job or goes to advertising within three years of his graduation. In one capacity or another, he had been drawing public money for twenty years; and meant to continue in the same occupation for twenty years more. His strong point was dignity, a dignity much resembling a safety night lamp; for no matter how often it was tipped over, it always righted itself, to gleam austerely from the doctor's bald forehead and patriarchal whiskers. At this particular inquest, the doctor's dignity lacked something of its usual calm. It was not a case in which the public would willingly accept the "person or persons unknown" verdict; and yet for the life of him, the coroner could not see how any other verdict was possible.

However, we still cling to the coroner as a necessary and desirable member of our detective fiction family, and we feel that we could better spare a better man.

2. The Inquest

THE INQUEST, IN DETECTIVE FICTION, came in with "The Murders in the Rue Morgue," where it is used as a vehicle for telling much of the story. Since then, the inquest has been a prominent incident in most of the murder stories of detective fiction; and as it can be made to present all manner of thrilling and exciting scenes, and also as it is most useful in leading or misleading the reader, it will probably remain with us.

In a short-story, the inquest is seldom if ever described in detail, because of lack of space. But in a full book the inquest provides several chapters of interesting and instructive reading.

Poe, ruled as ever by his exact economy of attention, and moreover, because his story is a short one after all, gives merely the gist of the inquest; listing the witnesses in descriptive fashion and tersely reporting their depositions.

I. Zangwill, in "The Big Bow Mystery," takes advantage of his inquest scene to indulge in sarcastic humor and veiled innuendos.

Anna Katharine Green is conscientious and straightforward in her inquest recitals; while the earlier French authors are diffuse and elaborate in their descriptions.

Taken by and large, the inquest is invaluable to the Detective Story writer. It affords such necessary opportunities for cataloging details without seeming to do so; for convincing the reader that the innocent are the criminals; for introducing and characterizing the actors; and for setting the stage with the necessary properties for the future scenes of the drama.

3. The Witnesses

THE PRINCIPAL ELEMENT OF THE inquest is, of course, the witnesses and their testimony. Few realize that the nursery tale of Cock Robin partakes of the nature of an inquest. In the first line, "Who killed Cock Robin?" we are informed as to the crime and the victim. This is immediately followed by the complete confession of the criminal and the disclosure of the weapon:

> *"I," said the sparrow,*
> *"With my bow and arrow;*
> *I killed Cock Robin"*

This is a frank enough confession, and doubtless true; but even a confession must have corroborative witness, and, an eye witness, if possible. Hence we read:

Who saw him die?

> *"I," said the fly,*
> *"With my little eye,*
> *I saw him die."*

And this investigation, this testimony of an eye witness, presented in an entertaining manner, is the reason for the introduction of the inquest in our story.

The witnesses are naturally the characters of the book. The jurymen are but transients, and are not heard of again after their verdict is rendered. But the witnesses comprise the chief movers of the machinery and it is in their power to make or mar the plot. For if the plot of a detective story is the knot and its unraveling, the evidence of the witnesses constitutes the strands of the skein.

The plot is the skeleton, but the evidence and the deductions therefrom are the muscle and sinew. On the value and presentation of the evidence does the reader's interest depend. No matter how absorbing the puzzle, if the evidence and deduction be not full of action and surprise the story palls.

4. Presentation of the Evidence

INDEED IT IS THE CHAIN of evidences, all more or less surprising, that holds the reader's interest through the five hundred pages of "The Moonstone," where the puzzle is only a jewel robbery. And here is one reason why real murder trials are not as interesting as fictional ones. For the newspaper reports are plain accounts of the evidence found, whether entertaining or not; but the wily detective author need introduce no evidence that is not picturesque or exciting.

The author should know exhaustively the truth about evidence, its real value and meaning; and knowing this, utilize such knowledge at will.

Learn too, the difference between vital and incidental evidence. Sherlock Holmes remarks:

It is of the highest importance in the art of detection to be able to recognize, out of a number of facts, which are incidental and which vital. Otherwise your energy and attention must be dissipated instead of being concentrated. Now, in this case there was not the slightest doubt in my mind from the first that the key of the whole matter must be looked for in the scrap of paper in the dead man's hand.

Of course; since the scrap of paper was put there by the author for that very purpose. But a close study of Conan Doyle's stories will prove the best lesson in collating and understanding evidence.

5. Circumstantial Evidence

LEARN, TOO, THE DIFFERENCE BETWEEN circumstantial evidence and the testimony of an eye witness. Remember, circumstantial evidence must be strong and well attested to convict a murderer. Remember, too, how rarely it is the case that a murderer allows an audience when he commits his crime. Learn to adjust for yourself the harmonization of these statements.

This point is reduced to an absurdity in Melville D. Post's story, "The Corpus Delicti." In this story an atrocious murder is committed, but with diabolical cleverness the criminal utterly destroys the body of his victim by the use of chemicals. When the trial is on, and overwhelming circumstantial evidence proves the crime, the counsel for the prosecution says:

"Men may lie, but circumstances cannot. The thousand hopes and fears and passions of men may delude, or bias the witness. Yet it is beyond the human mind to conceive that a clear, complete chain of concatenated circumstances can be in error. Hence it is that the greatest jurists have declared that such evidence, being rarely liable to delusion or fraud, is safest and most powerful. The machinery of human justice cannot guard against the remote and improbable doubt. The inference is persistent in the affairs of men. It is the only means by which the human mind reaches the truth. If you forbid the jury to exercise it, you bid them work after first striking off their hands. Rule out the irresistible inference, and the end of justice is come in this land; and you may as well leave the spider to weave his web through the abandoned court room."

This is rational and straightforward, but the counsel for the defence reports:

"I care not if the circumstantial evidence in this case were so strong and irresistible as to be overpowering; if the judge on the bench, if the jury, if every man within sound of my voice, were convinced of the guilt of the prisoner to the degree of certainty that is absolute; if the circumstantial evidence left in the mind no shadow of the remotest improbable doubt; yet, in the absence of the eyewitness, this prisoner cannot be punished, and this Court must compel the jury to acquit him."

This is unanswerable and after much hesitation the judge spoke thus:

"In this case the body has not been found and there is no direct proof of criminal agency on the part of the prisoner, although the chain of circumstantial evidence is complete and irresistible in the highest degree. Nevertheless, it is all circumstantial evidence, and under the laws of New York the prisoner cannot be punished. I have no right of discretion. The law does not permit a conviction in this case, although everyone of us may be morally certain of the prisoner's guilt. I am, therefore, gentlemen of the jury, compelled to direct you to find the prisoner not guilty."

This is an erratic plot, but founded on absolute knowledge of the law, and resulting in a most picturesque use of circumstantial evidence.

In this connection we might refer to a speech of Jacques Futrelle's hero detective who thus delivers himself:

"Circumstantial fiddlesticks!" snapped The Thinking Machine. "I wouldn't convict a yellow dog of stealing jam on circumstantial evidence alone, even if he had jam all over his nose." He squinted truculently at Hatch for a moment. "In the first place, well-behaved dogs don't eat jam," he added more mildly.

Indeed, most detective stories are simply the case of the dog with the jam on his nose and the plot is mostly concerned with proving that that particular dog is not the criminal after all.

6. Deductions from Evidence

THE EVIDENCE, WHETHER AT THE inquest or at a trial, must be carefully chosen, not only for its own attractive or surprising character but with a view to its material for deduction and analysis. A burnt match on the stairs of an elevated railroad station offers the casual observer little clue; but a burnt match of a particular style, on those same stairs, proving the hour when the criminal lit his "big black cigar," is of immense importance in leading to a conclusion, foregone in the author's mind but not in the reader's.

Remember, it is re-solution that counts. The interest depends on the fact of that match being a beacon light and proving its illuminative power as the tale goes on. No burnt match has a right to be in a detective story unless it is a lamp to the feet of the detective; and a light to a path, either right or wrong, but intentionally so.

Though circumstantial evidence may depend on personal testimony, it is oftener deduction from inanimate clues, preferably small ones, but always unexpected or incongruous ones.

In one of the "Astro" stories, the reader's interest is at once aroused by an unknown baby found in the street playing with a priceless fire opal and a black dead hand. Had the child held a rattle and a doll no curiosity would be felt as to the situation. This, of course, goes back to the accepted principle of the value of the bizarre.

7. Deductions from Clues

BUT EVEN MORE ADVANTAGEOUS THAN this is the use of the infinitesimal clue. When not irrationally lugged in, shreds, ravelings, scrapings of dust from boot heels, or scraps of paper are all much prized as fictional evidence.

In one of the best recent Detective Stories a red shoe button figures as the clue to a murderer. In one of Ottolengui's stories a waistcoat button is the clue. Of course buttons are a favorite clue as they can conveniently drop off and stay behind on the scene of the crime; or can even be pulled off the criminal's clothing by the frantic clutch of the victim.

A story by Melville D. Post, entitled "The Missing Link," hinges upon the loss of a cuff link. But this particular clue is rather hackneyed, and it even cropped up again in "The Trevor Case," a very popular recent novel; and also plays its part in "The Circular Staircase."

The great Sergeant Cuff, in "The Moonstone," first describes the value of a tiny clue by way of instructing his reader; and then goes on to work up a small smear on a freshly painted door into a clue of immense importance.

In "The Silent Bullet" the clue is so minute as to require a very powerful microscope to discern it. The paragraph quoted below describes the impression of the threads of woven material on a leaden bullet; which, though scientifically possible, is certainly a novel and ingenious bit of evidence for a Detective Story.

"Every leaden bullet, as I have said, which has struck such fabric bears an impression of the threads which is recognizable even when the bullet has penetrated deeply into the body. It is only obliterated partially or entirely when the bullet has been flattened by striking a bone or other hard object. Even then, as in this case, if only a part of the bullet is flattened the remainder may still show the marks of the fabric. A heavy warp, say of cotton velvet or, as I have here, homespun, will be imprinted well on the bullet, but even a fine batiste, containing one hundred threads to the inch, will show marks. Even layers of goods such as a coat, shirt, and undershirt may each leave their marks, but that does not concern us in this case. Now I have here a piece of pongee silk, cut from a woman's automobile-coat. I discharge the bullet through it— so. I compare the bullet now with the others and with the one probed from the neck of Mr. Parker. I find that the marks on the fatal bullet correspond precisely with those on the bullet fired through the pongee coat."

Nearly all of the Sherlock Holmes stories depend on the deductions from tiny clues, so finely drawn as to be sometimes a strain on the reader's credulity; but the credulity of the experienced reader of detective fiction becomes exceedingly agile; and he can believe any number of impossible things from before breakfast until long after midnight.

Of course this use of tiny clues is the direct result of the principle of microscopic observation, and it is inseparable from the work of the Transcendent Detective.

In "That Affair Next Door," the astute Miss Butterworth finds for a clue a small black pin: "A small matter," she declares to the reader, "but it points in the right direction."

In a story of Ashton-Kirk, the clue is the tiny, but symmetrically-shaped bit of pasteboard punched from a railroad ticket. Indeed, all Detective Stories fairly bristle with these tiny clues. But there are plenty yet unused. The alert Detective Story writer can find many that will serve his purpose. A single shred of excelsior found on the floor of a room, where no carefully packed bit of china or bric-a-brac has been unwrapped, will prove the presence of the only man under suspicion who received such a box by recent parcel delivery. Or a tiny, shiny spangle may lead as unerringly to a certain evening gown of a certain grande dame, as a grain of rice in a hat brim proves a bride, or straws in the hair, a farmer.

But these things must have some sort of a subtly indicative interest. Nobody wants to read of a dead leaf fallen from a tree, merely to prove that it is autumn. And so it is the author's work to provide clues that lead to something, and that pique the reader into endeavoring to find out for himself what it is.

8. Evidence by Applied Psychology

A NEW KIND OF EVIDENCE has appeared of late in Detective Stories that is not deduced from an inanimate clue or voluntarily spoken by a witness. It is the scientific procedure known as applied psychology. It necessitates apparatus with such impressive names as kymographs and tachistoscopes and ergographs; and it may be learned in its general plan from Professor Münsterberg's book, "On the Witness Stand."

This science aims to assist and serve such fields of practical life as education, medicine, art, economics and law. But the book in question considers only problems in which psychology and law come in contact. They deal essentially with the mind of the witness on the witness stand and their purpose is to turn the attention of serious men to this science.

The detective writer who wishes to make a point of the credibility of testimony of witnesses cannot do better than to make a close study of the principles set forth in this book.

9. Direct Observation

As a matter of fact, the inquest or trial scene in detective fiction makes a great point of the testimony of eye witnesses. Yet really the utter unreliability of eye witnesses has often been remarked upon; and Hawthorne, in his "Note-Book," says:

"Every day of my life makes me feel more and more how seldom a fact is accurately stated; how, almost invariably, when a story has passed through the mind of a third person it becomes, so far as regards the impression that it makes in further repetitions, little better than a falsehood, and this, too, though the narrator be the most truth-seeking person in existence. How marvelous the tendency is. Is truth a fantasy which we are to pursue forever and never grasp?"

Now, it is sufficient to pay attention to the conversations in which we take part everyday to discover that the worth of evidence depends to a very small degree on the good faith or the moral value of the witness. Who is there who has not seen for himself to what an extent accounts of the same fact may differ, even when related by serious witnesses endeavouring to keep scrupulously to the truth?

Nothing, indeed, is more difficult than to tell the truth; that is to say, to recount the past, to make a deposition upon some fact, even if the fact be one which has come a great number of times under our own eyes.

To prove that this is so, let the reader make the following simple experiment. Without any preliminary, ask a number of persons kindly to draw from memory the figure which indicates six o'clock, exactly as it appears on the dials of their watches. You will find that some of these persons will simply write the figure VI or 6; others, sharper, remembering that the figures take their line of direction from the centre of the dial, will write the symbol upside down, IX or 9. Everybody, however, will be quite convinced that his particular testimony is correct, and ready to swear to it on oath. Now ask them to take out their watches and look at them. Most of them will discover to their stupefaction that the figure VI or IX which they saw so clearly at the foot of the imaginary watch floating before their mind's eye has no existence at all on the dial of the real watch, where its place is taken by the small seconds-hand dial!

Here, then, we have a great number of inaccurate depositions; and yet, how often in the course of a day do most people look at their watches! There is no doubt, moreover, that all these people whom you have thus proved to be wrong acted in perfect good faith; not one of them had any wilful intention of deceiving.

Again, it is not uncommon to find a man who has owned his watch for many years, utterly unable to state whether the hours on the dial are indicated by Roman numerals or Arabic figures. This means only lack of observation, but quite as common is mistaken observation.

An amusing practical test of this is thus related of Professor Dueck. In order to test the memory and susceptibility to suggestion of his pupils he performed the following experiment on forty-eight boys between the ages of fourteen and seventeen. He passed a silver coin about the size of a fifty-cent piece around the class, instructing each boy to examine it carefully, but giving no further indications as to the purpose of his action. At the end of the lesson, which in other respects proceeded as usual, Professor Dueck, having again taken possession of the coin, addressed the class as follows:

"You have no doubt observed that the coin which I handed around had a hole in it; now I should like to test your powers of observation. I am, therefore, going to ask each of you to indicate the point on the coin where the hole is found. Just take a piece of paper, draw a circle upon it, and indicate roughly the position of the head on the coin and of the hole which you observed."

As a matter of fact there was no hole in the coin at all. Nevertheless no fewer than forty-four out of the forty-eight pupils indicated the position of the alleged hole in the coin, some even indicating the position of two holes. Of the four remaining pupils, only one positively asserted that there was no hole in the coin, the other three merely said that they had not observed the hole.

This alone is interesting enough, but there were several other features in the case which are well worth recording. In the first place the one and only individual who had not been open to suggestion was a boy who had previously shown his independence by giving considerable difficulty in matters of discipline. Furthermore, several of the younger boys, even after they were told that there was no hole in the coin, absolutely refused to admit this.

The Scientific American, commenting upon this experiment, remarks:

"It hardly needs to be pointed out how significant an observation of this character is in its bearing on legal testimony. We must not be surprised that the witness may under certain circumstances not merely make a certain statement incompatible with facts, but may even insist in his erroneous belief in the face of overwhelming evidence against it—and all this in perfectly good faith."

Once an observer of a magnificent military parade noted the exact and well-trained marching of the soldiers; and in describing it afterward, said positively, "And every man was exactly the same height." Which was far from being true, as the soldiers were of varying heights, but the strong impressions of harmony and precision, had given an unconscious effect of uniformity of height. All of which goes to prove that with the best intentions in the world, false testimony may be given.

Further than this, if desired, false testimony may be induced by suggestion of the questioner. Indeed in the giving of evidence suggestion plays a most important part. The simple fact of questioning a witness, of pressing him to answer, enormously increases the risk of errors in his evidence. The form of the question also influences the value of the reply that is made to it. This has given rise to the well-known prohibition of "leading questions" in courts of law.

Let us suppose, for instance; that some persons are questioned about the colour of a certain dog. The replies are likely to be much more correct if we ask the witnesses, "What is the colour of the dog?" than if we were to say to them, "Was the dog white, or was it brown?" The question will be positively suggestive if we ask, "Was the dog white?" To such a question the answer is probably of no value. In questioning witnesses—that is to say, in pressing them and forcing their memory— we may obtain, it is true, a much more extensive deposition than if we leave them free to answer spontaneously. Any advantage thus obtained, however, is problematical, since we lose in fidelity whatever we may gain in extent of information. A trained observation takes things in at a glance, and correctly, too.

M. Robert Houdin gives this interesting description of training his own eye, as quoted in "The Lock and Key Library":

"My son and I passed rapidly before a toy-shop, or any other displaying a variety of wares, and cast an attentive glance upon it. A few steps farther on we drew pencil and paper from our pockets, and tried which could describe the greater number of objects seen in passing. I must own that my son reached a perfection far greater than mine, for he could often write down forty objects, while I could scarce reach thirty. Often feeling vexed at this defeat, I would return to the shop and verify his statement, but he rarely made a mistake.

"My male readers will certainly understand the possibility of this, but they will recognize the difficulty. As for my lady readers, I am convinced beforehand they will not be of the same opinion, for they daily perform far more astounding feats. Thus, for instance, I can safely assert that a lady seeing another pass at full speed in a carriage, will have had time to analyze her toilet from her bonnet to her shoes, and be able to describe not only the fashion and quality of the stuffs, but also say if the lace be real or only machine made. I have known ladies to do this."

Zangwill in "Big Bow Mystery" thus argues the worthlessness of most casual observation:

"Sir, everything depends on our getting down to the root of the matter. What percentage of average evidence should you think is thorough, plain, simple, unvarnished fact, 'the truth, the whole truth, and nothing but the truth?'"

"Fifty?" said the Minister, humoring him a little.

"Not five. I say nothing of lapses of memory, or inborn defects of observational power—though in the suspiciously precise recollection of dates and events possessed by ordinary witnesses in important trials taking place years after the occurrences involved, is one of the most amazing things in the curiosities of modern jurisprudence. I defy you, sir, to tell me what you had for dinner last Monday or what exactly you were saying and doing at five o'clock last Tuesday afternoon. Nobody whose life does not run in mechanical grooves can do anything of the sort; unless, of course, the facts have been very impressive. But this by the way. The great obstacle to veracious observation is the element of prepossession in all vision. Has it ever struck you, sir, that we never see anyone more than once if that? The first time we meet a man we may possibly see him as he is; the second time our vision is colored and modified by the memory of the first. Do our friends appear to us as they appear to strangers? Do our rooms, our furniture, our pipes strike our eye as they would strike the eye of an outsider, looking on them for the first time?

"Can a mother see her baby's ugliness, or a lover his mistress' shortcomings though they stare everybody else in the face? Can we see ourselves as others see us? No; habit, prepossession changes all. The mind is a large factor of every so-called external fact. The eye sees, sometimes, what it wishes to see, more often what it expects to see. You follow me, sir?"

10. Exactness of Detail

IN THIS CONNECTION WE ARE not discussing the value of evidence, per se, but merely for what it is worth in the construction of a Detective Story. The bringing forth of false evidence to complicate the mysteries of the story, is entirely permissible, if fairly done. And to do this fairly and properly it is wise to make a study of evidence and its relative value.

As we have seen, the average citizen is not observant. He rarely could tell the details of an incident he has witnessed, unless he were already familiar with the conditions. There fore the author of a worth-while Detective Story must make it his business to familiarize himself perfectly and accurately with the conditions he is describing. A lack of this familiarity with details is often seen in our best artists who portray scenes of whose especial characteristics they are carelessly unobservant. An amusing instance of this sort is remarked in this letter, which appeared in one of our popular periodicals:

DEAR SIR

Your "Ministers' Number" has just come to hand. I assume that some degree of accuracy is desirable even in a cartoon. Most of the clergy at whom your shafts of wit are aimed seem to be of the Episcopal Church, and I guess we can stand it, but what hurts is the vesture in which you attempt to garb us.

For instance, "Charley, the Assistant Minister at St. Joseph's"—and by the way $1,200 is a large salary for Charley; from his looks I should not say he was worth as much as that, at least he would not be as assistant to me—is dressed in a long old-fashioned surplice with bishop sleeves. Young assistants sometimes have Episcopal bees in their bonnets, but never Episcopal sleeves in their surplices. Again, Charley has around his neck what appears to be a feather boa or a tippet. Twelve hundred dollars would not allow him to sport such luxury. Lastly, Charley, who is apparently meant to be a very high churchman, at least he looks like it, is wearing Geneva bands! What a combination! A long surplice with bishop sleeves, fur collar, and Geneva bands is not to be found in the heavens above or the earth beneath—it might be in the other place, but I have my doubts.

If any of your artists ever went to church for any purpose—incidentally it might benefit them and raise the moral tone of the paper!—they would see what kind of garments a minister does wear, and their fun would have added force and pungency, I think. I am sure LIFE always wants to be correct, even in its humor.

What I have said about Mr. Walker's little picture applies with equal force to Mr. Flagg's extraordinarily vested parson. Really, to what church does he belong? They say we Episcopalians never disturb the peace. Can it be that Mr. Flagg has the idea that Presbyterians, with their strenuous views on predestination and the election, are vested that way?

Very sincerely yours,
CYRUS TOWNSEND BRADY,
Rector
KANSAS CITY, MO,
September 25, 1912

11. Theories of Evidence

IF IT IS NECESSARY, THEN, for an artist to attend carefully to the costuming of his models, how much more necessary is it for the writer of a Detective Story to be carefully accurate even to the tiniest detail of his work. And as evidence is part and parcel of every Detective Story, let the earnest young writer make a close study of it from the best examples in literature.

Read Poe; "The Murders in the Rue Morgue" is all evidence. Read Gaboriau; he understood the fine points of testimony. Read Conan Doyle. Read Anna Katharine Green. And then compare and connote and contrast their presentation and treatment of evidence.

This subject is well summed up in the following quotation from "The Man in the Corner," in which the author both entertains and instructs us with his theories.

"But supposing it were of paramount importance that you should give an accurate description of a man who sat next to you for half an hour today, how would you proceed?"

"I should say that he was of medium height—"

"Five foot eight, nine, or ten?" he interrupted quietly.

"How can one tell to an inch or two?" rejoined Polly, crossly. "He was between colours."

"What's that?" he inquired blandly.

"Neither fair nor dark—his nose—"

"Well, what was his nose like? Will you sketch it?"

"I am not an artist. His nose was fairly straight—his eyes—"

"Were neither dark nor light—his hair had the same striking peculiarity—he was neither short nor tall—his nose was neither aquiline nor snub—" he recapitulated, sarcastically.

"No," she retorted; "he was just ordinary looking."

"Would you know him again—say tomorrow, and among a number of other men who were 'neither tall nor short, dark nor fair, aquiline nor snub-nosed,' etc.?"

"I don't know—I might—he was certainly not striking enough to be specially remembered."

"Exactly," he said, while he leant forward excitedly, for all the world like a Jack-in-the-box let loose. "Precisely; and you are a journalist call yourself one, at least—and it should be part of your business to notice and describe people. I don't mean only the wonderful personage with the clear Saxon features, the fine blue eyes, the noble brow and classic face, but the ordinary person—the person who represents ninety out of every hundred of his own kind—the average Englishman, say of the middle classes, who is neither very tall nor very short, who wears a moustache which is neither fair nor dark, but which masks his mouth, and a top hat which hides the shape of his head and brow, a man in fact, who dresses like hundreds of his fellow-creatures, moves like them, speaks like them, has no peculiarity.

"Try to describe him, to recognize him, say a week hence, among his other eighty-nine doubles; worse still, to swear his life away, if he happened to be implicated in some crime, wherein your recognition of him would place the halter round his neck.

"Try that, I say, and having utterly failed you will more readily understand how one of the greatest scoundrels unhung is still at large, and why the mystery on the Underground Railway was never cleared up."

Two paragraphs from "The Whispering Man" give another twist to the theory of evidence, and whether absolutely true or not, it is interesting and convincing.

Jeffrey caught the word out of my mouth. "Evidence? There was evidence against every single innocent person in this case—Pomeroy, Armstrong, Gwendolen Carr. The only person against whom there wasn't any was the guilty man himself. No, evidence doesn't amount to much until it's tied on behind the right guess.

"What does the best evidence in the world amount to, anyway, when it comes to that?" he concluded. "It's utterly meaningless, except when it's tied on behind some theory, like the tail on a kite. As for expert testimony, there's only one kind of true expert, and he's just an inspired guesser, no more, no less."

A contrast or discussion of the merits of circumstantial evidence and the testimony of an eye witness is always provocative of interest. Though like many other discussions it is really futile, it carries a certain weight if cleverly set down.

Sherlock Holmes thus remarks upon it:

"I could hardly imagine a more damning case," I remarked. "If ever circumstantial evidence pointed to a criminal it does so here."

"Circumstantial evidence is a very tricky thing," answered Holmes, thoughtfully. "It may seem to point very straight to one thing, but if you shift your own point of view a little, you may find it pointing in an equally uncompromising manner to something entirely different."

And seemingly opposed to this, is the opinion of the great detective John W. Murray, who says:

"I believe in circumstantial evidence. I have found it surer than direct evidence in many, many cases. Where circumstantial evidence and direct evidence unite, of course, the result is most satisfactory. There are those who say that circumstances may combine in a false conclusion. This is far less apt to occur than the falsity of direct evidence given by a witness who lies point blank, and who cannot be contradicted save by a judgment of his falsity through the manner of his lying. Few people are good liars. Many of them make their lies too probable; they outdo truth itself. To detect a liar is a great gift. It is a greater gift to detect the lie. I have known instances where, by good fortune, I detected the liar then the lie, and learned the whole truth simply by listening to the lie, and thereby judging the truth. There is no hard and fast rule for this detection. The ability to do it rests with the man. It is largely a matter of instinct."

While Mary E. Wilkins in "The Long Arm" voices the same theory with equal cleverness:

"Crime detection is not a secret art; anybody can do it if he has the writs and the time, and patience to get at all the facts, and if he knows enough of the ways of men and women. It sounds like boasting to say so much, but it isn't; we all fail too often to be vain, and when I fail, I always say, 'I couldn't get at all the facts,' or, 'I didn't know enough about the sort of people concerned.'"

Zangwill, too, states these principles clearly:

"Pray do not consider me impertinent, but have you ever given any attention to the science of evidence?"

"How do you mean?" asked the Home Secretary, rather puzzled, adding with a melancholy smile, "I have had to lately. Of course, I've never been a criminal lawyer, like some of my predecessors. But I should hardly speak of it as a science; I look upon it as a question of common-sense."

"Pardon me, sir. It is the most subtle and difficult of all the sciences. It is, indeed, rather the science of the sciences. What is the whole of Inductive logic, as laid down, say, by Bacon and Mill, but an attempt to appraise the value of evidence, the said evidence being the trails left by the Creator, so to speak? The Creator has—I say it in all reverence drawn a myriad red herrings across the track, but the true scientist refuses to be baffled by superficial appearances in detecting the secrets of Nature. The vulgar herd catches at the gross apparent fact, but the man of insight knows that what lies on the surface does lie."

So, realizing the importance of the presentation of evidence as one of the prime factors in our work, let us endeavor to gain a working comprehension of the subject and use it with discrimination and discernment.

XXIII

Structure

I n the construction of our story we must consider the question of

1. Length

First, and in the opinion of many authorities best, there is the short-story. With exceptions, the best mystery stories are short-stories. A short-story lends itself peculiarly to a mystery plot, principally because it is not easy to keep wonder and curiosity alive through a long story.

Again, many detective stories fall naturally into the length of a novelette—say 30,000 words.

Then there is a two-or three-part story, which differs from the novelette in construction, even when of the same length.

Another form is the serial, in which each installment must have its own climax, all leading to the final surprise.

And last of all, there is the full-sized book, where the interest may or may not be broken before the dénouement and solution.

2. The Short-Story and the Novel

Of making many books concerning and dissecting the short-story there is no end. As many probably there are regarding the construction of the novel; and between these two forms they tell us there is a great gulf fixed. But the fixing of this gulf is largely a matter of opinion, and the opinions are somewhat diversified.

One writer explains the intrinsic difference between a short-story and a story that is merely short. He holds that a short-story is by no means a condensed novel, but is different in kind from a novel. The novelette, however, he contends is a brief novel.

Another writer, following this distinction, goes so far as to say that were the novelette condensed to one half or less of its usually accepted length it would still be a novel and not a short-story.

Conversely, were a short-story expanded indefinitely it could never become a novel.

The foundation of this distinction lies in the principle that a short-story is founded on a unity of impression. It relates, more or less definitely, a single episode; while a novel is a series of correlated episodes, bearing on a single motive. The number of words in a piece of fiction has absolutely no part in determining its nomenclature.

Poe's distinction that a novel cannot be read at a sitting and a short-story can, is not entirely valid. For "a sitting" is surely a most uncertain division of time. To the busy man a sitting may be a half an hour; to the idle woman it may be half a day; while to the "shut-in" it is continuous and interminable. Moreover, in the case of a thrilling Mystery Story, a reader's sitting would be prolonged, even in spite of imperative duty calls, because of the desire to reach the solution of the mystery.

Again, as a distinction, we are told that the novel is expansive and the short-story intensive. Perhaps an illustration might be made by likening the novel to a map of the United States, and the short-story to a single state on the map viewed under a magnifying glass.

But these differentiations regarding short-stories and novels are fully explained and discussed in books exclusively devoted to such technique. And though the fine distinctions therein drawn are of highest importance to other branches of fiction, they are almost, if not entirely, negligible in the case of Detective Stories. For the inherent difference between a novel and a short-story is one of plot. Whereas, since Detective Stories have but one solitary plot,—"the problem and its solution,"—the difference in the detective short-story or the detective novel is merely that of length.

3. Singleness of Plot in the Detective Story

THE SINGLE PLOT THAT MAKES a Detective Story may be likened to an accordion; it may be pulled out to an extraordinary length, or compressed to a minimum. A detective novel may have minor complications, more characterization and more elaborate setting; but the plot must not vary from the plot of a detective short-story, being only the propounding of the riddle and the revealing of its answer. The longer the story the more numerous and bewildering the conditions of the riddle and the windings of the maze, but all tend definitely to the one end,—the answer.

In a short-story the plot rushes on breathlessly, bare and straight to its end. In a novelette there is more room for sidelights, more time for slower development, and more scope for minor issues; while a full-sized book still further amplifies these possibilities. But in these three forms the main thread must go on, without halt, in an ever rising crescendo of interest to the climax.

If the work is to be published in two or three parts, or if it is a longer serial, then the plan is so far changed as to present a definite climax at the end of each installment. But these must be all minor climaxes and all bearing successively and cumulatively on the final revelation.

4. The Question of Length

Now, IN WRITING DETECTIVE FICTION, unlike other kinds, the length of his story is entirely at the option of the author. For the detective plot possesses the characteristics of a piece of string; it differs from its fellows only in length. The story of "The Moonstone" could have been told in a hundred pages, but Wilkie Collins gives it five hundred. "The Murders in the Rue Morgue" could have been a full-sized book as well as "The Leavenworth Case." The inquest scene in the latter fills seventy pages, while Poe's story details the inquest in six pages.

Conan Doyle's stories are short because he uses the single incident of the crime and the single impression of its solution, with an absence of any detail not absolutely necessary. Sherlock Holmes himself, who is often a medium for his author's views, says that he could do in twenty-four hours detective work on which Lecoq occupied six months. This is true enough, but the reason is that, as we have previously pointed out, Lecoq figured in a novel while Sherlock had to do his work expeditiously in the confines of a short-story.

Gaboriau chose to write novels, and so in connection with the problem and its solution he makes use of side issues of all sorts; even including the past history of his characters, subordinate plots, and various byways of conjecture or misleadings.

So we see the length of a Mystery Story is entirely at the pleasure of the performer, without the hampering rules laid down for the writers of other types of fiction. Say the plot depends upon a cypher interest. Conan Doyle did the story of the "Dancing Men" in a short-story; Poe's "Gold Bug" is a novelette; while James DeMille's "The Cryptogram" is a very long book.

It may be because Detective Stories are the work of artisans rather than artists that they can be fitted to such a Procrustean bed of literature. But though a sponge may be the size of your head or compressed to the size of your fist, it is the same sponge and comprises and includes the same material and value.

Of course this general principle must be taken with limitations. Some of Conan Doyle's short-stories could not be made into satisfactory books, while others could easily be. As in other fiction, a slight incident is not enough for a novel, but a great incident is. A missing Christmas goose might not be of sufficient interest to fill a book, when a murder mystery is. Perhaps we may say a simple mystery indicates a short-story length, while a complex riddle, or one made complex by side issues means a novel.

And yet it is here that art steps in. A master hand can make a great interest out of a simple mystery, where a tyro could not succeed. Generally speaking, the short-story must differ from the novel in scope and structure. In detective fiction it differs in scope only; for the main structure is always the same.

Writers of the technique of fiction tell us that another difference between the short-story and the novel lies in the fact that the novel must be a love story, while the short-story need not deal with romance at all. Applied to detective fiction, this may be adapted to mean that a love interest is possible, though not imperative in a novel or a novelette; but a short-story has no reason for romance and no room for it, unless it is a necessary premise to the conditions of the story.

As a matter of absolute measurement, perhaps we may call four thousand words an ideal length for a short-story. A novelette should be thirty or thirty-five thousand words long; while a book may run as near as you wish to one hundred thousand words.

The length of Poe's "Gold Bug," nearly fifteen thousand words, would not be an acceptable size to editors of the present day. And though great writers may be a law unto themselves in this matter, it is wise to arrange a story in accordance with the editors' preferences.

Houdin, the magician, in speaking of his own principles of legerdemain, said: "It is more difficult to support admiration than to excite it," and so it is more difficult to hold an intellectual curiosity than to arouse it.

In his introduction to an excellent collection of mystery stories, Mr. Julian Hawthorne has written so discerningly on this subject that we quote from his article:

"I need hardly point out that there is a distinction and a difference between short riddle stories and long ones—novels. The former require far more technical art for their proper development; the enigma cannot be posed in so many ways, but must be stated once for all; there cannot be false scents, or but a few of them; there can be small opportunity for character drawing, and all kinds of ornament and comment must be reduced to their very lowest terms. Here, indeed, as everywhere, genius will have its way; and while a merely talented writer would deem it impossible to tell the story of 'The Gold Bug' in less than a volume, Poe could do it in a few thousand words, and yet appear to have said everything worth saying. In the case of the Sherlock Holmes tales, they form a series, and our previous knowledge of the hero enables the writer to dispense with much description and accompaniment that would be necessary had that eminent personage been presented in only a single complication of events. Each special episode of the great analyst's career can therefore be handled with the utmost economy, and yet fill all the requirements of intelligent interest and comprehension. But, as a rule, the riddle novel approaches its theme in a spirit essentially other than that which inspires the short tale. We are given, as it were, a wide landscape instead of a detailed genre picture. The number of the dramatis personae is much larger, and the parts given to many of them may be very small, though each should have his or her necessary function in the general plan. It is much easier to create perplexity on these terms; but on the other hand, the riddle novel demands a power of vivid character portrayal and of telling description which are not indispensable in the briefer narrative.

"The fault of all riddle novels is that they inevitably involve two kinds of interest, and can seldom balance these so perfectly that one or the other of them shall not suffer. The mind of the reader becomes weary in its frequent journeys between human characters on one side and the mysterious events on the other, and would prefer the more single-eyed treatment of the short tale. Wonder too is a very tender and short-lived emotion, and sometimes perishes after a few pages. Curiosity is tougher; but that, too, may be baffled too long, and end by tiring of the pursuit while it is yet in its early stages. Many excellent plots, admirable from the constructive point of view, have been wasted by stringing them out too far; the reader recognizes their merit, but loses his enthusiasm on account of a sort of monotony of strain; he wickedly turns to the concluding chapter, and the game is up.

"'The Woman in White,' by Wilkie Collins, was published about 1860, I think, in weekly installments, and certainly they were devoured with insatiable appetite by many thousands of readers. But I doubt whether a book of similar merit could command such a following today; and I will even confess that I have myself never read the concluding parts, and do not know to this day who the woman was or what were the wrongs from which she so poignantly suffered."

Stories which ought to be shorter are sometimes made into novels by long and often tedious interpolations.

"A Study in Scarlet," one of Conan Doyle's best stories, is unduly spun out by an interpolation which lasts from page 110 to 184. Likewise Gaboriau's "The Mystery of Orcival" has an interpolation from page 104 to 188. These extraneous narratives usually go back and tell of an episode that happened years before the scene of the story, and they are both uninteresting and inartistic.

As a rule, an author of detective fiction writes either short-stories or novels, but rarely both. Conan Doyle's only mystery novel is "The Hound of the Baskervilles"; while Gaboriau and Anna Katharine Green invariably write novels.

So we conclude that length is a matter of taste, and the detective fiction writer may use his own judgment as to the length of his works.

5. The Narrator in the Detective Story

THE TELLER OF THE DETECTIVE Story is an important factor in its technique. Many a good plot is spoiled because it is narrated by the wrong person.

Poe, with his quick sense of fitness, chose the narrator best calculated for the exploitation of his clever Dupin. This was a stroke of real genius, for the reader becomes acquainted with the principal through the subordinate. He is taught to look upon the work of a detective intelligently; taught to appreciate and understand it. He knows when it is time to applaud, because the narrator tells him. It is a pity that this narrator is nameless, for as Mrs. Harris, with even less personality, is a household word, so his name would have been. It is this narrator who rouses our interest, tantalizes our impatience, and piques our curiosity, in harmony with his own halting almost unbelieving observance of the marvels revealed to him. He teaches us to be amazed at the proper time and then at the proper time he explains what so amazed us.

Dr. Watson, narrator of the Sherlock Holmes stories, is a parallel character, though in no sense an imitation or plagiarism. The conditions of the revelations to be made require just such a person to make them; and without a doubt, Sherlock Holmes would have had his Dr. Watson even if Dupin had never had his.

Aside from the glory and honor cast upon the hero by this humble but adoring satellite, this means of narration has another decided advantage. Since the detective confides in his friend or not, as he chooses, the author can reveal or conceal facts as he chooses, and so mislead the reader at will. What the subordinate does not know he can not tell, and thus is the secret preserved. Again, the subordinate being but fallible, may surmise mistakenly. So then does the reader, and again the author's ends are served.

Sometimes the author prefers that the tale be told in the third person, but even so, the character of "Harris" is still usually in evidence. Often he is a reporter, for this gives him opportunity to go uninvited, yet free from the stigma of idle curiosity into the scenes of interest. A reporter eager for a "scoop" for his paper, sets a fine example of alert interest and close scrutiny for the reader to profit by.

In the foreword to "The Silent Bullet" the hero detective picks out his reporter and tells him how useful he will be to him in his work. "The Thinking Machine" has the reporter "Hutchinson Hatch," while "Rouletabille" has a clever reporter named "Sainclair."

Of course the story may be told directly from the mouth of the author. But the proportion of this manner of telling is not so large in Detective Story work as in other fiction; because there are secrets to be preserved. Not only the main secret of the mystery, but also the secrets of what the strange proceedings of the detective may mean. And if the author is telling the tale, it is manifestly difficult for him to preserve an ingenuous and veracious manner, though this may be done if the author maintains a certain aloofness and an arbitrary standard of what to tell and what not.

Gaboriau's stories are all told in the third person; so are DuBoisgobey's and many of Anna Katharine Green's. Gaston Leroux uses this form and so does Mr. Webster in "The Whispering Man."

"The Moonstone" is a conglomeration of forms. The narrator is changed to suit the needs of the author, and the book is made up of the stories of the diaries of several people interested; "The Woman in White" follows the same narrative method. "The Leavenworth Case" is also told by various people, and sometimes in diary form.

While not always effective in other fiction, the diary is a most useful form for Detective Stories. For secrets can be confided to a diary, and though thus revealed to the reader, they are not disclosed to the other characters in the book; which is frequently a necessary condition. While never used for the whole book, the diary form often appears on certain pages of the story. "The Mystery of the Yellow Room," "The Hound of the Baskervilles," and many of our best authors' works show more or less of the useful and often necessary diary form.

But whatever narrator is chosen, let the choice be made after careful consideration of the conditions of the story. If there is a great surprise which must be concealed until the end, the narrator must be kept in ignorance of it until the end. If the story hinges on the marvelous brain work of a transcendent detective, give him a Dr. Watson to expatiate on it and to be awed by it. If a scientific or other straightforward recital of procedure, it may be told by the author. These points can best be learned and understood by reading the works of the best authors and noting what kind of narrator they choose and why.

6. The Setting

THE SETTING OF THE STORY will of course depend on the plot; but, other things being equal, do not choose too low life for your scenes. The facts of a murder are in themselves sufficiently unattractive to make it unnecessary to add to the distastefulness of the story by unpleasant surroundings. Let the people in your story be at least fairly well to do, of at least moderately good position and of a decent education. Unless absolutely necessary to have it otherwise, let the house or the scene of the crime be attractive or interesting, and let even the subordinate characters be of refined and intelligent type. For one reader who enjoys tales of slum life there are a dozen who prefer ladies and gentlemen, if not lords and ladies.

It may be argued that murders or other crimes do not occur in high life as frequently as among the lower classes. This point may be open to discussion; but it would make no difference what the decision might be. Detective Stories are not realistic, and if the author choose to have his murder committed in a community of gentle-folk, he is entirely at liberty to do so.

It goes without saying that the locality and social customs of the story must be those with which the author is familiar. A Detective Story depends so much on the logic and plausibility of its conditions, that a vague or uncertain touch on the practical or material details greatly mars the effect.

Let us see to it, then, that our setting and our atmosphere are free from mistake or anachronism. Economy of attention demands that we keep the reader's mind wholly intent on the solution of the problem; and this may not be done if we allow questionable or contradictory work on the minor interests.

XXIV

Plots

1. The Plot is the Story

As we have seen, the detective story, short or long, has but one plot—the problem and its solution. No matter what elaboration may be introduced, the skeleton of the plot is the same; and it is this simplicity of construction, this straight and narrow path of procedure, that makes the writing of detective stories both easy and hard.

Mr. Bliss Perry eliminates the necessity in some stories, and by some writers for any characterization or setting whatever. He says, in "A Study of Prose Fiction":

"If its plot be sufficiently entertaining, comical, novel, thrilling, the characters may be the merest lay figures and yet the story remains an admirable work of art. Poe's tales of ratiocination, as he loved to call them, like "The Gold Bug," "The Purloined Letter," or his tales of pseudo-science, like "A Descent into the Maelstrom," are dependent for none of their power upon any interest attaching to character. The exercise of the pure logical faculty, or the wonder and the terror of the natural world, gives scope enough for that consummate craftsman."

And in his "Talks on Writing English" Arlo Bates observes:

"There is a crude popular idea that the refinements of literary art are wasted, at any rate upon the general reader. So many books succeed, at least temporarily, which can make no slightest pretence to any grace of manner, and which have not even the merit of reasonable accuracy, that the student is apt to feel that these things are superfluous."

But we have shown earlier in the book that while a detective story, even if poorly written, may interest and amuse, it is not literature unless it shows that superiority of intellectual attainment demanded by the critics or scholars.

2. Constructing the Plot

BUT REFERRING NOW TO THE plot, let the young writer be careful that he plans his story with absolute logic and sequence. Poe tells us that it was his "design to render it manifest that no one point in its composition is referable either to accident or intuition; that the work proceeded, step by step, to its completion with the precision and rigid consequence of a mathematical problem."

We accept Poe as the master in this field of fiction, and we can do no better than to study both his own stories and his essays in criticism of them. He makes this definite statement regarding the plotting of a story:

"Nothing is more clear than that every plot, worth the name, must be elaborated to its denouement before anything be attempted with the pen. It is only with the denouement constantly in view that we can give a plot its indispensable air of consequence, or causation, by making the incidents, and especially the tone at all points, tend to the development of the intention."

In building a story, then, let us construct it entirely from start to finish before beginning its actual diction. Construct the plot backward, if need be; but see to it that every incident and every episode, every speech of the characters and every hint of the author have their direct bearing on the statement of the problem or the quest of its solution.

Here is another valuable point in construction given us by Poe:

"The design of mystery, however, being once determined upon by an author, it becomes imperative, first that no undue or inartistical means be employed to conceal the secret of the plot; and, secondly, that the secret be well kept. Now, when, at page 16, we read that "the body of poor Mr. Rudge, the steward, was found" months after the outrage, etc., we see that Mr. Dickens has been guilty of no misdemeanor against art in stating what was not the fact; since the falsehood is put into the mouth of Solomon Daisy, and given merely as the impression of thus individual and of the public. The writer has not asserted it in his own person, but ingeniously conveyed an idea (false in itself, yet a belief in which is necessary for the effect of the tale) by the mouth of one of his characters. The case is different, however, when Mrs. Rudge is repeatedly denominated "the widow." It is the author who, himself, frequently so terms her. This is disingenuous and inartistical; accidentally so, of course."

An exactly parallel idea to this may be noticed in "The Leavenworth Case." Harwell, the private secretary, is a witness at the inquest. Also, he is the murderer. In the very beginning of the book the question is put to him:

"You are the person who last saw Mr. Leavenworth alive, are you not?"

We are then told that the young man raised his head with a haughty gesture that well nigh transfigured it, and replied: "Certainly not; as I am not the man who killed him!"

Now, he was the man who killed him, and had the author told the reader he was not, it would have been infringing on the rights of the reader. But it is perfectly legitimate that the character in the book should make this false statement, by way of not incriminating himself. By this device the reader is not only convinced that this Harwell is innocent, but feels a warming sympathy toward the suspected man. Harwell's status now being established in the reader's mind, as that of injured innocence, he is at liberty to figure prominently all through the book, yet never arouse the reader's sleeping suspicion until the author so wills it.

This point is a strong one to a conscientious writer of detective fiction—to learn at the end of the volume that the real culprit is the person who has been before you throughout, but whom you never have dreamed of suspecting.

Anna Katharine Green is an adept in the use of this plan, and surpasses most other writers in her ability to carry her unsuspected criminal straight through the book to the last page. In reading "Hand and Ring," who would guess that Lawyer Orcutt was the murderer of Mrs. Clemmens? The thrilling story goes on, and the reader successively suspects Hildreth, Mansell, or any character in the book rather than Orcutt, the grave and aristocratic lawyer.

It is this surprise, when at last the identity of the criminal is learned, that is the crux of the Detective Story. Observation and deduction, though important in interest, are side issues of the plot—which must bend all else to the final surprise.

In "The Whispering Man," who would guess or even deduce that the clever detective is himself the criminal? Note how deftly he is introduced to the reader, because "he is destined to play a large and most romantic part in the solution of the mystery, and his queer, brilliant, eccentric personality is to appear very often in the ensuing pages."

But this hint gives the reader no suspicion that the man thus introduced is really the criminal, nor does he suspect it until the very last. This book is rather more subtly constructed than "Hand and Ring," in that the motive for the crime is shown in the beginning of the book; though so skilfully veiled that even an experienced reader might be excused for not discerning it. The author, Henry Kitchell Webster, calls this his favorite of all the books he has written. He says, and very truly, that "he has played fair with his readers, given them every bit of information—all the clues to the identity of the person who committed the crime—that he himself has, but managing to lead their attention away from the real culprit until the desired moment for climax and revelation has arrived.

"In this kind of story when the big smash comes the reader should be able to go back in the story, and having reread all that goes up to the climax be able to unravel each clue which leads to the climax."

This is the true spirit of the writer of detective fiction.

3. Maintaining Suspense

ANOTHER AND VERY NECESSARY POINT to remember is that the mystery must be of sufficient interest to be worth unraveling. To quote Anna Katharine Green on her methods of construction:

"I must have a central idea which appeals to my imagination; and an end of such point or interest that the reader will feel that it justifies the intricacies which are introduced to hold it back. In other words the heart of the labyrinth must be worth reaching."

This of course refers especially to books, where more intricacies must be introduced than in a short-story. Mr. Burton E. Stevenson, a successful writer of detective fiction, professes these principles:

"First, to play fair with the reader, the cards must all lie on the table. It isn't honest to keep any up your sleeve; and the problem is to surprise the reader by the unexpected way in which you combine them. The reader must have before him all the facts which the solver of the mystery has, and then the 'Solver' must get there first. I also refuse to make any person act suspiciously without cause. If the person is innocent there is no reason why he should behave as though he were guilty.

"I think perhaps my particular trick is to keep the reader in suspense not so much as to what is going to happen as to how it is going to happen. I may add that it also seems necessary to me that every mystery should be approached from at least two angles; say, an amateur detective and a professional one, for instance; and that a great part of the interest of the story lies in the conflict between them, victory leaning first toward one and then toward the other. When I start a story I write it clear through, working regularly everyday, (though it takes the lash sometimes) and then going back to do the dovetailing. There must be no loose ends; every joint must fit and there must be no superfluous lumber. A detective story ought to run a swift, straight course from start to finish. It isn't a leisurely stroll through the country, it's a hundred yard dash! And you may have noted that in "The Boule Cabinet" there isn't a hint of love interest; love interest is dead weight unless it is an essential part of the plot; and one can't carry much dead weight and win a hundred yard dash."

Mr. Stevenson succinctly expresses the true principles of detective fiction; and by adhering to these, the young writer is travelling in the right path.

Dr. Nevil Monroe Hopkins—whose detective, "Mason Brant," operates in "The Strange Case of Dr. North," and other novelettes—writes thus on the same subject:

"I endeavor to start right off with action and to maintain it throughout, introducing such interesting characters and atmosphere as I can. I try to have a novel plot and to make most of the characters talk to each other in a direct manner; and to have some of the meeting-places, at least, rather gruesome. I endeavor also to have a golden thread of love and romance running from start to finish, upon which to string the more unwholesome elements which are necessary to contribute effectively to the phases of mystery. I believe always in writing deductively, in visiting queer places, and in accumulating acquaintances among police officials, doctors, lawyers, coroners, and the like."

So we see that the advisability of romance in detective stories is a matter of opinion, and opinions differ among the authorities. But the love interest, if not overdone, may be left to the discretion of the author, remembering that the mystery is the primary interest.

Henry Kitchell Webster gives perhaps a more definite formula than those above quoted:

4. Planning the Story

BEFORE WRITING: 1. PLAN ORIGINAL crime, method, and motive of the murderer. 2. Create, with this as a nucleus, sub-plots relating to several persons who by coincidence are drawn to the place or are connected with the victim, in different ways.

THEN WRITE. 1. Introduction. 2. Murder discovery. 3. Then take up the least likely suspect first, followed by others. 4. Hero Detective enters, decides, arrests and explains.

Mr. Gelett Burgess constructs his stories by architectural diagrams. The first story in his book, "The Master of Mysteries," (published anonymously) is "The Missing John Hudson"—We subjoin its preliminary plan:

Another well-known writer gives this very definite formula:

1. Preliminaries. Status quo. Introduction of dramatis personae.
2. Birth of Plot. Assembly of actors and assignment of parts.
3. Tentative separation of sheep from goats, intentionally misleading.
4. The Crime,—shot into the story like a bomb.
5. Gropings for murderer, on part of the police, coroner, friends, relatives and amateur detective.
6. Failure of everybody. Call in Transcendent Detective.
7. He glances about, announces that the facts are thus and so and proves that the facts are thus and so.
8. Discreet removal of the villain by suicide, accident or otherwise.
9. Marriage of the girl to the amateur detective. (This is invariable and imperative!)

The last item is in satiric vein, for among our best writers it is not considered imperative!

All of the foregoing formulae, kindly contributed by their authors, cannot fail to be of use to the beginning writer of Detective Stories. They all agree in the principal points, and are quite in line with Poe's strict laws.

The rights of the reader must be kept in mind by the author. It is not fair to mislead the reader until he is up against a blank wall. A false clue must lead in an obvious and seemingly logical direction. Then the false clue must be detected, as a natural consequence of the mistaken lead, and the right clues brought into view. It is not fair to make an innocent character appear guilty or vice versa, but it is quite right if the character make himself appear so. A witness who stammers and hesitates, may be guilty or may be innocently embarrassed. That is for the reader to judge.

And just in proportion to the cleverness and subtlety of the author's inventive genius, will the reader be duly and rightfully bewildered, or misled, and the game be well played.

Prof. Max Dessoir, in a very fine article on "The Psychology of Conjuring," writes as follows: "By awakening interest in some unimportant detail, the conjurer concentrates that attention on some false point, or negatively, diverts it from the main object, and we all know the senses of an inattentive person are pretty dull. . . When causing the disappearance of some object, the conjurer counts one, two, three, because, the attention of the public being diverted to three, they do not notice what happens at one and two. . . A specially successful method of diversion is founded on the human craze for imitation. . . The conjurer counts on this in many cases. He always looks in the direction where he wants the attention of the public, and does everything himself which he wants the public to do. . . If the trick is in the left hand, the conjurer turns sharply to the person to the right, presuming correctly that the spectators will make the same movement, and will not notice what is going on in the left hand. . . Every sharp, short remark will, for a moment, at least, divert the eyes from the hands and direct them to the mouth, according to the above-mentioned law of imitation."

These most valuable directions may be helpfully adapted to the writing of Detective Stories. The author is, in a way, a conjuror, with an avowed intent to hoodwink his audience.

Detective Stories call for logic, plausibility and a true sense of proportion. Literary ability is to be desired; but before that, there must be power of deduction and a perfect sense of values.

5. The Question of Humor

IF ROMANCE IS OUT OF place in a detective story, humor is even more so. With the exception of the whimsical De Quincey and the waggish Zangwill, few can write or read about murder with any touch of humor. The best Detective Stories are absolutely void of it, and except in the hands of a whimsical genius it is entirely out of place.

Mr. Zangwill wrote only one Detective Story, but that one is unique; and in plot far and away cleverer than any tale of a Transcendent Detective. Though professing to care little for this Detective Story of his, he says in the preface to its second edition:

"'Big Bow Mystery' seems to me an excellent murder story, as murder stories go, for, while as sensational as the most of them, it contains more humor and character creation than the best. Indeed, the humor is too abundant. Mysteries should be sedate and sober. There should be a pervasive atmosphere of horror and awe such as Poe manages to create. Humor is out of tone; it would be more artistic to preserve a somber note throughout. But I was a realist in those days, and in real life mysteries occur to real persons with their individual humors, and mysterious circumstances are apt to be complicated by comic."

6. Some Unique Devices

A UNIQUE PLOT IN WHICH the unsuspected criminal is ever before us is "The Mystery of the Yellow Room," by Gaston Leroux. This astonishing story depends on two absolutely original propositions. One, that the attempt at murder in an inaccessible room occurred long before it was supposed to have done so. The other that the great and celebrated detective who condescends to take the case is really the criminal. But the workmanship of this story and the several and perfect surprises can only be appreciated by reading it.

It was in all probability the great desire of the detective writer to choose for his criminal the character least likely to be suspected, that first suggested making the criminal of the story the detective also. Surely the last person the reader would suspect would be the detective. This has been frequently done of late, indeed so frequently as to cause great danger of this plot's losing its effectiveness. For the astute reader, always ready to learn the latest trick, has even now begun to suspect the least likely one for the criminal.

In "The Accomplice," by F.T. Hill, the criminal is the prosecuting attorney, which is in itself a clever idea, and gives scope for beautifully misleading incidents.

In a word, then, marshal your characters tentatively and select the one seemingly impossible as a criminal. Give him a plausible and adequate motive. Give him opportunity. Give him intelligence and ability to hide his traces; and then go on, using every sidelight and every tiny clue possible, gently to persuade your reader, but never to force him, to a false conclusion; and then at the last spring your surprise suddenly and drop the curtain at once.

Nothing is more annoying to the trained reader than a long chapter of explanation after the revelation. We have sometimes more than one chapter of the dead criminal's written confession, and our wonder and curiosity also being dead, we take little interest in the perusal.

Unless this post-mortem confession is inevitable to your plot, so arrange it that the motives and methods are explained just before the climax instead of just after.

Conan Doyle beautifully escaped this situation in "A Study in Scarlet," by reserving Sherlock Holmes' explanation of his own work until after the long and wearisome interpolation revealing the motive of the crime. The reader waded through, or skimmed through those chapters, because spurred on by his desire to learn the re-solution of the problem, to which he knew the answer.

But Conan Doyle is not at his best in mystery novels. The short-story is his forte. In "The Hound of the Baskervilles" the author realizes often that the action must be retarded, and Sherlock Holmes for once in his life is obliged to bungle. About a third of the way through the book, Holmes indulges in a shrug and a rueful smile. "Snap goes our third thread, and we end where we began," said he.

Never in a short-story would he have made his third thread snap, nor would he, indeed, have had any third thread; the first would have led to the desired goal. But in a book, threads must be multiplied and snapped and tangled to make the larger web. In "The Hound of the Baskervilles" we are treated to descriptions of scenery. We learn that "Rolling pasture lands curved upwards on either side of us, and old gabled houses peeped out from amid the thick green foliage, but behind the peaceful and sunlit country-side there rose, ever dark against the evening sky, the long, gloomy curve of the moor, broken by the jagged and sinister hills." In a short-story these things would have been left to the imagination, for lack of room.

A further consideration is that, in the book, unnecessary though acceptable characters had to be introduced, such as Selden and his wife's brother. A love interest is introduced around the beautiful Miss Stapleton. The device of Watson's diary report is introduced to delay the decisions of Sherlock Holmes. And the mysterious "L.L." is invented for the same reason. But so accustomed is Conan Doyle to the quick action of a short-story that these forced delays hamper him.

He is, however, exceedingly clever in palming off his own desires for delay upon his characters; as for instance in the following detail of Holmes' character:

One of Sherlock Holmes's defects—if, indeed, one may call it a defect—was that he was exceedingly loath to communicate his full plans to any other person until the instant of their fulfillment. Partly it came no doubt from his own masterful nature, which loved to dominate and surprise those who were around him. Partly also from his professional caution, which urged him never to take any chances. The result, however, was very trying for those who were acting as his agents and assistants. I had often suffered under it, but never more so than during that long drive in the darkness. The great ordeal was in front of us; at last we were about to make our final effort, and yet Holmes had said nothing, and I could only surmise what his course of action would be.

Now, of course, the real reason for Holmes' silence during that long, dark drive was because if he had told all he knew, the story would have ended then and there.

As is characteristic of Conan Doyle, the dénouement of this story entirely satisfies the reader. The exceedingly bizarre conception of this supernatural hound is logically and rationally explained. Moreover, and the young writer would do well to note this point, the criminal is summarily and inconspicuously disposed of.

It is always unpleasant to contemplate the hanging or the electrocuting of the fiction criminal. For this reason he not infrequently takes poison (which he has ready in his pocket), as soon as he is discovered, and dies peacefully, close upon the last words of his confession. This is one of the conventions adopted to spare the reader's feelings. For a criminal that can hold the reader's interest throughout the story is often too attractive a character to be permitted a horrible taking off.

But these conventions and devices and unwritten laws of the technique of the Mystery Story can only be learned—or, at least, can best be learned—from the thoughtful reading of the works of the masters in this field. The beauty and value of these creations cannot be appreciated by the casual or untrained reader. Only a connoisseur in the art of detective fiction can appreciate and intelligently enjoy the skill with which a great author plays with his readers. It may be likened to the skilled fisherman playing with trout. Or perhaps it is better symbolized by these remarks of the Great Herrman when speaking of his handcuff tricks:

"Common sense alone does not entitle a person to judge competently of the safety of fetters; only the man who is familiar with the technique of knots and the different ways of tying can express an opinion. To decide whether a closure is right or not, requires technical knowledge. Most people imagine that they can go unprepared to a spiritualistic seance, and pass a correct opinion on the existence or nonexistence of prestidigitation. This standpoint is as childish as when a layman expresses himself on the genuineness of the seal of the middle ages or on the nature of a nervous affection."

And so, the reader who is unversed in the arts and crafts of detective fiction cannot be expected to value the skill shown in the great presentations of The Problem and its Solution.

XXV

FURTHER ADVICES

The Use of Coincidences
The Use of Melodrama
Dullness
Unique Plots and their Solubility
Women as Writers of Detective Stories

1. The Use of Coincidences

AN ERROR INTO WHICH THE beginning author easily falls is the too lavish use of coincidences. While perhaps the majority of detective stories are founded upon coincidences, they must be made so plausible, so seemingly inevitable, that they shall not appear to be mere coincidences. A modern fiction detective thus frankly admits the value of coincidences in his work:

"Don't forget the fortunate coincidences," replied Average Jones modestly. "They're about half of it. In fact, detective work, for all that is said on the other side, is mostly the ability to recognize and connect coincidences."

But the reader cannot agree that a frankly announced coincidence makes as good a mystery problem as one where that element is left out. For instance in "The Adventure of Black Peter," in his confession, the criminal relates: "Like a fool I left my baccy-pouch upon the table."

The pouch, so obligingly, even necessarily, left on the table was of course the clue to the criminal. As a further coincidence this remarkable pouch bore the initials "P.C.," which quite conveniently pointed to a suspect named Peter Carey, as well as to the real criminal, Patrick Cairns. This being discovered, Sherlock Holmes says naively, "I was convinced that the initials P.C. upon the pouch were a coincidence and not those of Peter Carey, since he seldom smoked and no pipe was found in his cabin."

All of this shows too clearly the author's dependence on a coincidence. In the completed structure the literary architect should not let his framework show, for it dispels illusion and either prevents or mars surprise.

But the whole question of coincidence is too deep and too really scientific to attempt its discussion here. Poe knew it to its last and finest degree, but not everyone could follow its ramifications with the accuracy of his peculiar mind. He says in one instance:

"Coincidences ten times as remarkable as this (the delivery of the money, and murder committed within three days upon the party receiving it) happen to all of us every hour of our lives, without attracting even momentary notice. Coincidences, in general, are great stumbling-blocks in the way of that class of thinkers who have been educated to know nothing of the theory of probabilities: that theory to which the most glorious objects of human research are indebted for the most glorious of illustrations."

Though the theory of probabilities is too abstruse for any but scholars, a general knowledge of the relative values of coincidences is most useful to the writer of detective fiction.

Poe says further:

"There are few persons, even among the calmest thinkers, who have not occasionally been startled into a vague yet thrilling half credence in the supernatural, by coincidences of so seemingly marvellous a character that, as mere coincidences, the intellect has been unable to receive them. Such sentiments—for the half credences of which I speak have never the full force of thought—are seldom thoroughly stifled unless by reference to the doctrine of chance, or, as it is technically termed, the Calculus of Probabilities. Now this Calculus is, in its essence, purely mathematical; and thus we have the anomaly of the most rigidly exact in science applied to the shadow and spirituality of the most intangible in speculation."

The avenues of thought opened to our minds by these suggestions are fascinatingly attractive, and could we study the matter seriously it would soon put an end to many widespread fallacies of coincidence—such as receiving a letter from a friend one has been thinking of and ascribing it to telepathy—and like matters.

Gaboriau appreciated the futility of depending upon the coincidence:

"Don't forget," replied Lecoq, "that the field of conjecture is boundless. Imagine whatever complication you like, I am ready to maintain that such a complication has occurred or will present itself some day. Lieuben, a German lunatic, bet that he would succeed in turning up a pack of cards in a certain order stated in a written agreement. He turned and turned ten hours per day for twenty years. He had repeated the operation 4,246,028 times when he succeeded."

But leaving aside these deeper doctrines, let us use coincidence when necessary, carefully veiling it, however, with plausibility. Work up to the coincidence until it seems to occur naturally. Invent causes to produce the effects that otherwise would have seemed pure coincidence.

2. The Use of Melodrama

ANOTHER FAULT TO BE AVOIDED is the use of melodramatic speech or incident. The day is past when readers are thrilled by the sort of diction that charmed Pomona of "Rudder Grange," as she read aloud, "Ha—Ha—Lord—Marmont—thundered—thou—too—shalt—suffer!" And yet, in "A Scandal in Bohemia" we read: "'And the papers?' asked the king, hoarsely; 'all is lost!'"

It is difficult to discover a loss of "the papers" without melodramatic exclamation; but moderate the speech of your characters at the time of the appalling discovery as much as possible.

Avoid, too, the use of sentiment. Romance is not now referred to; but other sentiments which though acceptable in the "story of manners," tend to distract the reader of detective fiction. This field recognizes few emotions and no moral; and as a human document it depends for its success upon the primitive instincts of mankind and the material indications thereof.

3. Dullness

AVOID DULL AND PROSY DESCRIPTION. If any type of story depends on action and excitement, it is the type we are discussing. Keep before you always the question of your reader's attitude towards your work. Arrest their attention, rouse their curiosity, awake their interest, and you have made your start. Continue to stimulate all these to the highest pitch, and your story is written. Let your final explanation more than satisfy their anticipation, and you have made a success.

Build everything toward the final climax, using minor surprises as stepping-stones by the way. Continually produce the unexpected Persistently lead the reader to believe one thing and then suddenly convince him that he ought to have known it was another! Use every art and craft that in you lies to mislead him, but in such a way that when he is turned back to the right path he will vow he misled himself.

Remember the two great principles: to have your facts as straight and true as a mathematical proposition; and to have your fancies as fascinating and elusive as a fairy tale. In a word, the ideal writer of detective fiction should be the child of Euclid and Scheherazade.

4. Unique Plots and Their Solubility

DISDAINING OR TIRING OF THE regulation plot, some writers have branched off into erratic forms. This may be done with wonderfully fine effect if done perfectly. But only a genius, and an experienced one at that, should attempt it.

Perhaps the most brilliant achievement of this sort is Zangwill's "Big Bow Mystery." As this book is now out of print, it may be well to state briefly its plot.

A widowed landlady, a Mrs. Drabdump, after repeated knockings on the bolted bedroom door of her lodger, Arthur Constant, fails to awaken him. Terrified by vague fears of tragedy, she rushes across the street to implore the help of a neighbor, Mr. Grodman. He returns with her, and together they break in the bolted door of Constant's bedroom. A horrible sight meets Mrs. Drabdump's eyes, as she discovers the young man dead in his bed with his throat cut from ear to ear. Both windows are fastened; the door, until burst in, was both locked and bolted; and there is no other opening in the room. Add to this the fact that no razor or weapon of any sort can be found, and the problem seems insoluble. What is probably the best jury scene in fiction concludes logically that since the room could not have been entered by any intruder it could not be murder and must be suicide. It also concludes logically that since no weapon is found and the doctors declare that the wound could not have been self-inflicted, it could not be suicide and must be murder! This ingenious deadlock forms the nucleus of the story which is elaborated with cunning skill and marvelous subtlety.

The most experienced reader is not prepared for the surprising dénouement, which shows that the murder was committed by Mr. Grodman, after he broke open the door, and had been deliberately planned for by him, beforehand.

Stated thus barely, the plot seems incredible; but as written by Mr. Zangwill, it is plausible, convincing, and intensely interesting.

After all, Detective Stories depend upon the ingenuity of the author—in the best, intellect is paramount. Characters, judged by other standards, may seem unreal without disturbing the reader's equanimity, provided the chain of causation is kept logically perfect. The disregard of this axiom has resulted in many failures. Gaboriau, not content to write a mere tale of mystery, tried to convert it into a well-rounded novel. But the most notable recent instance of the thing was the endeavor of Gaston Leroux in "The Perfume of the Lady in Black," the sequel to "The Mystery of the Yellow Room." Without knowing quite why, readers found their interest in it flagging. In some respects it is the subtlest story of its kind. The shifting semi-tropical atmosphere is finely caught and ought a priori to add intensity to the central mystery of doubtful identity. The mystery itself is developed with rare psychological insight, and the relation between a mother and son is so acutely defined as to make a certain noticeable halt in the process of detection seem perfectly natural. Yet impatience with the story is inevitable. From habit the reader holds his attention in readiness for running down a crime—for that and nothing more—and his mind relaxes when outlying material is brought in.

Dr. Harry Thurston Peck says:

"The indispensable condition of a good mystery is that it should be able and unable to be solved by the reader, and that the writer's solution should satisfy. Many a mystery runs on breathlessly enough till the dénouement is reached, only to leave the reader with the sense of having been robbed of his breath under false pretences. And not only must the solution be adequate, but all its data must be given in the body of the story. The author must not suddenly spring a new person or a new circumstance upon the reader at the end. Thus, if a friend were to ask me to guess who dined with him yesterday, it would be fatuous if he had in mind somebody of whom he knew I had never heard."

Irrespective of all else, it is the mystery that arouses curiosity to the pitch of demanding explanation that counts. By few has it been played with a skill like that of Wilkie Collins, who, with little characterization or sentiment, without creating individuals of fiction whom we remember, or whose sayings we quote, could hold the attention of the novel-reading world with his "Woman in White," or set them eagerly agog to find the whereabouts of the mysterious diamond taken from its Eastern sanctuary. For ingenuity of construction, blind leads, bafflings, and sustained interest "The Moonstone" stands high in the catalogue of the mysteries of fiction; and the reader was penetrating to a degree who fastened upon Mr. Godfrey Ablewhite the theft.

5. Women as Writers of Detective Stories

NOT A FEW AMONG THE best writers of detective fiction are women. That perspicacious critic, Julian Hawthorne, observes:

"I have often marvelled that women so seldom attempt this form of literature; many of them possess a good constructive faculty, and their love of detail and of mystery is notorious. Perhaps they are too fond of sentiment; and sentiment must be handled with caution in riddle stories."

And a contemporary English essayist thus compliments our foremost American detective story writer:

"It may seem curious that women should be successful in a branch of fiction which many would be disposed to pronounce a masculine specialty. Perhaps Mrs. Green has herself supplied the explanation. In one of her best stories, 'That Affair Next Door,' she introduces us to a very commonplace old maid, like most old maids curious, secretive, keenly observant of her neighbours' affairs, and fond of speculating about other people's business. Circumstances throw her into the very centre of a mysterious crime, and suddenly reveal in her all the qualities of a great detective. All the characteristics which made her a nuisance to her neighbours make her an invaluable ally to the police. The conception is a daring, and, I think, a true one. I fancy that the two faculties which the great Sherlock declared to be the prime necessities of a detective, observation and deduction, are feminine rather than masculine faculties. It will hardly be disputed that it is so in regard to the former; while, as to the latter, what man ever discovered as much about the inhabitants of the house opposite as any woman will deduce from the shape of their window blinds. Most women quite habitually indulge in the sort of ratiocination that Holmes practiced over the old hat. Be that as it may, Mrs. A.K. Green herself has certainly as much right as any contemporary writer to claim the mantle of Gaboriau for stories the excellent technique of which should put some popular writers on this side of the Atlantic to shame."

Anna Katharine Green, who is Mrs. Charles Rohlfs in real life, is far and away the best in our home field. She is entirely conversant with all the rules of detective fiction, and her long list of books stands alone on the top shelf. She, herself, tells an amusing story in connection with her first book, the celebrated "Leavenworth Case." She wrote this story when quite young; and, becoming absorbed in the work, wrote wherever she happened to be, using any kind of stationery that might be at hand, from finest letter paper to backs of old envelopes or torn out ledger leaves. Unheeding the growing length of her story, she kept on until she had every drawer of an old bureau overflowing with its manuscript. Concluding at last, she stuffed all her papers into a large suit-case, and sallied forth to a publisher. The first publisher she called upon eagerly accepted the story; but to her regret, the young author was obliged to cut out more than forty thousand words of her manuscript. But the result was the most popular and the best-written detective novel by an American.

Other feminine authors have succeeded in this field. Mary E. Wilkins' short-story, "The Long Arm," conforms to all the conditions required by the unwritten law. Natalie Lincoln, in "The Trevor Case," and Mary Roberts Rinehart, in "The Circular Staircase," have done admirable work, as has also Stella M. Düring in "Love's Privilege." "That Mainwaring Affair," by A.M. Barbour, is among the masterpieces of construction, and Florence Warden may be accounted among the best authors of mystery stories in England. The series of short-stories by Baroness d'Orczy, and Augusta Gröner, are as clever as any written by men.

But of whatever sex the writer, or of whatever manner or style the setting, the one end and aim of the author must be curiosity aroused, increased and gratified. Other stories, other manners; but the Detective Story depends solely on this principle.

And ever remember Mr. Zangwill's dictum:

"The mystery-story is just the one species of story that can not be told impromptu or altered at the last moment, seeing that it demands the most careful piecing together and the most elaborate dove-tailing."

XXVI

Final Advices

General Qualities of the Detective Story
Correctness
Names
Titles

U ntil lately the Detective Story has not been looked upon as worthy of serious consideration from a technical point of view. But in the minds of many it has now risen to a place where it calls for standardization. Detective Stories in the last half century have progressed in two directions, good and bad. In fact they have fairly mushroomed out in all grades of quality. And so, to meet the growing appreciation of a good Detective Story, it is worth while to do one's best in writing them as they should be written.

True, hundreds of them are published every year, whose authors belong to "The mob of gentlemen who wrote with ease."

But although Pope made that very expressive line, he said also:

> *"True ease in writing, comes from art, not chance,*
> *As those move easiest who have learned to dance."*

In a recent book on the subject of the game of Bridge, the author cleverly designates the grades of Bridge players thus: Idiots, Butchers, Tinkers, Artists, and Necromancers. The student of Detective Stories will at once recognize that these designations very aptly describe writers of detective fiction.

As Poe was the master of this sort of technique, he was of course a necromancer; but the other names to be put in his class are exceedingly few. We have many Artists writing detective stories, and many more who may be called Tinkers. The lower grades, though voluminous their output, we will not consider here.

1. General Qualities of the Detective Story

BUT AS A KEYNOTE TO the story we would write let us remember that its success depends first of all upon the interest of the mystery. Perhaps the voice of the public as expressed by the literary critic best tells us what is desired. To quote from the review of a very recent Detective Story:

"The new physician sets about a stealthy investigation. He finds that in the neighboring house, behind the blue wall, something odd is in progress—the doors are locked against him. The eager question which keeps the reader hurrying through the four hundred pages is 'What will he discover?' As often happens, the solution scarcely supports the weight of the mystery. The story is a fantastic tangle, written with polished literary craftsmanship. But it is too ingenious in its opening to live up to its promises. It leaves one disappointed."

It is a blot on our escutcheon that we should be accused of often presenting an explanation too slight to support the mystery. Even polished literary craftsmanship cannot make up for the unpardonable sin of a disappointing solution. But this by no means disparages the value of literary excellence. This ought ye to have done, but not to leave the other undone. With all the power that in you lies make for literary craftsmanship; but strive equally hard to perfect a plot which though built on accepted even if hackneyed models, has a few points of absolute originality.

Notice in Anna Katharine Green's books how there is invariably some clever original touch which has never been used before. In, for instance, "Initials Only," the young woman is shot, fatally, but no bullet can be found. As we discover later, instead of a bullet, the assassin used an icicle! Could anything be more unexpected? The sharp needle of ice pierced her heart and of course melted immediately and left no trace.

But the novel and original touches, though greatly desirable, are incidental to the plot, which should be built on the strong and rational foundations used by our best writers.

As examples of excellent construction, read, "Hand and Ring," "The Mystery of a Hansom Cab," "The DeBercy Affair," "That Mainwaring Affair," or "The Accomplice." All of these are plotted entirely in accordance with the best usage, and may serve as models of construction.

In the case of short-stories, such definite and careful building of the plot is less imperative, as the author has room only for the single incident of the crime, and a short and swift account of its solution.

Specially ingenious plots, like "Big Bow Mystery" or "The mystery of the Yellow Room," may not be achieved by everyone; but all may pay heed to the soundness of construction required by even the simplest plot.

2. Correctness

AS IN EVERYTHING ELSE, THE writer should be careful of his diction. In a way, the detective story demands accurate English even more than polished expression. We have seen the word suspicion used as a verb, in a story by an educated author. Even Sir Conan Doyle allows his wonderful work to be marred by such slips as inferred for implied; relation for relative; and even an absolute grammatical error, when Holmes says, "It would be robbing you of the credit of the case if I was to presume to help you."

Again, one frequently meets with such errors as a reference to a "Frankenstein," when what they really mean is Frankenstein's Monster.

All of these things are unpardonable, and especially so in a field of literature where accuracy is a prime element.

Without overworking the poor words, learn to use intelligently and correctly—deduce, connote; vital, and incidental; fact, and truth; and all of the catch words that belong to the peculiar conditions of our subject,—even ratiocination.

3. Names

ESPECIAL ATTENTION SHOULD BE PAID to the names of the characters in our story.

If the influence of a right name is felt in real life, how much more so in fiction! In real life it is a matter of chance or of lucky accident if the baptismal name prove a just and congruous one, suited to the character and the circumstances of the owner. The natural parent may claim forgiveness for error on the score that he could not foresee the possible career of the child whom he may have handicapped at the altar. The author of a work of fiction can make no such plea. His characters should take form in his brain, like Minerva in the skull of Jupiter; they should be armed at all points, and the most vulnerable point of their equipment is an unworthy name. Yet knowledge of the thing desired does not necessarily lead to its easy discovery. It is a matter for thought, for research, for studious inquiry. Great skill and nicety of perception must be called into play. The effect must not be too crudely palpable. Suggestion, not insistence, is needed. The good old trick which pleased our simpler forefathers, that which consists in merely labelling a character,—all ingenuous, but not ingenious, stratagem,—has had its day. It was carried to an extreme in the early English drama, where even Shakespeare gives us such names among his minor characters as Mouldy, Feeble, Shadow, Shallow, etc., and it retained its hold on the comic stage down to the time of the Lydia Languishes, the Sneerwells, the Mrs. Malaprops of Sheridan, the Sir Fopling Flutters of Vanbrugh.

While such definitely descriptive names are perhaps not to be used, let us at least choose names that will seem to connote the effect intended.

"Scientific Sprague" is a good name because it is especially descriptive; and perhaps also because it is alliterative. We remember that name when we would not remember "Ledroit Conners" who figures in an equally good series of stories. "Craig Kennedy" does not stick in our memory like the "Thinking Machine," and "Rouletabille," though expressive in intent, has not the arrestiveness of "Raffles."

4. Titles

AND IF THE NAMES OF the characters are in their way important, how much more so is the title of the story. When Poe began his stories, no titles were hackneyed and he was at liberty to use "The Murders in the Rue Morgue" and "The Mystery of Marie Roget" without being trite.

But as both these titles have been borrowed hundreds of times, it is wise for the young writer to endeavor to think up an original title. Conan Doyle was an artist at this, and though all of his titles were "The Adventure of—," the rest of the phrase was so striking as to command interest at once. Whose curiosity would not be aroused by "The Adventure of the Speckled Band," or "The Adventure of the Five Orange Pips"? Incidentally, Conan Doyle has mentioned a dozen or more attractive titles, to which he has never yet written stories. We wish we might read of "The Adventure of the Paradol Chamber," "The Singular Tragedy of the Atkinson Brothers at Trincomalee," and many others of this list of equally fascinating titles:

"The Darlington Substitution Scandal," "The Arnsworth Castle Affair," "The Affair of the Amateur Mendicant Society," "The Loss of the 'Sophy Anderson'," "The Adventure of the Grice Patersons in Uffa,"

"The Camberwell Poisoning Case," "The Dundas Separation Case," "The Affair of the Reigning Family of Holland," "The Adventure of the Tired Captain," "The Trepoff Murder," "The Affair of the Netherland Sumatra Company," "The Tankerville Club Scandal," "The Case of Mrs. Etheredge," "The Affair of the King of Scandinavia," "The Manor House Case," "The Tarleton Murder," "The Affair of the Aluminum Crutch," "The Case of Vamberry, the Wine Merchant," "Ricoletti of the Club Foot and His Abominable Wife," "The Adventure of the Old Russian Woman."

But many authors content themselves with "The Mystery of Maple Hollow," or "The Connolly Case." Such titles as, "That Mainwaring Affair," "That Affair at Elizabeth," "That Affair Next door" are good in their way, but the phrase has been overworked.

Some titles are so obvious that they are repeated, probably unwittingly, by various authors. "The Long Arm" has been chosen as a title by Samuel N. Gardenhire, E. Phillips Oppenheim, Richard Harding Davis, and Mary E. Wilkins.

"A Mysterious Disappearance," appealed to the taste of three or four authors, while "The Corpus Delicti" took the fancy of two or three more.

Such titles as "The Scales of Justice," or "Vengeance is Mine" are entirely legitimate, though not novel. Titles like those chosen by Anna Katharine Green are much more to be commended: "The Woman in the Alcove," "The Doctor, his Wife and the Clock," "Initials Only" or "One of my Sons," are unique and therefore arrestive.

"The Trevor Case," is a hackneyed style of title, while "The Circular Staircase" is not.

As a general rule avoid unpleasant words in a title. Omit the words Murder, Crime, or Blood. These words are inevitable in your text, but unattractive in your title.

In fine, do your best to make both matter and manner of your story the best that in you lies; and never for a moment commit the error of thinking that because you are writing a detective story you may scamp your efforts to achieve good literature.

We quote by permission the following advice by Mr. Arlo Bates. Though written for the benefit of young authors in all fields of literature, it may be applied especially to writers of detective fiction.

"A youth who decides to follow a life of letters will not do amiss to be frank with himself at the start. He may say to his inner self: 'I can make money with my pen. It is a business, like another. I should find it pleasant, to be sure, to try to produce literature; but I see that it does not pay. I prefer the flesh pots of Egypt, hot, well filled, highly spiced, to any vague promises of the delights of a far-off and rather doubtful Canaan of art. I will write what people will buy; and I will take my reward as I go, in pleasant applause and good hard cash.' Or if he be of another mind, he may have the hardihood to say to himself something of this sort: 'It is true that if I do the best I can in literature, I shall be hard put to it to pay the butcher and the baker. The candlestick-maker will dwell in abundance, while by the glimmer of a tallow dip set in the meanest of his wares I wearily and very likely hungrily write that which not one man in a thousand would care to read, and not one woman in ten thousand would think of taking out of the circulating library. There is, moreover, the gravest doubt whether, even after I am dead and cannot enjoy it if it comes, reputation will crown my work. Yet in spite of all this, I am so constituted that the delight of doing my best, the pleasure of serving my art, will make up to me for all that I forego in choosing to strive toward literary perfection. I elect to walk while others ride, to be splashed by mud from the carriage wheels of the wife of the man whose rubbish is sold by the million copies and given away with the popular brand of soap; I will starve if it must be, but I will live my own life.' Something of one of these decisions it will be well to adopt at the start.

"When the decision is made, it is to be abided by. A man has no more right to complain at the loss of the thing he deliberately let go than he has to be angry that two and two make four. It is true that few are able to make the higher choice without some secret thought,—that unacknowledged hope which, all intangible as it is, is one of the most comforting delusions of life; that hope not put into word even in the most secret chamber of the heart, yet without which so many heroisms would be impossible—some deeply hidden conviction that fortune will to them be so propitious that all discouraging precedents will be violated. It is so hard for youth to believe that anything it desires is impossible. The ardent young author, working steadfastly in his attic, has a firm faith that fame and fortune will one day be his in abundance. That this dream is so often false is profoundly pathetic; but it is not a vital misfortune if the man be virile enough not to be soured by disappointment and disillusion. Character is the great stake for which one plays the game of life; and if this is won, the rest is of less, no matter how grave, weight. The failure of literary aspirations is bitter, but the worst is escaped as long as one is able firmly to say: 'I chose the pleasure of an unviolated literary conscience, the delight of serving art with my best endeavor, rather than the rewards of meretricious work. I have had what I bargained for; and I stand by that ungrudgingly. If I hoped for a bonus at the hand of Fortune and have not got it, at least I have received the price which I stipulated.'

"The price stipulated in such a bargain with life is at least sure. He who elects to serve literature and to do his best for the pleasure of such doing, cannot be robbed of his reward; while he who works for other advantages may and often does fail of securing them. He who makes the pleasure of being true to his best instincts his purpose, is secure of the satisfaction which comes of nobility of intention and consciousness of high aim, while the man who seeks money and notoriety often comes to grief. A writer may even be willing to stoop to any and every low device to gain popularity, and yet may miss it. It is one thing for a mail to be willing to sell himself to the devil, and quite another to induce the devil to pay his price.

"No man devotes his life to any work without some more or less clearly defined idea of what he shall gain from such a muse The reward of literature is not money, although occasionally that will come in abundance, and in these days usually rewards in moderation any literary labor done at all well. The reward is not reputation, albeit that cannot but be pleasant to any man who wins it, for no sane human being can remain totally indifferent to the approval and applause of his follows. These things are good, but they are not the true guerdons of art. The real reward of literature is the joy of producing it. There are few earthly delights which can compare with the pleasure of artistic creation: to feel a work grow in the mind and take shape under the hand; to look on a new found idea as a 'watcher of the skies when a new planet swims into his ken;' to be lifted above whatever is small or petty or annoying, whatever is unsatisfactory in human life, by the power of the creative impulse,— that is the true good of the literary worker; and it is a good so great that all others may well seem petty beside it. There is much else which is attractive and desirable,—contact with alert minds, familiarity with the thought of the world, and the enjoyment of an artistic atmosphere,— but these are less certain, and are really of less importance. The most admirable return for all one's labors that he hath under the sun, is the joy of a congenial pursuit and the inspiration of creative effort.

"This may seem somewhat far from the standards of a workaday world. It is certain that no transports of literary creation will pay the coal bill or settle an account at the grocer's. Necessity knows no law, and a man may be forced to drudgery with the pen as with the pickaxe. To him, however, who is willing and able to sacrifice material to intellectual ends, what I have said is of actual and practical application."

A Note About the Author

Carolyn Wells (1862–1942) was an American poet, librarian, and mystery writer. Born in Rahway, New Jersey, Wells began her career as a children's author with such works as *At the Sign of the Sphinx* (1896), *The Jingle Book* (1899), and *The Story of Betty* (1899). After reading a mystery novel by Anna Katharine Green, Wells began focusing her efforts on the genre and found success with her popular Detective Fleming Stone stories. *The Clue* (1909), her most critically acclaimed work, cemented her reputation as a leading mystery writer of the early twentieth century. In 1918, Wells married Hadwin Houghton, the heir of the Houghton-Mifflin publishing fortune, and remained throughout her life an avid collector of rare and important poetry volumes.

A Note from the Publisher

Spanning many genres, from non-fiction essays to literature classics to children's books and lyric poetry, Mint Edition books showcase the master works of our time in a modern new package. The text is freshly typeset, is clean and easy to read, and features a new note about the author in each volume. Many books also include exclusive new introductory material. Every book boasts a striking new cover, which makes it as appropriate for collecting as it is for gift giving. Mint Edition books are only printed when a reader orders them, so natural resources are not wasted. We're proud that our books are never manufactured in excess and exist only in the exact quantity they need to be read and enjoyed.

Discover more of your favorite classics with Bookfinity™.

- Track your reading with custom book lists.
- Get great book recommendations for your personalized Reader Type.
- Add reviews for your favorite books.
- AND MUCH MORE!

Visit **bookfinity.com** and take the fun Reader Type quiz to get started.

Enjoy our classic and modern companion pairings!

Printed in the USA
CPSIA information can be obtained
at www.ICGtesting.com
LVHW041628070224
771245LV00029B/272